THE MENDELSSOHNS

Three Generations of Genius

Also by Herbert Kupferberg

THOSE FABULOUS PHILADELPHIANS:
The Life and Times of a Great Orchestra

THE

MENDELSSOHNS

Three Generations of Genius

Herbert Kupferberg

Charles Scribner's Sons
New York

                         She was not made
Through years or moons the inner weight to bear,
   Which colder hearts endure till they are laid
By age in earth: her days and pleasures were
   Brief, but delightful—such as had not staid
Long with her destiny; but she sleeps well
By the sea-shore, whereon she loved to dwell.

                         —BYRON, *Don Juan*

Contents

Illustrations

Introduction

The Mendelssohns were the Rothschilds of culture. Like the famous family of bankers, they came out of the ghetto to become one of the leading German-Jewish clans of the eighteenth and nineteenth centuries, with an influence and a progeny that extended throughout the world.

Like the Rothschilds, they were noted for their financial acumen and established a famous banking house, Mendelssohn and Company, which became the leading private bank in Berlin until its liquidation in 1939.

But the real wealth of the Mendelssohns lay in the realms of religion, literature, and music. The most famous of all was, of course, Felix Mendelssohn, who became the dominant composer of his time in Europe and whose music remains an integral part of today's concert repertory. But Felix was the product of a family celebrated long before him for its contributions to European culture and thought.

The founder of the line, Moses Mendelssohn, an impoverished, bright-eyed hunchback, emerged from the Dessau ghetto to become the most celebrated Jew in five hundred years, attaining a European vogue as a philosopher and litterateur, writing the most popular book of his day, and, most important of all, setting in motion forces which, although he did not intend them that way, led to a modernization of Jewish religious practices and helped create Reform Judaism as we know it today.

So thoroughly did Moses Mendelssohn emancipate the Jews that many of his own descendants forswore their religion and, while still retaining their ancestral traditions and outlook, underwent conversion. Moses produced sons who were conservative bankers, but also free-thinking daughters who were in the forefront of the women's liberation movement of their day and one of whom, Dorothea Mendelssohn, scandalized Europe with her writings and her *amours*.

Although I hope I have not stinted Moses Mendelssohn's contributions as a religious reformer and philosopher or Felix's achievements as a musician, I have tried to put my emphasis on the family as human beings. The Mendelssohn story, it seems to me, has validity in terms of Moses' dramatic climb from poverty to fame, Abraham's deep internal struggle over his religious doubts and scruples, Henrietta's curious career as a Parisian governess and its grisly aftermath, Felix's response to the conflicting pulls of professionalism and domesticity and his strongly individual relationships with the women in his life, from his tragic sister Fanny to his ambitious protégée Jenny Lind. And I have tried to carry the story of this remarkable family and its enterprises down to our own time and to explore the fate not only of the Mendelssohn descendants but of the Mendelssohn reputation.

Many people have helped in my researches and reading. I would like to express especial gratitude to Ilse and Stephan Dobbs for help with translations and for much valuable background information, to Dr. Rudolf Elvers for data on the prewar and postwar periods, to Professor Felix Gilbert for genealogical facts and other family material, to Dr. Joseph L. Gottesman for medical data, to Francesco von Mendelssohn for family information, to Hedy and Ludwig Moses for translation assistance, and to Rabbi Irwin Sanders for material and insights on Moses Mendelssohn. The following libraries and institutions were of invaluable aid, whether knowingly or unknowingly: the Mendelssohn Archive of the Prussian State Library in Berlin, the Music and Theater Divisions of the New York Public Library at Lincoln Center and the Jewish Division in the main library, the Jewish Theological Seminary Library, the Leo Baeck Institute, and the Forest Hills Jewish Center Library. To all go my thanks, together with my absolution for any errors that may have occurred. Finally, again to my family I express my deep appreciation for the encouragement, assistance, and occasional interludes of quiet which helped in the writing of this book.

HERBERT KUPFERBERG

THE MENDELSSOHNS

Three Generations of Genius

Part I

MOSES

LAY BROTHER:
By God, you are a Christian!
There never was a better Christian than you!
NATHAN:
That which makes me in your eyes a Christian
makes you a Jew in mine.

—LESSING,
Nathan the Wise

I The Stranger from Dessau

In September of 1743, a fourteen-year-old boy carrying his belongings in a small pack on his back walked eighty miles from the town of Dessau in central Germany to Berlin, the capital of the kingdom of Prussia. He was small, humpbacked, and spoke with a stammer. His name, taken from his native city, was Moses Dessau. Few people who passed him during the five days he walked on that dusty road could have regarded him as a figure of much account, yet as Moses Mendelssohn, he was to become one of the most famous Europeans of his day and the forebear of a remarkable family whose history, achievements, and tragedies form the story of this book.

As he approached Berlin, he headed for the checkpoint known as the Rosenthaler Gate, the only one through which Jews were permitted to enter. When he got there, according to one legend, the watchman asked him what his name was. "Moses," he replied. The next question was what he wanted to do in Berlin. "To learn," the boy blurted out. The watchman laughed. "Go, Moses," he said with an ironic wave, "the sea has opened before you."

Whether or not Moses actually spoke the word *lernen,* which tradition ascribes to him, there is no doubt that it clearly represented his intent. History has known few youths as hungry for learning, or more in need of it. In his fourteen years he had absorbed as much as Dessau had to offer, and he was now at an age when he would either have to settle for one of the few available Jewish trades—probably that of a peddler—or seek new teachers and other schooling in Berlin.

Moses' father, Mendel Dessau, ran a small Hebrew day school for the Jewish boys of the town, all of whom came from families as impoverished as his own. He earned a little extra income from his labors as a religious scribe, copying out passages from the Bible onto strips of parchment which were encased in the *mezuzoth* his coreligionists affixed to their doorposts and in the *tephillin* they wore during their morning prayers. Both Moses and his younger brother Saul helped their father in this copying work. From it Moses developed a beautiful calligraphy that became a family characteristic, turning up in his son Abraham's neat banking entries and in his grandson Felix's precise musical notation. Of Moses' mother little is known, except that her name was Suschen, that she died before her son attained prominence, and that he always remembered her as a patient, long-suffering woman. Indeed, it is hard to see how she could have been otherwise, living in her cramped and squalid surroundings.

The horrors of the modern world have perhaps given us a new perspective on the iniquities of the medieval. The ancient ghettos of Dessau and Berlin, for all the misery they saw, never witnessed the systematic exterminations of our time. Life was penurious and precarious, but it was life; somehow, people managed to exist and endure and, occasionally, escape. Nevertheless, every ghetto dweller was constantly aware of his state of isolation, insecurity, and humiliation—compelled to doff his hat whenever a non-Jew demanded it, subject to outbreaks of brutal violence, barred by law from nearly all the trades and professions, and, save in exceptional cases, forced to dwell in the most wretched and unwholesome part of town.

Johann Wolfgang von Goethe, who years later was to entertain Moses Mendelssohn's grandson Felix at his mansion in Weimar, wrote as a boy of eleven of a visit to the Frankfurt ghetto: "It consisted of little more than a single street that in early times was apparently squeezed in like an animal-run between the city wall and the moat. The closeness, the dirt, the swarming folk, the accent of an ugly language—all these together made the most unpleasant impression when one only glanced through the gate in passing. It was long before I ventured to enter, and I did not find it easy to return there. . . ."

The Dessau ghetto, where Moses Mendelssohn was born on September 6, 1729, was no better. But the town, which had about 150 Jewish families among its population of 9,500, was considered a minor center of learning and even had its own Hebrew printing press. Mendelssohn always retained an affection for it; to his dying day, he used a seal inscribed in Hebrew: "Moses, the Stranger from Dessau."

For a ghetto child whose father eked out a living by transcribing the Pentateuch, learning started early. Mendel Dessau would rouse his seven-year-old son at three or four in the morning, wrap an old cloak about him, and carry him through the streets to the Hebrew school where he and other scholars of similar age were taught, in the words of an early and somewhat indignant biographer,* "to prattle mechanically the Mishna and Gemara concerning the laws of betrothing, divorce, legal damages, sacerdotal functions and other similar matters above their comprehension before they were able to read out and understand a single text of Scripture correctly."

This kind of learning was the only type purveyed in the ghetto schools, for the wall not only separated the Jews from physical and social contact with their neighbors; it also cut them off from the mainstream of European culture and civilization. Jewish children in Germany learned neither the German language nor literature, and the only Hebrew they knew was in the liturgy for prayers, much as an American choirboy today "knows" Latin. Their every-

*M. Samuels, whose *Memoirs of Moses Mendelssohn, the Jewish Philosopher,* published in London in 1827, was the first English biography of Mendelssohn.

day language was Yiddish, that admixture of German, Polish, and Hebraic words, written in Hebrew lettering, which produced the "ugly accents" that assailed Goethe's youthful ears.

Moreover, the ghetto schools did not even put major emphasis on the Jewish people's incomparable literary and moral legacy, the Old Testament itself. Instead of reading the Bible, the children were taught from the various books of exegesis, commentary, and legalistic quibbling produced by hundreds of inward-turned rabbis and scholars during generations of dispersal and isolation. If there was a world of the mind beyond the Mishna and Gemara, these young Talmudic students knew little about it.

Moses, brighter and quicker than his fellow pupils, soon began to supplement by his own studies the endless doctrinal formulas pronounced daily by a bearded sage named Rabbi Hirsch, who was in charge of the class. He decided to learn Hebrew by grammar rather than rote, and he came to understand it so well that by the age of ten, he was writing his own Hebrew poetry. Later on he concluded he was no poet: "I have no genius for poetry. My mind is more disposed to penetrate into the deeper recesses of the understanding than to roam in the lighter regions of fancy."

About the same time that he was experimenting with verse, a book fell into his hands that left a permanent mark on him physically no less than spiritually. The chief rabbi of the town, David Frankel, with whom he now began to study, presented him with a copy of Moses Maimonides's *A Guide to the Perplexed.* Written in 1190, this work was one of the earliest (and most successful) books addressed, in its author's words, "to thinkers whose studies have brought them into collision with religion." An attempt to demonstrate the compatibility of reason and faith, it has always represented an epochal step in man's long effort to make ancient religious principles retain their validity in a changing world.

The young student received it with ecstasy, finding in it meanings and messages that far transcended the semantic and legalistic hairsplitting of his Talmudic researches. Night after night, he sat by an oil lamp, reading, studying, remembering. He had always been frail and undersized, and now as he bent over the book's thousand pages, his spine developed a permanent curvature. "Maimon gave me my hump," he later wrote, "but still I dote on him for the many hours of dejection he converted into rapture. . . . He weakened my body, but invigorated my soul."

Shortly after Moses underwent his bar-mitzvah ritual at the age of thirteen, his tutor Rabbi Frankel was called to Berlin to become chief rabbi there. For Frankel this was a considerable advancement: Berlin was the chief city of the rising kingdom of Prussia, with a population of well over 100,000; Frederick the Great ruled from nearby Potsdam; and there were perhaps 1,500 Jews within the city. For young Moses, however, Frankel's departure was a calamity, and he stood on a hillside weeping as his teacher left the city. Gone was the only man in Dessau with whom he could discuss Maimonides. Besides, since he was now at an age that Jews then regarded literally as the beginning of manhood, he would have to see about earning a living. He knew no trade and had no skills, so the path seemed clearly marked out for him to become a peddler, frail physique notwithstanding. It was not a prospect that pleased him, and after weeks of discussion with his reluctant parents, he finally persuaded them to let him journey to Berlin and seek out Rabbi Frankel for further studies. His father gave him his blessing, and his mother, a gold ducat; and with little more than these, he set out for the Prussian capital.

Berlin, like any other large German town, had its *Judengasse,* and Mendelssohn headed straight toward it once he had been approved by the watchman at the Rosenthaler Gate and paid the *Leibzoll,* or "body tax," which was levied on all Jews entering a city or crossing a frontier. His immediate objective was the dwelling of Rabbi Frankel, which he quickly found. His old teacher was surprised to see him, but speedily did what he could to help. He had recently completed the manuscript of a commentary to the Jerusalem Talmud and, being acquainted with Moses' fine handwriting, paid him small sums to copy portions of it. He also introduced him to a merchant named Herman Bamberg, who gave him sleeping space in his attic. Twice a week the Bambergs invited him to share their evening meal, and on Sabbath and festival days he was a table guest of Rabbi Frankel. But for seven years, his basic diet consisted of a loaf of bread, which he divided into seven portions with notches to make sure that it would last him the week. His life, not entirely to his liking, closely resembled that described by the Talmud for serious study: "Eat bread with salt, drink water by measure, sleep upon the hard earth, lead a life of privation, and busy thyself with the Law."

But Moses busied himself with other preoccupations besides the Law. Although he faithfully attended Frankel's rabbinic lectures, he also plunged into the seas of secular learning from which, as an inmate of the ghetto, he had been kept stranded. His first conquest was the German language itself; not only did he learn it quickly and thoroughly; he became its stylistic master. His knowledge of German in turn opened up new areas to him. One of the first German books he read was a history of Protestantism, which opened his eyes to worlds of religion besides his own. Until then, he had been totally ignorant of Christian theology. Similarly, there were other discoveries to be made: literature, philosophy, science, languages. He decided to teach himself Latin and bought a secondhand dictionary from his earnings as a copyist. With its help, he tackled declensions and verb forms. He read Locke's *Essay on Human Understanding* in a Latin translation, piecing it out word by word, and found it fascinating; after that, the Latin classics offered him no trouble.

Soon word began to spread through the Jewish community in Berlin of the young scholar from Dessau so insatiable for knowledge, and others began to assist him in his quest. A young Jewish physician from Prague named Abraham Kisch helped with his Latin. English and French he studied with Solomon Gumpertz, a well-to-do medical student who had achieved the feat, unprecedented for a Jew, of taking a degree at the University of Königsberg. A brilliant young mathematician named Israel Zamosz, who had left Poland because his independent religious views had incurred the wrath of the local rabbis, arrived in Berlin with no place to live; Mendelssohn invited him to share his garret lodgings in return for lessons in logic and Euclidean geometry. Zamosz also had some knowledge of the fine arts, a field of which Mendelssohn was almost totally ignorant, and the two young men spent hours discussing the principles of esthetics. But Mendelssohn himself was his own best teacher and in afteryears could truthfully write: "I have never been to any university, neither have I ever heard a classroom lecture, and one of the greatest difficulties I had to surmount was that I had to obtain everything by my own effort and industry."

One subject alone failed to interest him, and that was history. Later on he explained his deficiency by saying that "one who had no country of his own could not profit by history," and that "I always yawn when I have to read something historical, unless the style enlivens the writing." Whatever his reasoning, throughout his life it was always man's ideas, rather than his actions, that most stimulated his mind.

Even a philosopher must eat, and by the age of twenty-one, Mendelssohn was looking for steady employment. He might easily have followed in Frankel's footsteps and become a rabbi, but his secular studies, which gradually replaced his Talmudic perusals, drove any thought of a religious career from his mind. He was fortunate in the job he finally found. In 1750, a wealthy Jewish merchant, Isaac Bernhard, engaged him as tutor to his four children. This meant he could give up his garret for a comfortable room in the Bernhard house, that he would receive a regular stipend, and that he would still have time to spend in study. With his new-found income he began to take music lessons and make occasional visits to concerts and the theater.

Bernhard, who owned a silk factory, was one of the leading Jews of Berlin. Eighteenth-century Germany was not a country but a mass of petty principalities, each with its own ruler, court, and hierarchy of officials. In some of these, Jews of business acumen and versatility had managed to find places as financial agents or merchants, thus leaving the ghetto behind them. The Prussian court of Frederick the Great divided all Jews into three classifications: "Court Jews," who lived virtually without restrictions and who were often employed by the king as business advisers, financial go-betweens, or even as mint officials; "Protected Jews," who were guaranteed at least the right of residence in a given city; and "Tolerated Jews," the great mass of the people, who lacked any civil rights or legal standing at all and who could be expelled without notice or excuse. Bernhard was in the first class; Mendelssohn, in the third; indeed, it was only as a dependent of the silk merchant that he was able to reside unmolested in Berlin.

For four years, Mendelssohn remained in Bernhard's house, teaching his children in both secular and religious subjects. When they had all passed school age and Mendelssohn's tutorial function was ended, Bernhard offered him a job in his silk factory as a bookkeeper, a post in which he quickly put to good use his ready mind, his mathematical ability, and his excellent handwriting. Eventually, Mendelssohn became Bernhard's manager and finally his partner, so that as a successful businessman, he had a decent income for the rest of his life. But although he worked conscientiously at silks, he never really liked it. "A good bookkeeper," he wrote ruefully to a friend, "certainly is an uncommon creature and deserves a very high reward, for he must resign wit, perception and sense, and become a mere block of wood in order to keep books properly."

On another occasion he complained: "The whole day I hear so much useless talk, hear and do so many frivolous, tiring, stupefying things, that it is no small benefit to me in the evening to be able to converse with a sensible being. . . . This tiresome, oppressive business! It drags me down and devours the strength of my best years. Like a mule, I plod through life with a load on my back; and unfortunately my self-esteem keeps whispering to me that perhaps I was intended by nature to be a race-horse." How many bookkeepers since have arrived at the same conclusion!

II *A Literary and Social Lion*

Will Durant has written that "a Jewish merchant is a dead scholar." Moses Mendelssohn, for all his protestations, managed to live a flourishing life as both. He even found it possible to turn his commercial activities to literary use. In his first year working at Bernhard's factory, he had to deliver a consignment of silk samples to a government official's home. Kept waiting in the courtyard for an hour, he began to observe the contours of the building's façade, judge its proportions, and study its decorations; then, using the parcel of silks as a desk, and remembering his garret discussions on the arts with Israel Zamosz, he jotted down ideas for a short treatise on esthetics, which was eventually published under the title *Letters on the Emotions.*

Shortly after, a Swiss visitor named Johann Caspar Lavater left this picture of the busy scholar-merchant: "The Jew Mendelssohn, author of the philosophical *Letters on the Emotions,* we found in his office, busy with silk goods. A companionable, brilliant soul, with pleasing ideas; the body of an Aesop; a man of keen insight, exquisite taste and wide erudition. He is a great venerator of all thinking minds and himself a metaphysician; an impartial judge of all works of talent and taste; frank and openhearted in intercourse, more modest in his speech than in his writings, unaffected by praise. . . ."

Thus, almost simultaneously with his entry into the silk business, Mendelssohn launched himself on a career as a critic and writer. Possibly no Jew before him had ever used the German language with such fluency and elegance, and certainly none had attempted to build a career around it. Mendelssohn was a master of languages and could converse equally readily with an English nobleman, a French revolutionist, and a Polish ghetto refugee; but for him, the preferred tongue always was German. He spoke it at home and among his friends; he wrote his books in it and taught it to his children. When he decided to stop using the name Moses Dessau, with which he had come to Berlin, and to be known instead in the Jewish manner as the son of his father, he did not use the Hebraic form Moshe ben Mendel, but the Germanic Moses Mendelssohn.

In becoming a literary man, Mendelssohn had considerable assistance. A number of independent-minded young writers and editors, themselves Christians, took an interest in the work and ideas of the brilliant Jewish bookkeeper who seemed so eager to explore the worlds of philosophy and learning. Among them was Gotthold Ephraim Lessing, whose friendship with Mendelssohn makes for one of the most deeply human episodes in the literary history of any country—above all, that of Germany.

Lessing was then twenty-five years old, the same age as Mendelssohn. He was at the outset of a career that was to make him one of the leading literary figures of the German Enlightenment and had not yet written his most famous play, *Nathan the Wise;* indeed, it could never have been written without Moses Mendelssohn, for he was to serve as the model for its main character. But seven years earlier, Lessing, the son of a pastor and one of the greatest apostles of tolerance ever produced in Germany, had written a curious play called *The Jew*, whose hero rescues a Christian nobleman from a murderous assault by robbers, only to be reviled when he reveals his Hebraic origins. Critics had received the play with skepticism or derision, Professor Johann Michaelis, a well-known Göttingen theologian, declaring flatly: "A noble Jew is a poetic impossibility." Lessing replied that his intention had indeed been to combat prejudice—"a prejudice which can only flow from hatred and pride and makes the Jew not only a boor, but a pariah of mankind."

In his youthful play, Lessing had created a fictitious Jew of character and refinement; now, in Moses Mendelssohn, he met a real one. They were introduced to one another by Gumpertz, the medical student who had taught Mendelssohn English and French; Lessing was looking for a good chess player to give him a match, and Gumpertz suggested Mendelssohn. And so the two young men met over the chessboard, just as Nathan the Wise and Saladin were to meet twenty-five years later in Lessing's play.

Before long, their friendship turned into a close literary partnership. Mendelssohn had written a set of *Philosophical Observations,* a work in which he called on Germans to discard French influences (then prevalent at the court of Frederick the Great, where Voltaire was a practically permanent resident) and to follow instead their own natural bent in philosophy. Mendelssohn showed his manuscript to Lessing and asked him for his opinion; Lessing promptly took it to a printer and had it published. Although the *Philosophical Observations* at first appeared anonymously, Mendelssohn quickly became known as its author, and it created a minor sensation, going through three printings. No Jew previously had had a book published in the German language.

There followed an even more direct collaboration between Lessing and Mendelssohn. The Berlin Academy, the official Prussian literary and scientific directorate sponsored by Frederick the Great, in 1755 offered a prize for the best essay on "The Philosophical System of Alexander Pope," specifically on the question of whether the English poet had been correct in making his famous assertion "Whatever is, is right" in his *Essay on Man.*

It was a typically pedantic, literary-academy kind of competition, and the subject struck both Lessing and Mendelssohn as nonsensical, especially since Pope himself had warned his readers "not to laugh at my gravity, but permit me to wear the beard of a philosopher till I pull it off and make a jest of it myself." Lessing and Mendelssohn didn't enter the competition directly; instead, they published a paper ironically entitled *Pope, a Metaphysician!* in which they derided the whole affair. Once again, the initial publication was anonymous, but the identity of the authors became known. Curiously, no offense was taken at the court of *le roi philosophe;* in fact, several of Frederick's courtiers asked to meet "the young Hebrew who wrote in German," and Mendelssohn was presented to the French mathematician Maupertuis, the head of the Berlin Academy.

Mendelssohn was well qualified to write on Pope because he knew the poet's works well and throughout his life maintained a keen interest in English literature. Long before the famous translations by Schlegel and Tieck started a great wave of popularity for Shakespeare in Germany, Moses Mendelssohn was systematically reading the plays in English for himself—and making a few translations of his own. Among the Shakespearean passages he put into German were Ariel's song "Where the bee sucks," from *The Tempest;* "You spotted snakes," from *A Midsummer Night's Dream;* and, inevitably, Hamlet's soliloquy "To be or not to be," which in Moses Mendelssohn's published version reads:

> Sein oder Nichtsein, dieses ist die Frage!
> Ist's edler, im Gemüt des Schicksals Wut
> Und giftiges Geschoß zu dulden; oder
> Sein ganzes Heer von Qualen zu bekämpfen
> Und kämpfend zu vergehen?—Vergehen?—Schlafen!
> Mehr heißt es nicht. Ein süßer Schlummer ist's,
> Der uns von tausend Herzensangst befreit,
> Die dieses Fleisches Erbteil sind.—Wie würdig
> Des frommen Wunsches ist vergehen, schlafen!—
> Doch schlafen?—Nicht auch träumen? Ach, hier liegt
> Der Knoten; Träume, die im Todesschlaf
> Uns schrecken, wenn einst dies Fleisch verwest,
> Sind furchtbar. Diese lehren uns geduldig
> Des langen Lebens schweres Joch ertragen.
> Wer litte sonst des Glückes Schmach und Geißel,

Der Stolzen Übermut, die Tyrannei
Der Mächtigen, die Qual verschmähter Liebe,
Den Mißbrauch der Gesetze, und jedes Schalks
Verspottung der Verdienste, mit Geduld?
Könnt' uns ein bloßer Dolch die Ruhe schenken,
Wo ist der Tor, der unter dieser Bürde
Des Lebens länger seufzte?—Allein
Die Furcht vor dem, was nach dem Tode folgt,
Das Land, von da kein Reisender zurück
Auf Erden kam, entwaffnen unsern Mut.
Wir leiden lieber hier bewußte Qual,
Eh' wir in jene Ungewißheit fliehen.—
So macht uns alle das Gewissen feige!
Die Überlegung kränkt mit bleicher Farbe
Das Angesicht des feurigsten Entschlusses,
Dies unterbricht die größte Unternehmung
In ihrem Lauf, und jede wichtige Tat
Erstirbt.

Mendelssohn's knowledge of English literature was among the bonds that linked him to Lessing, who had similar tastes. Soon both men were part of a literary circle that included Frederick Nicolai, an energetic bookdealer and publisher, and Thomas Abbt, a brilliant university professor, who was to die prematurely at the age of twenty-eight. Nicolai joined Mendelssohn in taking Greek lessons from a local churchman, and the young men spent their evenings together eagerly talking about literature, philosophy and esthetics, and playing chess. Mendelssohn and Nicolai also belonged to an informal organization called the "Learned Coffee-House," a group of young scholars in which each member presented a philosophical or mathematical paper once a month. Mendelssohn had never lost his stammer and, when it came his turn, invariably asked another member to read for him. But he had no difficulty at all, his ghetto upbringing notwithstanding, in bearing himself with pride and dignity among these young men —all of them Christians and most from well-to-do families—who were striving to bring a new vitality to German literature and philosophy. And they, for their part, welcomed the stooped and stammering Jew with the enthusiasm of youth and the camaraderie of the republic of letters. On one occasion, when each member was asked to describe his own defects in verse, Mendelssohn wrote a poem that went:

> Great you call Demosthenes,
>   Stuttering orator of Greece;
> Hunchbacked Aesop you deem wise;—
>   In your circle I surmise
> I am doubly wise and great.
>   What in each was separate
> You in me united find,—
>   Hump and heavy tongue combined.

Nicolai, besides being a publisher, was a wide-ranging author, writing everything from philosophical novels to a treatise on the *Use of Artificial Hair and Wigs.* But his most signal contribution to German letters probably came in several periodicals he edited with the help of Mendelssohn. One of these, launched in 1759, was a literary journal called *Letters About Literature,* in which Mendelssohn, Lessing, and Nicolai regularly set forth their views on poetry, philosophy, and art. Reviews of this kind were uncommon in eighteenth-century Germany, and those as independent and outspoken as *Letters About Literature* were virtually nonexistent. Specifically, the publication conducted a campaign against the persistent French cultural orientation of Frederick and his court.

The Prussian king, who had reigned since 1740, was a contradictory ruler. In military matters, he displayed true Teutonic vigor; but in literary and social matters, he tried to be a thoroughgoing Frenchman. He called his Potsdam palace Sans Souci; he invariably spoke and wrote in French; he surrounded himself with French literary and scientific figures like Voltaire and Maupertuis. "In our own country," he wrote in an essay entitled *De la Littérature allemande,* "I hear a jargon devoid of any grace, and which each person manipulates as he pleases, with no discrimination. . . . Let us admit sincerely and frankly that up to this time literature has not flourished on our soil. . . . To convince yourself of the bad taste that reigns in Germany, you have only to frequent the theater. You will see the awful plays of Shakespeare translated into our language, and the whole audience transported with delight by these absurd farces, fit only for the savages of Canada. . . ." The mass of people may have shrugged off Frederick's outlook as merely one more idiosyncrasy of royalty, but the young literary generation of Germans was furious about it, and their resentment found its outlet in the columns of *Letters About Literature.*

Frederick's artistic propensities extended to playing and composing music for the flute and writing poetry in French. A volume of his collected verse entitled *Poésies diverses* was published just as *Letters About Literature* came into existence. The poems, of course, were entirely in French, and Frederick even apologized lightly for the way he used the language in an opening snatch of verse that ran:

> Ma Muse tudesque et bizarre
> Jargonnant un français barbare
> Dit les choses comme elle peut.*

The book was obviously one that called for review in the pages of *Letters About Literature* and, equally obviously, one that a reviewer might naturally approach with a certain amount of hesitation. The assignment fell to Mendelssohn, and it cannot be said that he shirked it. Politely but unmistakably, he took the king to task for writing his poems in French. Frederick's apologia about his *"Muse tudesque,"* he wrote, was "beneath the dignity of the august author," and added, "What a loss to our mother tongue that this Prince makes a more fluent use of French!" Moses also

---

*My Germanic and bizarre Muse
Jargonizing a barbaric French
Says things as best she can.

criticized the king's philosophic outlook, commenting on a poem that denied the immortality of the soul: "A Frederick who does not believe in the soul's immortality is a mere chimera, a round square, a square circle."

For a Jew from Dessau to lecture the ruler of Prussia about "our mother tongue" was a bit too much for the royal court. A formal complaint was drawn up by a cleric named von Justi, who had also written a work that received an unfavorable notice in *Letters About Literature.* Von Justi's indictment charged that "this Jew disregarded proper reverence for the King's all-highest, sanctified person, and impudently passed judgment on his poetry." The journal was forthwith suspended, and Mendelssohn was ordered to appear at court to explain himself.

The day selected for the appointment happening to fall on the Sabbath, upon which Jews are forbidden to ride, Mendelssohn applied to his friend Rabbi Frankel for a dispensation permitting him to travel to Potsdam. A large turn-out was on hand, since many in Frederick's court besides the king were curious to see *"le Juif de Berlin."* Faced with at least a royal reprimand, and possibly expulsion from the city, Mendelssohn explained gravely to the king: "Writing poetry is like bowling, and whoever bowls, be he king or peasant, must have the pinboy tell him his score." It was a clever and gracious riposte, perhaps calculated to win the admiration of a sophisticated Frenchman, such as Frederick imagined himself to be. In any case, the "explanation" was accepted, Mendelssohn was dismissed unscathed, and the ban against the publication was lifted.

Frederick the Great's feelings toward his Jewish subjects were decidedly antipathetic. He had his Court Jews, as which European monarch did not; but he was chary of giving out too many patents of Protected rank, and the great mass of Jewry in his domains continued to live without the most basic legal protections and under a constant threat of expulsion. His general attitude was expressed in an instruction to his administrators: "The more the Jews can be excluded from commerce the better," with the added proviso that he wanted "all bad and unimportant Jews in the small towns" removed. When he conquered Silesia, inadvertently bringing many additional Jews under his control, he solved the problem by ordering most of them to leave. In the city of Breslau, for example, only twelve Jewish families were permitted to remain.

In 1750, when Moses Mendelssohn was twenty-one years old, Frederick promulgated a charter setting forth the rules governing the life of all Jews in Prussia. In addition to the three broad classifications of Court, Protected and Tolerated Jews, the charter limited the numbers of semi-official functionaries permitted in Berlin—one rabbi, two cantors, six grave-diggers, three slaughterers, three butchers, three bakers, one physician, two printers, two teachers for girls, both of whom were required to be married, and sundry others. Severe limitations were put on the numbers of Jewish marriages, and only first-born sons of the upper categories were permitted the right of settlement. Lending money for interest was closely regulated, and business activities and manual trades limited to a few fields. Even peddling in cities was prohibited except at the time of fairs. Jewish beggars were totally barred. The entire community was held responsible for the failure of an individual to pay taxes. It was, Count Mirabeau wrote in France, "a law worthy of a cannibal."

Frederick even put restrictions on the lot of the Protected Jews *(Schutz-Juden)* of Berlin. Under his decree Protected Jews were divided into two types, "Regular" and "Irregular." The former were permitted to lead a fairly normal life without fear of expulsion, although they could neither farm nor own homes. They could even have as many children as they wished. Irregular Protected Jews, however, were officially not permitted to have children, meaning that all their offspring faced the choice of either illegitimacy or emigration. And most Jews, of course, remained as before, without any official status at all and permitted in the city only on sufferance.

Mendelssohn all along had remained in this last category, being neither a Court Jew nor a Protected one. However, sometime after his appearance before Frederick, some of his Christian friends decided it was time to seek for him at least the status of a *Schutz-Jude.* Their spokesman was one of Frederick's most esteemed French courtiers, Jean-Baptiste de Boyer, the Marquis d'Argens, a worldly, well-traveled, and enlightened writer, who had lived in Berlin for a decade and was one of the luminaries of the Royal Academy. D'Argens came to see Mendelssohn and urged him to phrase the petition to the king himself. Moses at first declined, saying he would not "beg for that permission to exist which is the natural right of every human being who lives as a peaceful citizen." Mendelssohn's friends persisted, however, until he reluctantly consented to draw up the formal document. D'Argens himself presented it to the king, endorsing it with this gracious note: "A bad Catholic philosopher begs a bad Protestant philosopher to grant the Privilege to a bad Jewish philosopher. There is too much philosophy in all this for right not to be on the side of the request." Nevertheless, Frederick held back, and after a time it was given out that the petition had been accidentally mislaid. In any event, it was not until 1763, a year after Mendelssohn had married, that he was raised to the status of Protected Jew, and then only of Irregular rank. It remained for Frederick's successor, Frederick William II, to confer similar rights on his posterity in 1787.

Although efforts have been made to depict Moses and Frederick as being on a fairly familiar basis, there is little evidence to substantiate such a notion. The king may have regarded the philosopher, however dubiously, as something of an adornment to his realm and as handy proof of such tendencies toward tolerance as he acknowledged. Mendelssohn, for his part, accepted Frederick as his legally constituted ruler, and in after years, when he became a kind of unofficial spokesman for the Berlin Jewish community, even composed a commemorative sermon (which Rabbi Frankel read to the synagogue congregation) extolling the royal victory over the Austrians at Rossbach in the Seven Years' War, although he privately wrote to Lessing that things had reached a fine state of affairs when he found himself "writing a sermon and praising a king."*

Nevertheless, legends grew about the supposed conversations between the king and Mendelssohn—exchanges in which Mendelssohn always had the last word—and they persist to this day in Jewish folklore. One story tells how Mendelssohn is summoned to Potsdam by Frederick, who is urgently in need of his advice. A haughty officer, seeing the stooped and poorly dressed Jew at the door, asks him who he might be and why he wishes to see the king. Sizing up his interrogator, Mendelssohn replies: "I am a sleight-of-hand artist," and is promptly admitted. When he recounts the story to Frederick, the king asks: "But why did you tell him that?" "Because," replies Mendelssohn, "I know it is easier for a juggler to get into your palace than a philosopher." Another tale tells of the king encountering the philosopher out for a stroll on the street one day. "Good morning, Mr. Mendelssohn, where are you going?" asks the monarch. "I don't know," replies Mendelssohn. "How dare you make such an answer to me!" shouts Frederick. "Guard! take this man to prison!" Says Mendelssohn as the guard prepares to lead him off: "You see, Your Majesty? Did I know I was going to prison?" The king chuckles and lets him off.

So, at least, go the stories—not the least of the tributes paid by his contemporaries to a man they regarded not only as a scholar and philosopher but as a shrewd and sage human being.

---

*The sermon was delivered at the Berlin synagogue on December 10, 1757, five days after the battle. The following year, it was published in London, the first of Mendelssohn's works to be translated into English. The sermon, after likening Frederick to various Biblical heroes and praising him for saving Prussia from the "perfidious machinations" of its adversaries, cautioned its hearers against taking delight in slaughter or in exulting over a fallen foe. It concluded: "Lord of Hosts, thou hast glorified thy servant Frederick, and, for his sake, hast thou done mighty things. Continue to give him his heart's desire. O grant that the sword of destruction may be sheathed; and say to the Angel of Death, hold thy hand. May the Shepherds of thy people, the Princes of the earth, live before thee in peace and tranquility, and may truth and the knowledge of the Lord fill the earth as the waters cover the sea. . . . Help thy people, the remains of thy Israel; and in our days may the Redeemer come to Zion. Amen."

III *The German Socrates*

By the age of thirty-three, Moses Mendelssohn lived independently, had faithful friends, and held a growing reputation as a thinker and writer. In fact, he possessed all that a philosopher needs, and more than many attain, except that he had no wife. During Passover week especially, he told Lessing, he felt cross and out of sorts because he lacked a family of his own with which to celebrate the holiday. Efforts had been made by Frankel, Bernhard and others to bring him together with a number of eligible Jewish girls, but none proved fruitful.

In 1762, on a visit to Hamburg, he met a twenty-four-year-old blonde, blue-eyed girl named Fromet Gugenheim, the daughter of a merchant. According to the story handed down in the family, he was much taken with her; and she, of course, knew of his reputation—her father, who was eager for the match, had seen to that. However, when she laid eyes for the first time on his stunted, misshapen figure, she burst into tears. Afterward, Mendelssohn sat down with her alone.

"Is it my hump?" he asked.

She nodded.

"Let me tell you a story, then," Mendelssohn said. "When a Jewish child is born, proclamation is made in heaven of the name of the person that he or she is to marry. When I was born, my future wife was also named, but at the same time it was said that she herself would be humpbacked. 'O God,' I said, 'a deformed girl will become embittered and unhappy. Dear Lord, let me have the humpback, and make the maiden flawless and beautiful.' "

It would have taken a more cynical young woman than Fromet Gugenheim to resist such wooing, and in June, 1762, they were married. At that time, under one of Frederick's decrees, every Jew getting married was required to make a substantial purchase from the royal pottery works recently established by the king.* Little selection was offered by the manager of the factory to his reluctant Jewish customers; accordingly, Moses and Fromet Mendelssohn became the possessors of twenty life-sized porcelain apes, which they forthwith distributed around their Berlin house. Many of them remained in the family for years.

Mendelssohn had confided his marriage plans to Lessing, who, like himself, was a bachelor. In Hamburg, he wrote, he had gone to the theater, conversed with learned men, and "committed the folly of falling in love."

"The woman I am about to marry," he told his friend, "has no property, is neither learned nor beautiful, yet nevertheless I, infatuated fool, am so wrapped up in her that I believe I shall be able to live happily with her."

Philosophic candor was all very well for Lessing, but with Fromet herself, Mendelssohn adopted a different tone, properly romantic, yet with an elegant banter. In a letter shortly after their engagement was announced, he wrote: "Dearest Fromet: In your father's letter I have made a discovery which pleased me not a little. The kind man assures me that his daughter Fromet is as fair as she is virtuous. What do you think? May we take the honest man's word for it? This good Mr. Abraham Gugenheim must surely know that even philosophers are fond of beautiful things. . . . As long as we have to be separated, we must not miss an opportunity to think of one another. It gives me no little pleasure when I can think: now Fromet reads my letters, now Fromet writes

---

*This represented something of an advance over a regulation established by Frederick's father, Frederick William I, that each newlywed Jew must buy a carcass of a wild boar killed on a royal hunt.

to me, now she is vexed because she is disturbed, and now she is happy because she has found the right word. . . ."

Mendelssohn never achieved real wealth. But thanks to his position at Bernhard's silk house, he had far more economic security than most of his fellow religionists, and his home was comfortable, despite the china apes that peered out of every corner. Soon it began to be filled with a growing family. The Mendelssohns' first child, a girl, died before she was a year old. Moses wrote to his friend Thomas Abbt:

Death has knocked at my door and robbed me of a child, which has lived but eleven innocent months; but God be praised, her short life was happy and full of bright promise. My friend, the dear child did not live these eleven months in vain. Her mind had even in that short time made an astonishing progress; from a little animal that wept and slept, she grew into the bud of a reasoning creature. As the points of the young blades of grass press through the hard earth in the spring, one could see in her the emergence of the first passions. She showed pity, hatred, love and admiration; she understood the language of those who spoke, and endeavored to make known her thoughts to them. Is no trace of all this left in the whole of nature? You will laugh at my simplicity, and see in this talk the weakness of a man who, seeking comfort, finds it nowhere but in his own imagination. It may be; yet I cannot believe that God has set us on his earth like foam on the wave.

About the same time that his daughter died, Mendelssohn received word of the death of his father in Dessau. Another son was to die at the age of twelve, but three sons and three daughters survived, so that the Mendelssohn house on Spandau Street was always noisy with children and with the tutors engaged to instruct them. Poor relatives, both his and Fromet's, had a way of stopping by, too, so perhaps it was no accident that Mendelssohn became a philosopher who thrived on companionship rather than solitude.

As did most other people in the centuries prior to adequate artificial illumination, Mendelssohn rose daily at or before dawn. He recited his morning prayers and then had an hour or so to himself—usually his only solitude of the day. At 8 A.M., he was in his office, meeting customers ("tiresome people!" he once exclaimed in a letter to Lessing), balancing accounts, supervising the workers, inspecting merchandise. Frequently he would slip a book of poetry into his pocket, to read in case he had an idle moment. At four in the afternoon, his day really began, for then he left his business behind him and returned home, usually to a house full of friends, relatives, and visitors, some of whom came from abroad to seek conversation with the famous Jew of Berlin.

For by now, the Mendelssohn house had become a focal point of the intellectual and cultural life of the city. Fromet put out raisins and almonds (one of her descendants, Sebastian Hensel, recorded that she was frugal to the point of actually counting them out) or sometimes a light supper, and all who wished to come were invited. Mendelssohn generally sat in his armchair as a kind of umpire for the discussions, listening rather than talking, and generally seeking to reconcile opposing points of view. When, as often happened, his guests were Christians who sought to engage him in religious discussion, he did his best to move to other subjects, for he disliked confrontations and, when he could, avoided controversies. At such moments he was fond of quoting the reply of the ancient Jewish teacher Hillel to a heathen who had asked him to recite the entire Law while standing on one foot: "My son, love thy neighbor as thyself. That is the entire Law; the rest is commentary."

A poor young Jewish scholar from Lithuania named Solomon Maimon, who had traveled to Berlin to see Mendelssohn, was overawed by the distinguished atmosphere he found: "When I opened Mendelssohn's door and saw him and the other gentlefolk who were there, as well as the beautiful rooms and elegant furniture, I shrank back. . . . Mendelssohn, however, had observed me. He came out and spoke to me very kindly, led me into his room, placed himself beside me at the window, and paid me many compliments about my writing. . . . Not satisfied with this, the worthy man looked after my maintenance also and recommended me to the most eminent, enlightened and wealthy Jews, who made provision for my board and other wants. . . ."

Mendelssohn, however, could be brusque with those of his own faith who tried to test him on the more recondite points of Orthodoxy or to show off their own superior knowledge. To a self-styled rabbinic expert who questioned him about an obscure passage in the writings of Ibn Ezra, eleventh-century Spanish philosopher and poet, Mendelssohn replied: "I do not comprehend the meaning of it myself, but in order to ascertain this fine point, it would be best to contemplate the works of God, and his goodness and mercy to all his creatures. Then it will be time enough to study Ibn Ezra." Told by one of his visitors that three Christians named Trescho, Ziegra, and Bahrdt had expressed doubt that Jews could possess the power of reasoning philosophically, he replied drily: "Happy for us that God is more merciful than Trescho, Ziegra and Bahrdt."

Meanwhile, Mendelssohn continued to produce articles, reviews, essays, and books. He wrote a short treatise on the physical and mathematical foundation of music. He translated from the French Jean Jacques Rousseau's *Discourse on Inequality Among Men* and wrote an introduction and explanatory notes for it, dedicating the entire project to Lessing. While on his honeymoon, he entered an essay contest set by the Academy of Sciences on the question of whether mathematical proofs could be applied to philosophy. Mendelssohn won the prize of fifty ducats and a gold medal, although the competitors included Immanuel Kant, who subsequently became his friend and admirer.

But the work which, above all others, carried Mendelssohn's name throughout Europe was a curious book called *Phaedon, or the Immortality of the Soul,* which was published in 1767. This was the fruit of Mendelssohn's long hours of reading in Greek, and it was nothing less than an attempt to carry Plato into the eighteenth century. It was to be a popular, not an abstruse, work, so Mendelssohn cast it, as Plato had, in the form of a dialogue; but his Socrates reasoned like a modern German, not an ancient Greek, philosopher.

The first part of the book was purely Mendelssohn's translation, into smooth and graceful German, of Plato's original *Phaedo,* the conversation of Socrates and his friends on the last day of his life. However, as the dialogue proceeded, Mendelssohn began to add his own arguments in favor of immortality, while still maintaining the Socratic form. Some of his ideas were original, some stemmed from such thinkers as Leibniz and Christian von Wolff, but Mendelssohn's presentation gave them new crispness and cogency.

According to Mendelssohn's Socrates, when things perish, they do not pass into nothingness but are dissolved into their elements; consequently the soul, a simple, indivisible essence, cannot be destroyed. Besides, since God has implanted in man the concept of immortality of the soul, can he then be guilty of deception? "If our soul is mortal, then reason is a dream which Jupiter has sent to deceive a set of wretches, and virtue loses all the splendor which makes it godly in our eyes. . . . Then we are sent here like the beasts, to search for food, and die."

For intellectuals and the thoughtful German public, many of whom were looking for rational arguments to bolster their waning faith in immortality and afterlife, Mendelssohn's work was a godsend. Its logical presentation was eagerly seized upon, quoted, and discussed wherever people of culture gathered; and although it was fated, in its turn, to be made obsolete by changing beliefs and newer philosophies, it produced a profound effect upon its generation.

Phaedon became the most widely read book of its time. That it had been written by a Jew added to its allure, almost as if an Australian bushman of today should suddenly produce a masterpiece of philosophic thought. Mendelssohn's work was praised not only for the lucidity of its ideas but for the elegance and grace of its language. It went through three large German editions within two years and was translated into English, French, Dutch, Italian, Danish, Russian, Polish, Hungarian, and Hebrew. Mendelssohn became known as "the German Socrates" and "the modern Plato." The ruler of a nearby principality, the duke of Brunswick, attempted to persuade him to move to his court. The sister of Frederick the Great discoursed with him about death and immortality and hung his portrait on her wall. Two Benedictine friars sought his advice on the future moral and philosophical conduct of their order. The Jewish community of Berlin, as a mark of their esteem, exempted him from payment of all future communal taxes. Goethe and Herder praised him to the skies; Kant wrote him that "a genius such as you will succeed in creating a new epoch in philosophy." Lessing had already called him "a second Spinoza, who would do honor to his nation"; now, however, the comparison was carried back four hundred years beyond the Dutch lensmaker, and he was hailed throughout Europe as the greatest Jew since Maimonides and "the third Moses."* The nightly gathering of intellectuals at his home became more distinguished than ever, with even Frederick's courtiers among them, and he was raised to the status almost of a Berlin institution, to be pointed out to visitors along with the other famous sights of the city.

And yet one honor eluded him. Shortly after *Phaedon* appeared, the Royal Academy of Sciences proposed Mendelssohn's admission to its philosophical division. He would have been its first Jewish member. But Frederick the Great struck his name from the list. Catherine the Great of Russia was also a candidate that year, and Frederick, it seemed, preferred not to give her a Jewish colleague upon her entry.† So Catherine was formally inducted and Mendelssohn excluded, without, however, making her any the more of a philosopher, or him any the less.

---

*The first, of course, being the original Lawgiver.

†Told that the Academy had chosen him but that the king had not confirmed him, Mendelssohn commented: "Better than if the king had chosen me and the Academy not confirmed me."

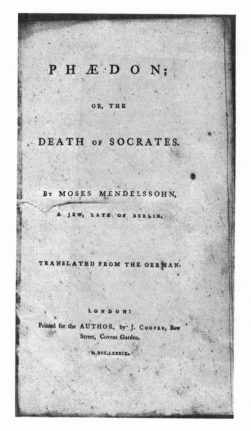

PHÆDON;

OR, THE

DEATH OF SOCRATES.

BY MOSES MENDELSSOHN,

A JEW, LATE OF BERLIN.

TRANSLATED FROM THE GERMAN.

LONDON:

Printed for the AUTHOR, by J. COOPER, Bow
Street, Covent Garden.

M.DCC.LXXXIX.

Moses Mendelssohn's Phaedon
*became the best-selling book
of its day, with many translations from the original German. These are title pages of
English and French editions,
with the Dutch on following
page.*

PHÉDON,
OU
ENTRETIENS
SUR LA SPIRITUALITÉ
ET
L'IMMORTALITÉ DE L'AME.

Par M. MOSÈS MENDELS-SOHN, *Juif à Berlin.*
TRADUIT DE L'ALLEMAND,
Par M. JUNKER, *de l'Académie des Belles-Lettres
de Gottingen.*

Cum in manu jam mortiferum illud teneret poculum, ita locu-
tus est, ut non ad mortem trudi, verùm in cœlum videretur
afcendere. CICERO, *Tufc. Quæft.* lib. 1.

A PARIS,
Chez LE BOUCHER, Libraire, Quai des
Augustins, à la Prudence.

M. D. CC. LXXIII.
Avec Approbation & Privilége du Roi.

PHEDON

OF OVER DE

ONSTERFLYKHEID

D E R

Z I E L E,

IN DRIE TZAMENSPRAAKEN,

D O O R

MOSES MENDELSZOON.

NAAR DEN TWEEDEN VERBETERDEN DRUK,

UIT HET HOOGDUITSCH VERTAALD.

IN 's GRAAVENHAAGE,

By PIETER van CLEEF,

M. DCC. LXIX.

IV *The Great Lavater Controversy*

Mendelssohn's aversion to religious controversy was well known to and respected by his friends, most of whom forbore to involve him in questions of Christianity versus Judaism. A similar reticence marked his writings; with the exception of a short-lived periodical called *The Moral Preacher,* which he edited at the outset of his career, he wrote little publicly on Judaism or on his own religious beliefs. Although the treatment of Jews by the civil authorities, including the restrictions he was subject to personally, rankled him, he preferred not to raise the matter for public discussion, but he did make his feelings known to his friends. To a Benedictine brother, he wrote:

> Everywhere in this so-called tolerant land, I live so isolated through real intolerance, so beset on every side, that, out of love for my own children I lock myself up in a silk factory, as in a cloister. Of an evening I take a walk with my wife and children. "Father," asks one of them innocently, "what are those boys calling us? Why do they throw stones at us? What have we done to them?" "Yes," says another, "they always follow us on the streets and shout 'Jew-boy, Jew-boy!' Is it a disgrace in their eyes to be a Jew? And what does it matter to them?" . . . Ah, I close my eyes, stifle a sigh, and exclaim: "Poor humanity! You have indeed brought things to a sorry pass!"

To Gumpertz, he commented early in his career that while he realized that the common people among Christians regarded Jews as beneath contempt, he was surprised to find that "cultivated

31

people" held the same opinion: "What a humiliation for our oppressed nation!" Still, he saw no reason to step forward as a defender of the faith, preferring to practice his religion and pursue his secular studies alike—in the peace of his household. Nothing was further from his mind than becoming a Jewish activist.

Now, however, into his busy but tranquil life a Christian divine named Johann Caspar Lavater dropped a bombshell. This was the same Lavater who some years back had called on Mendelssohn in his office at the silk factory and painted a rapturous picture of him as "a brilliant soul, with pleasing ideas." Lavater was one of the most notable eccentrics of the late eighteenth century, a poet, theologian, scientist, and mystic, who was the deacon of the Protestant church in Zurich, a city not noted for its hospitality to Jews —in fact, it barred them altogether.

Lavater, twelve years younger than Mendelssohn, had founded a new science that he called physiognomy, which, he said, could detect traits of character and intellect from a study of the facial features. He also was a preacher celebrated for his irresistible eloquence and his magnetic eyes, with a reputation for his ability to convert unbelievers to Christianity. In the famous Moses Mendelssohn, he saw an unprecedented opportunity to practice physiognomy and proselytization at the same time. On his first visit to Berlin, after impetuously rushing to Mendelssohn's business office, he eagerly accepted the philosopher's courteous invitation to join the evening discussion circle at his home. There, in repeated visits, the young deacon attempted to draw Mendelssohn into debate about the divinity of Jesus, the validity of the New Testament miracles, and the comparative merits of Judaism and Christianity, only to be turned gently aside.

Lavater also found Mendelssohn fascinating on purely physiognomic grounds, writing ecstatically in a book on the new "science" of the philosopher's dark complexion, curly black hair, vaulted brow, bright eyes, aquiline nose, small pointed beard, and smiling expression: "I rejoice to see these outlines. My glance descends from the noble curve of the forehead to the prominent bones of the eye. In the depth of this eye a Socratic soul resides. . . . Oh, how all this harmonizes and makes the divine truth of physiognomy sensible and visible." Lavater included in his book a silhouette of Mendelssohn's head and expressed his intention of having a plaster model of it made. However, he decided first to try not for his skull but for his soul.

A short time before, a Geneva professor named Charles Bonnet had written an apologia for revealed religion entitled *Inquiry into the Evidences of Christianity.* Lavater, much taken with the work, translated it from French into German in 1769 and decided to publish it with a dedication to Moses Mendelssohn.

However, it was as barbed a dedication as could be devised, and one which Mendelssohn must have read with horror. For, after saluting Mendelssohn—with what was presumably intended as a compliment—as "an Israelite in whom there is no guile," Lavater went on to invite him to read the book and then either publicly to refute its arguments on behalf of Christianity, or to accept them as binding upon himself and thus accept conversion.

Recalling that Mendelssohn, in a conversation with him, had spoken respectfully of Jesus Christ, Lavater wrote: "I beseech you and conjure you to read this work, I will not say with philosophic impartiality, which I am sure will be the case, but for the purpose of publicly refuting it, in case you should find the main arguments in support of the facts of Christianity untenable; or, should you find them conclusive, to do what policy, love of truth, and probity demand—what Socrates would doubtless have done, had *he* read the work and found it unanswerable."

For several months Mendelssohn debated his course. There never was a question of his converting to Christianity, although such a step could possibly have brought him a university post or acceptance at court and in the salons of the aristocracy. But he was torn between his desire to ignore Lavater's challenge and the need to answer it, on behalf of both himself and other Jews. Many

Christians, Bonnet among them, considered Lavater's demand to be rash and regrettable; but it engendered great excitement among the literary public, and bets on whether Mendelssohn would reply were actually made in several Berlin coffeehouses. Mendelssohn went to the Berlin Consistory, the ecclesiastical court charged with the function of censorship, whose imprimatur was necessary if a reply was to be published. He asked whether the consistory would wish to see his document page by page as it was printed or to wait until it was completed. He was told the court had confidence in his discretion and had no need to see his reply in advance at all.

On December 12, 1769, Mendelssohn made his answer public. His 4,000-word *Letter to Johann Caspar Lavater,* published as a pamphlet by his friend Nicolai and quickly reprinted throughout Europe, must surely rank as one of the most devastating documents in the annals of polemics.

Addressing his adversary courteously as "honored Philanthropist" and writing with the utmost politeness, Mendelssohn began by noting the alternatives given him by Lavater: either to refute Bonnet's pro-Christian arguments or to emulate Socrates—"which, I suppose, means to renounce the religion of my fathers and embrace that which Mr. Bonnet vindicates."

Mendelssohn then recalled how he had attempted, years before, to steer his discussions with Lavater away from religion "to more neutral topics" and also how he had exacted a promise that "no public use should ever be made" of their private talks on Christianity. "I would, of course, rather be mistaken in my recollection than tax you with a breach of promise," he added ironically.

"But let me assure you," Mendelssohn wrote, "that my scruples of engaging in religious controversy have never proceeded from timidity or bashfulness. It was not from the other day that I began searching into my religion. . . .

"I am unable to conceive what should keep me tied to a religion so excessively severe, and so commonly despised, if I were not convinced in my own heart of its truth. Whatever the result of my studies, I would have felt compelled to leave the faith of my fathers had I felt it was untrue. . . . However, inasmuch as my theological investigations have strengthened me in this faith, I was able to live in it with tranquillity, without feeling that I had to justify my convictions before the world.

"I do not deny that I have detected in my religion human additions and base alloy which tarnish its pristine beauty. But where is the friend of truth that can boast of having *his* religion free from similar corruptions? . . . Of the essentials of my religion I am as firmly, as irrefragably convinced as you, Sir, or Mr. Bonnet ever can be of those of yours, and I herewith declare in the presence of the God of Truth, who has created and sustained both you and me, in whose name you have challenged me in your dedication, that I will adhere to my principles so long as my soul remains unchanged. . . .

"I have never entered into a dispute about Judaism even when I have seen it unfairly attacked or held up to scorn. . . . I wanted to answer the world's demeaning opinion of the Jew by righteous living, not by pamphleteering. . . .

"Pursuant to the principles of my religion, I am not to seek to convert anyone who is not born into our faith. . . . Our rabbis are so far from proselytomania that they instruct us to dissuade, by forcible means, every one who comes forth to be converted. We are to lead him to reflect that, by such a step, he is subjecting himself needlessly to a most onerous burden. . . . We are to hold up to him a faithful picture of the misery, tribulation and obloquy in which our nation is now living, to guard him from a rash act which he might ultimately regret. . . . We do not send our missionaries to the two Indies or to Greenland to preach our doctrine to these remote people. . . .

"Suppose there were among my contemporaries a Confucius or a Solon, I could, consistently with my religious principles, love and admire the great man, but I should never entertain the extravagant idea of converting him. Why should I convert a Confucius or a Solon? As he does not belong to the Congregation of Jacob, my religious laws do not apply to him; and on doctrines we should soon come to an understanding. Do I think there is a chance of his being saved? I certainly believe that he who leads mankind on to virtue in this world cannot be damned in the next. . . .

"I am a member of an oppressed people who have to supplicate the shelter and protection of the ascendant nations; and these boons they do not obtain everywhere, indeed nowhere, without more or less of restriction. Rights granted to every other human being, my brethren in the faith willingly forgo, contented with being tolerated and protected; and they account it no small favor when a nation admits them under bearable conditions. Do the laws of your own town of Zurich permit your circumcised friend to visit you there? No. . . . Such considerations have motivated my desire to avoid religious controversies. . . . But when a Lavater solemnly calls upon me, I have no choice but to express my convictions in public, lest too stubborn a silence be misconstrued as disregard or acquiesence.

"I have read with attention your translation of Bonnet's work. Even considered in the abstract, as an apology for the Christian religion, I must own that it does not appear to me to possess the merit that you attach to it. I know Mr. Bonnet, from other works, as an excellent author; but I have read many vindications of the same religion, I will not only say by English writers but by our own German countrymen, which I thought more profound and philosophical than Mr. Bonnet's essay, which you are recommending for my conversion. . . . If you believe, as you say you do, that Socrates himself should have found Mr. Bonnet's arguments unanswerable, it can only mean that one of us is a remarkable instance of the dominion of prejudice and upbringing even over those who go, with an upright heart, in search of truth. . . .

"I have now stated to you the reasons why I so earnestly wish to have no more to do with religious controversy. . . . But if you insist, I shall have to lay aside my scruples and publish my arguments against Mr. Bonnet's work in the form of a *Counter-Inquiry.* I hope you will spare me from this irksome task, and rather give me leave to draw to that state of quietude which is more congenial to my disposition. . . . I should be sorry to be led into the temptation of breaking through those boundaries which I have, after mature deliberation, marked out to myself.

"I am, with most perfect respect,

Yours sincerely,

MOSES MENDELSSOHN."

Lavater was staggered by the reply. He had begun to have qualms about his challenge almost immediately after the dedication was published, and now, as he wrote Mendelssohn on February 14, 1770, there was little he could do except apologize. Acknowledging that he should have sought Mendelssohn's view privately and worded his dedication differently he wrote: "I retract my peremptory challenge, in which I was not sufficiently warranted. And here, before the public, I entreat you to forgive whatever is importunate, whatever is improper in my dedication."

Mendelssohn, heartened not only by the fullness of Lavater's apology but by the widespread sympathy he had received during public discussions of the affair, now began to think that perhaps he had been overly hard on the Swiss deacon. There was no need to crave his pardon, he wrote him: "An overhasty zeal for truth carries forgiveness with it." As for himself, "during the few evening hours of relaxation" that his business permitted him, he was resolved anew to stay out of all controversy: "Nature never intended me for a wrestler, either in a physical or moral sense."

So far as Lavater was concerned, the dispute was over; but others of his faction chose to renew it, some with elaborately phrased arguments, others with scurrilous attacks on the "Jewish bookkeeper," as one author spitefully called Mendelssohn.

Among those joining the fray was Bonnet himself. The professor had regretted Lavater's challenge when it was issued, but he became incensed when Mendelssohn, in his reply, not only denounced the dedication but disparaged the book. Consequently, in a new edition of his work, he issued a refutation of Mendelssohn's "trashy statements." This, naturally, brought forth another answer from Mendelssohn, in which he disputed Bonnet's belief in miracles as evidence of Christianity's truth. *Every* religion, argued Mendelssohn, had its own "signs and miracles to produce, and surely every one has a right to place confidence in those of his own forefathers." He concluded with a plea for both Christians and Jews to live up to the highest precepts of their own religions, quoting the prophet Jeremiah: "And they shall teach no more every man his neighbor, and every man his brother, saying: 'Know the Lord': for they shall all know me, from the least of them unto the greatest of them."

The Lavater controversy and its aftermath left Mendelssohn spiritually and physically exhausted. He suffered from weakness, headaches, and dizziness, and made several trips to a spa at Pyrmont. For several months in 1771, he was told by his physician to cut down as much as he could on his intellectual activity. He continued to go to his office several hours each day, but he abstained from reading and, as far as he could, from thinking. He even avoided serious conversation to the point of eliminating his evening gatherings for a while, and when someone asked him how he passed his time, he replied wryly: "By counting the rooftiles on the houses across the street." Gradually his health returned, and he was able to resume his accustomed activities.

And yet there was a difference. For the Lavater affair had brought about a profound change in the nature of his thought and the direction of his life. Hitherto he had been, although Jewish, a German philosopher and author, writing for a German public. Now Lavater, who had wanted to make him a Christian, had brought to him the realization that, whether he wished it or not, he had become the spokesman and the leader of the Jews of Germany, perhaps of all Europe. Gradually he accepted the idea that there was more for him to accomplish in such a role than there was in remaining one more philosopher in a country that already had too many. As his mind began functioning fully again and his vigor flowed back, he turned not to Plato or Leibniz for his studies, but to the Hebrew Bible.

V *Builder of Bridges*

Nearly a century before Moses Mendelssohn arrived in Berlin, another young Jewish philosopher, Baruch Spinoza, wrote: "The heaviest burden that men can lay upon us is not that they persecute us with their hatred and scorn, but that they thus plant hatred and scorn in our souls."

Seventeenth-century Amsterdam, where Spinoza lived, was far less restrictive against its Jews than eighteenth-century Berlin, but he nevertheless realized the real tragedy of the medieval ghetto for Jew and Gentile alike. The wall that shut off Jewry from all other people not only condemned them to isolation and humiliation; it also served as a barrier preventing any transmission of ideas or understanding. The medieval Jew was no less eager for knowledge or capable of advancement than the ancient or the modern, but cut off from normal pursuits and human contacts, he was forced to turn inwardly to pore over his Law and re-examine it minutely from every conceivable angle, and some inconceivable. It was a way to pass the centuries. Even the educated Christian, for his part, knew the Jew only as an unkempt and squalid ghetto denizen or as a bearded moneychanger who emerged at times to do the dirty work of kings or merchants. The best that the greatest literary genius who ever lived could do for the Jew was to make him a Shylock.

Moses Mendelssohn had written indignantly on several occasions of the physical and social humiliations visited upon his coreligionists, not to mention himself. On a trip to Dresden, he had been forced to pay, as a Jew, an entry fee into the city of twenty groschen, the same amount charged for livestock. The law, he remarked with grim humor, "appraised a German philosopher at the same value as a Polish cow." In this instance, when the authorities discovered Mendelssohn's identity, they remitted the fee; nevertheless, the tax remained on the books. On another occasion he went to Königsberg to hear his friend Kant lecture and, while seated in an anteroom, was jeered at by some students for his hump, pointed beard, and generally undistinguished appearance. "I am only waiting to hear Professor Kant's discourse," he explained patiently.

But such indignities bothered him less than the intellectual gap that separated Jews from Christians, for he foresaw that once this was closed, greater understanding and advancement would follow. Furthermore, he felt, with the knowledge born of his experience of both worlds, that if bridges were to be built, it would be up to the Jews to lay the first stones. Lavater's letter had served to clarify and focus his own religious feelings, and now, as he recovered from the aftereffects of the famous controversy, he prepared, like his Biblical namesake, to lead his people out of a desert, a desert of the mind. "My people have sunk to such a low cultural level," he wrote, "that one despairs of the possibility of effecting a change for the better."

His weapon in this battle was a new translation he undertook of the Bible from Hebrew into German. Luther, of course, had already made the standard German translations of both Old and New Testaments, but they were based on a Latin, rather than a Hebrew text, and in any case would certainly not be accepted by Jewish readers. Until Mendelssohn, no Jew read the Bible in German—and very few understandingly in Hebrew. Biblical instruction was largely in the hands of Polish rabbis and schoolmasters, who so encrusted the text with their own emendations that they made it all but unintelligible.

Mendelssohn said afterward that he intended his Bible translation primarily for the instruction of his own children; however, there is no doubt that he also designed it for the common reader everywhere among his own people; and eventually he concluded that "our rabbis need it even worse." For his translation was by no means accepted unreservedly by Jews; among Polish Talmudists, there was indignation that the sacred text should be rendered into a profane language, and even some German rabbis denounced it. Steps were taken to repress it by Jewish authorities in Prague, Altona, and Posen. The rabbi of the town of Fürth issued an edict excommunicating anyone found reading "the German Pentateuch of Moses Dessau"—the name by which Mendelssohn continued to be known among many of his fellow Jews. The great Talmudist Moses Sofer, chief rabbi of Pressburg, in his last will and testament exhorted his followers to shun not only Mendelssohn's Bible translation but his other writings as well.

So Mendelssohn, once more against his will, was drawn into a controversy with "those pugnacious proclaimers of peace," as he called the traditionalist rabbis who attacked him. But such voices this time were in a minority. For German Jews, and for some Russian and Polish Jews as well, Mendelssohn's Bible, published in 1779, did what John Wycliffe's had accomplished for Englishmen in 1382. And among Christians, the work was greeted almost as rapturously as *Phaedon* had been. The new translation found a public in England, France, and Holland; among the subscribers to the first edition was the king of Denmark.

Mendelssohn did not translate the complete Old Testament, nor did he work without assistance. Joining him in the project were four young scholars, Solomon Dubno, Hartwig Wessely, Aaron Jaroslav, and Herz Homberg. The original Hebrew and the German translation were printed side by side, the latter in Hebrew lettering, to make it easier for Jews to read. Each book was accompanied by a commentary on its historical, religious, and moral significance; and in preparing this, Mendelssohn consulted Christian as well as Hebraic sources, one of the factors that drew upon him the wrath of the Talmudists. In his preface to the Book of Ecclesiastes he answered them: "Because our wise men have counseled us to receive truth from whoever speaks it, I have also searched in the works of the commentators who are not of the sons of Israel; and wherever I found in their mouths a word of truth, I offered it to the Lord, and it became holy."

The task of translation took a decade, and encompassed the Pentateuch (the Five Books of Moses, which to Jews are the core of the Bible and the source of all Law), Ecclesiastes, the Psalms, and the Song of Solomon, which was not found until after Mendelssohn's death, among his papers. He took especial pleasure in working on the Psalms, which he rendered into German in a metrical translation. Wrote Mendelssohn's early English biographer, M. Samuel, admiringly: "Every chord touched by the royal Harper caused a responsive one to vibrate in the bosom of his translator." Mendelssohn's working method was simple, if leisurely; for ten years he carried a copy of the Hebrew Book of Psalms wherever he went, with blank sheets inserted between the pages, so that he could work on them whenever he had time. Rather than translating the Psalms in order, he selected whichever happened to suit his state of mind at a particular moment. In his preface to the published edition, he recommended that they be read in the same way.

Mendelssohn's translation of the Pentateuch almost single-handedly brought about the Jewish Enlightenment in Germany. For many, it made German rather than Yiddish their everyday language. Jewish youth turned to it eagerly, often as a result of their elders' efforts at suppression. It did more than open the Bible's meaning to those who wished to find it; it established the German language itself as a means of communication and literary expression for an entire generation that was ready to dismantle the ghetto's walls. Two centuries of distinguished writing by German Jews in philosophy, politics, drama, and fiction begin with Moses Mendelssohn's Pentateuch.

Along with his work toward religious and cultural enlightenment of the Jews went a new activism on Mendelssohn's part toward helping them win the civil and human rights so long withheld from them. Prior to the exchange with Lavater, he had held himself apart from any struggle against repression; he was a pacifist by nature and a fatalist by inclination. When his Christian friend Thomas Abbt, to whom he had dedicated his *Phaedon,* asked him, in 1764, what was to become of the Jews, he had answered coolly in language that might almost have come from a courtier of Frederick the Great: "You ask me concerning the destination of my countrymen. What countrymen? Those of Dessau or those of Jerusalem? Make yourself clearer and I shall say with Molière's Pancratius: *'Je m'en lave les mains. Je n'en sais rien. Il en sera ce qu'il pourra. Selon les aventures. . . .'* * With the composure of a German metaphysician I wrap myself in my threadbare cloak and I say like Pangloss: 'This is the best of all possible worlds.' "

But ten years later, Mendelssohn had accepted the role of being a Jewish ambassador-at-large to the Christian world. Time and again his fellow Jews called upon "Reb Moshe" to intervene on their behalf with the civil authorities. Many of them had an exaggerated notion of his standing in official circles, imagining him hobnobbing with courtiers and swapping philosophic observations in French with the great Frederick himself. And indeed, he did have connections of a sort, if less extensive than they supposed; and he now began to make use of them in an effort to correct glaring wrongs and combat persistent injustices.

One of his first opportunities came in 1775, when the only two towns in Switzerland that permitted permanent Jewish residents, Endingen and Lengnau, suddenly forbade them to marry. Remembering Mendelssohn's exchange with Zurich's Deacon

•

*"I wash my hands of it. I know nothing about it. He'll become what he can. However it works out. . . ."

Lavater, the Jews of the two towns wrote to Mendelssohn bidding him ask his old antagonist to intervene on their behalf. Mendelssohn had had little to do with Lavater in the six years that had passed since their controversy, and he may have found it irksome to ask a favor of him. Nevertheless, he did so, and the deacon responded nobly. He interceded with the authorities, and the regulation was rescinded.

Five years later, the entire Jewish population of Dresden, in a time of great economic stress, was ordered to leave the city unless they paid all outstanding taxes instantly. Once again, an appeal was made to Mendelssohn, who wrote to a friend at the court of the prince-elector: "The last post has just brought news that hundreds of my co-religionists are to be driven out of Dresden. . . . Where are these wretches to go with their innocent wives and children? Where are they to find shelter and protection if the country in which they have lost their means expels them? Expulsion is the hardest punishment for a Jew, harder than living in exile, almost equivalent to extermination from God's earth. . . . And human beings are to suffer this misfortune though they are not guilty of any crime, merely because they hold different convictions and have been impoverished by misfortune. . . ." This time, too, Mendelssohn's intervention had its effect, and the prince-elector canceled the order.

Mendelssohn's support was not given to Jewish causes automatically. When the Orthodox residents of the Mecklenburg-Schwerin region were ordered by the authorities to leave the bodies of their dead unburied three days to avoid the danger of premature burial, rather than interring them immediately, as was their custom, they turned to Mendelssohn, who promptly told them he regarded the regulation as quite sensible and urged them to build a mortuary in the cemetery.

Mendelssohn also was skeptical of plans, heard even then, for the establishment of a Jewish state in Palestine; he thought that the Jews of his time were not ready for it. "The greatest difficulty which stands in the way of the project," he wrote to a friend, "arises out of the character of my nation, which is not sufficiently prepared to undertake anything great. The oppression under which we have been living for so many centuries has robbed our spirit of all vigor. This is not our fault. Still, we cannot deny that the natural desire for liberty has with us lost its energy. It has changed into a monkish virtue which finds expression in prayer and suffering, but not in action. Considering how dispersed this nation is I cannot even hope for the spirit of union without which the most carefully studied project must fail."

Nevertheless, the idea of "an independent Jewish kingdom" in the Holy Land exercised a pull on him; he mused that it would call "for enormous sums of money," which the Jews lacked. In any case, he remarked with a certain prescience, it would become feasible only "at a time when the greatest European powers are involved in a general war in which each has to look after itself."

In 1778, Frederick the Great asked to see the Jewish code of civil laws in a language he could understand; and at the request of the chief rabbi of Berlin, Hirschel Lewin, Mendelssohn compiled a German digest of the *Hoshen hamishpat* ("Breastplate of Justice") dealing with Jewish laws of inheritance, property, and the like. The king had it published under the title *Ritual Laws of the Jews,* and it retained its authority in the Jewish communities of Berlin and elsewhere for years. Mendelssohn was also instrumental in persuading Frederick to abolish the government position of synagogue inspector, a petty official who kept Jewish worshippers under surveillance during religious services in order to detect any signs of political subversion or hostility to Christianity. The job was not a very distinguished one and usually went to a court hanger-on in need of an emolument. The synagogue inspectors were, of course, non-Jews and rarely knew enough Hebrew to understand the services, leaving them an easy prey for religious fanatics or meddlers.

An inspector in Königsberg filed a report with the Berlin authorities that one of the Sabbath prayers, the Alenu, contained a cabbalistic attack on Jesus Christ. The Alenu, which contains references to idolaters, had long incurred the suspicions of Christian fanatics; and the Königsberg inspector alleged that he had actually seen Jewish worshippers spitting as they pronounced the blasphemous words: "Glorify the Creator, who has not made us like the families of earth. He has not set our portion with theirs, nor our lot with the multitude, for they prostrate themselves before vanity and folly, and pray to a God who cannot help them."

Jewish leaders in Berlin, alarmed when word of the inspector's report leaked out, asked Mendelssohn to draw up a paper on the history and origins of the Alenu prayer. Mendelssohn quickly complied, citing references to show that Alenu, far from being an attack on Christianity, actually dated back to the Second Temple in the Roman era and referred to the pagan idolatry of those ancient times. Frederick promptly abolished the synagogue inspector sinecure, and Jews were relieved from the humiliation of conducting their services under official watch.

Mendelssohn's various intercessions did more than remedy a number of specific instances of intolerance; they led to a body of literature that raised the whole question of religious tolerance throughout Europe and set forth the Jewish case for equality with a directness with which it had never been stated before. The sequence of events started in 1780 when the Jews of Alsace (which at that time belonged to France, although many Germans lived there) decided to address themselves to King Louis XVI for an amelioration of their circumstances. The 15,000 or 20,000 Jews of the province lived in particularly inhuman conditions: they were confined rigorously in ghettos; they paid tribute money to king, bishop, and local ruler; they were forbidden to engage in handicrafts or trade; they were taxed on leaving the province and re-entering it; in Strasbourg, the capital, they were forbidden to remain overnight—the list was almost endless.

Led by a distinguished Alsatian Jew named Cerf Berr, the community wrote to Mendelssohn to ask his help in formulating their petition to the French king. Mendelssohn wanted to help, but he hesitated. At the age of fifty he was weary; his health, never robust, was deteriorating; visits to the spa at Pyrmont had failed to restore his energy. Besides, there were other voices now being raised in the same cause, younger, fresher, and not all of them Jewish. It was to one of these young Christian friends, a twenty-nine-year-old historian named Christian William Dohm, that he now delegated the task of drawing up a letter to Louis XVI on the subject of the Alsatian Jews. Dohm, a regular caller at the Mendelssohn house, had been given the title of councillor and appointed keeper of the royal archives by Frederick the Great. Now, in response to Mendelssohn's request, and probably in consultation with him, he produced a work entitled *Upon the Civil Amelioration of the Jews,* demanding equal rights for the oppressed minority not only in Alsace but everywhere.

So far as Alsace was concerned, Dohm's document brought only minimal improvement; it led to the abolition of the *impôt du pied forchu,* ("cloven-foot tax") levied on animals and Jews entering a town. However, the raising of a Christian voice on behalf of the Jews was a startling event and was avidly debated throughout the Continent; and although it left Louis XVI and Frederick the Great largely unmoved, it helped induce their Austrian counterpart, Joseph II, to issue a series of Edicts of Toleration permitting Jews to learn the arts and sciences, enter universities, cease paying "body taxes," and in general attain designation as "fellow men"—a milestone in their struggle for equality. Reading Dohm's pamphlet and surveying its impact, Mendelssohn could exclaim: "Blessed be Almighty God who has allowed me, at the end of my days, to see the happy time when the rights of humanity begin to be realized in their true extent."

However, there were portions in *Upon the Civil Amelioration of the Jews* that troubled Mendelssohn. One was Dohm's depiction of the Jews of the day as a generally coarse and shiftless lot who could be saved only by outside intervention. Mendelssohn felt that even the lowest level of Jews were no worse in character than Christians of similar class and upbringing. Noting that Jews had for centuries been forbidden from entering the arts and the sciences, he commented ironically: "They tie our hands, and blame us for not using them."

Mendelssohn was even more dubious about a suggestion made by Dohm that Judaism, like Christianity, be sanctioned by the government as an official religion, with the authority to expel or excommunicate dissenters or noncomformists. Mendelssohn strongly advocated separation of church and state, and he totally opposed the concept of excommunication, arguing that no man, including a rabbi or an elder of the synagogue, should have the power to punish another for his religious or philosophical beliefs: "What sensible person would pretend to reform his neighbor's thoughts, or to chasten his heart by coercion?"

These ideas Mendelssohn set down in a preface to a book published by another of his young associates, the physician Marcus Herz—a translation from the French of *Vindication of the Jews* by Menasseh ben Israel, a Dutch Jew who, on a visit to London in 1655, had sought to persuade Oliver Cromwell to readmit Jews to England. The text of Menasseh's original plea was powerful enough, but Mendelssohn's eloquent preface strengthened the argument further.

By now articles and pamphlets about the state of the Jews were coming out in profusion, with the entire question of religious liberty being avidly debated in private salons and the public prints. In the midst of the acrimonious controversy, Mendelssohn decided to set forth once and for all, for the benefit of his friends and enemies alike, his own philosophical ideas about Judaism. He did so in a little book called *Jerusalem,* in which he attempted to reconcile rationalism and religion, Europe and Sinai. To him, Mendelssohn wrote, Judaism represented not revealed religion but revealed law. Unlike Christianity, it had no dogma essential to salvation; it judged men by their actions rather than their beliefs; it did not say "You shall believe," but "You shall do." Jews, he held, should govern themselves by three laws: the laws of reason should guide their thoughts; those of the state, their political and social acts; and those of the Bible, their moral and religious lives.

In *Jerusalem,* Mendelssohn urged his fellow Jews to continue to observe their ancient rituals and ceremonies, since "what divine law has ordained cannot be repealed by reason, which is equally divine. . . . Adapt yourselves to the customs and constitution of the country in which you have been placed, but hold fast also to the religion of your fathers. Bear both burdens as best you can. . . . If we render unto Caesar what is Caesar's, let us also render unto God what is God's."

Jerusalem brought Mendelssohn additional acclaim, and he took particular satisfaction in a letter from Kant that said: "I consider this book to be the herald of a great reform, which will affect not only your people, but also others. You have succeeded in combining your religion with such a degree of freedom as was never imagined possible, and of which no other faith can boast. You have, at the same time, so thoroughly and clearly demonstrated the necessity of unlimited liberty of conscience in every religion, that ultimately our Church will also be led to reflect how to remove from its midst everything that disturbs and oppresses conscience, which will finally unite all men in their view of the essential points of religion."

Most Jews also praised and welcomed *Jerusalem,* the Orthodox because of its emphasis on religious ritual, the secularists because of its advocacy of free thought. Moses Mendelssohn was one of the rare souls who found it possible to feel simultaneously the exhilaration of both.

Moses Mendelssohn, who left the Dessau ghetto at the age of fourteen to become famous as a philosopher, author, and emancipator of the Jews.

Right, Lavater's silhouette of Moses Mendelssohn.

Below, Lavater attempts to convert Mendelssohn while Lessing waits at chess table and Fromet Mendelssohn brings in raisins and almonds. Picture is by Moritz Oppenheim, noted for Jewish family paintings.

Leah and Abraham Men-
delssohn, parents of Felix.
Drawings are by Wilhelm
Hensel, who married Felix's
sister Fanny after using his
artistic talents to overcome
Leah's opposition to the
match.

Frederick von Schlegel and Dorothea Mendelssohn, whose seven-year-long affair and subsequent marriage scandalized their contemporaries. Dorothea ran a salon, wrote a novel, and in her old age introduced her nephew Felix Mendelssohn to his bride. Both portraits are by Dorothea's artist-son, Johannes Veit.

Fanny (right) and Rebecca Mendelssohn, sisters of Felix, as drawn by Wilhelm Hensel.

Illustration from a Victorian biography depicts Felix (full name Jacob Ludwig Felix) as a boy directing a home musicale while sister Fanny sits by.

A cluster of Berlin musicians. Top row, Karl Friedrich Rungenhagen, Gasparo Spontini, Felix Mendelssohn. Bottom row, Friedrich Wollanck, Bernhard Klein (two minor composers of the day) and Carl Friedrich Zelter.

Felix Mendelssohn as an English dandy. Watercolor by J. W. Childe was made during the composer's first visit to London at the age of twenty.

Felix's wife Cecile, painted by Edward Magnus. She was eighteen at her marriage, and said to be one of the most beautiful girls in Frankfurt.

Fingal's Cave in the Hebrides Islands, from a nineteenth-century etching. For the music it inspired Felix to write on the spot, see page 141.

VI Moses the Wise

As Mendelssohn entered his fifties, there were other matters besides philosophy and the silk business to occupy his mind. For he had become the head of a large household and was neither the first nor the last philosopher to discover that family cares, the realities of illness and death, the burdens of raising children and educating them, all impinge upon the contemplative life.

Fromet Mendelssohn shared these problems and bore the additional burdens that stemmed from being the wife of a philosopher. She herself made no pretense to being an intellectual. When she was a girl in Hamburg, she studied French, and thinking her studies would please Mendelssohn, she told him proudly of her progress in the language while he was courting her. But to him, one scholar in the family was enough, and he wrote back to her: "You write about your diligence in studying French. Dearest Fromet! Please do not overdo this diligence, and protect your health. It is of much too great importance to me. I think I know your capabilities. You do not have to damage your body in order to improve your soul." He kept counseling her to read only by natural light in the summertime and warned her against the perils of excessive study: "Moderate learning becomes a lady, but not scholarship. A girl who has read her eyes red deserves to be laughed at."

So Fromet learned to be philosophical in other ways, mostly by putting up with the nightly procession of dignitaries and scholars who descended on her home to partake of her husband's conversation and her refreshments. Fromet seldom was a direct participant in the philosophical and theological discussions that went on into the night, but she refueled them discreetly with her tea and cakes, raisins and almonds. The visitors became gratefully aware of the unobtrusive blonde woman who saw to the table and the other minor amenities of an evening at the Mendelssohns. Her husband went through life with an open mind; she, with an open house; to maintain either requires strength of character.

It also was Fromet who saw to the daily religious ritual of the household. One writer who attended a Friday night gathering at the Mendelssohns reported that the guests suddenly missed seeing Mendelssohn and his wife in the room. Then, through an open door, the visitors saw in an adjoining chamber the gleam of Sabbath candles, with Fromet pronouncing the blessing over them and Mendelssohn standing beside her.

By 1783, the year *Jerusalem* was published, the Mendelssohns had six children, ranging in age from nineteen to two: Dorothea, Joseph, Abraham, Henrietta, Recha, and Nathan. Appraising them with a fine show of philosophic impartiality, Moses wrote a friend that all seemed to fit an old Jewish proverb: "Not short, not tall, not wise, not foolish."

Moses was content to let Fromet and the two servants he kept in the household see to the children's daily upbringing, but the direction of their education he reserved for himself. This, too, added to the hubbub of the house, for by now he had gathered a group of young disciples such as Solomon Dubno, Herz Homberg, and Solomon Maimon around him to assist in his Biblical translations and researches; and to them he also turned over the task of instructing his children in religion, philosophy, literature, and mathematics.

The two oldest children, Dorothea and Joseph, also received a special course of instruction directly from their famous father. Every morning he spent an hour or more with them discussing philosophy and religion. The hours between rising and going to his office he always regarded as the most precious of the day, since they offered virtually the only solitude he had. Now, in his waning years, he decided to devote them to educating those of his children who were old enough to understand him.

We do not know how the young people regarded these morning sessions; even a famous father can be a burden when he delivers homilies, particularly at daybreak. Yet they at least had some company, for Joseph was permitted to invite two of his friends, the Humboldt brothers—Alexander, sixteen, an explorer and naturalist in the making, and William, eighteen, later to become a noted philologist and diplomat. Both were young Christians who had become interested in Jewish matters to the point of learning Hebrew, and they welcomed their morning visits to the philosopher. Mendelssohn later published his family lectures in a little volume of religious reflections called *Morning Hours.*

The presence of Dorothea at the daily sessions is interesting, for it indicates that whatever doubts Mendelssohn may have had about the usefulness of academic learning to a woman, he at least did not exclude his daughters from his educational system. It cannot be said, however, that he held very advanced views upon the subject of women's emancipation in general, especially when it came to the right of selecting their own husbands. In accordance with the traditional ghetto view, he believed that the best matches were those arranged by parents.

He could point, if he wished, to the example of one of Dorothea's best friends, a beautiful girl named Henrietta de Lemos. When Henrietta reached the age of fifteen, her father, the foremost Jewish physician in Berlin, asked her whether she would rather marry a doctor or a rabbi. When she replied, possibly out of respect to her father, that she preferred a doctor, she was promptly married off to Dr. Marcus Herz, a distinguished practitioner and scientist (Moses Mendelssohn was among his patients), but a man seventeen years her senior, and whom she had scarcely ever met.

Dorothea was treated equally unceremoniously; at the age of nineteen, she was betrothed to Simon Veit, a young banker. She accepted her parents' choice dutifully but unenthusiastically, and they were married in April, 1783. Veit was invited forthwith to attend his father-in-law's Morning Hours lectures.

The same year saw the first stage production in Berlin of Lessing's play *Nathan the Wise,* whose central figure, a philosophical Jewish merchant living in Jerusalem at the time of the Crusades, was regarded universally as a portrayal of Moses Mendelssohn.

Mendelssohn and Lessing had drifted apart over the years, although they retained the warmest affection for each other and continued to correspond. While Mendelssohn stayed put in Berlin, surrounded by his growing family, Lessing had become a wanderer, producing books that were to lay the foundations of his fame, but encountering great difficulty in making ends meet. He married late in life, only to watch his wife die in childbirth; finally, he achieved a measure of security by accepting a post as librarian to the crown prince of Brunswick.

Lessing spent his life trying to plant the seeds of tolerance, enlightenment and free thought in a generally unfertile soil. In his *Wolfenbüttel Fragments* he ventured to offer an historical rather than a supernatural account of Jesus, and denied the miracles of the Bible, especially the Resurrection. He pleaded for "a religion of reason" rather than faith; in fact, he was a Christian counterpart of Moses Mendelssohn, attacking from the opposite side the wall of ignorance that divided Christians and Jews. It was no wonder that he was persecuted by proponents of orthodoxy and regarded with suspicion by the established order, and that his *Fragments* were confiscated by the government.

In 1779, he wrote *Nathan the Wise,* his dramatic masterpiece and the noblest plea for tolerance ever written in the German language. Lessing himself realized its significance, writing to Elise Reimarus, the daughter of a philosopher friend: "I am curious whether they [that is, the governmental authorities] will let me preach without interference from my old pulpit—the theater."

It was not until two years after Lessing's death that *Nathan the Wise* was produced in Berlin, and it renewed all the old quarrels about whether a noble Jew could be validly represented on the stage. In fact, the quarrel was broadened by the presence in the play of a noble Moslem, in the personage of the Sultan Saladin. Only the Christians were depicted by Lessing as mean-spirited and bigoted, so much so that he felt it necessary to explain in his preface: "If it should be said. . . . that it is inconceivable that such characters should have lived among Jews and Mussulmen, I will have it known that the Jews and Mussulmen were the only learned men at that time. . . ."

Although *Nathan the Wise* takes place in twelfth-century Palestine rather than eighteenth-century Germany, the parallels are clear. Like Moses Mendelssohn, Nathan is a merchant and a sage; again like him, he manages to maintain his religion, dignity, and honor in a hostile environment.

In the famous exchange in which the Lay Brother, realizing Nathan's worth, cries out to him, "By God, you are a Christian! There never was a better Christian than you!" and Nathan replies, "That which makes me in your eyes a Christian makes you a Jew in mine," there is an echo of the feeling Moses Mendelssohn once expressed to a traveling Christian missionary who sought out his views on religion: "Love man and you please God, whether you are Christian, Jew or heathen; for the name does not matter. On this I build my religion."

Mendelssohn himself was profoundly impressed with Lessing's play, thought it his finest work, and predicted, quite accurately, that posterity would appreciate its importance better than his contemporaries. If he knew that he himself had been Lessing's model, he gave no sign of it; but he reported with paternal pride in a letter to a friend that his youngest son, the four-year-old Nathan, had a habit of strutting around the house calling himself "Nathan the Wise."

Nathan the Wise was Lessing's swan song; he was just fifty years old when it was printed in 1779, but he was ill and exhausted, and the attacks and vituperation that followed its publication further distressed him. Lessing's last letter to Mendelssohn, written only a few months before his death on February 15, 1781, conveyed all the weariness felt by both of these old comrades in arms, their strength spent and their ends approaching. The occasion for Lessing's letter was to introduce to Mendelssohn a Jew named Alexander Davison, who had undergone persecution by both Christians and Jews.

"All he wants from you," Lessing wrote,

> is that you should show him the shortest and safest road to some European country where there are neither Christians nor Jews. I hate to lose him, but as soon as he has safely arrived there I shall be the first to follow him. I am still chewing and enjoying the letter you sent me. . . . Dear friend, I need such letters from time to time if I am not to become altogether morose. You know that I am not a man who is hungering for praise. But the coldness with which the world is wont to treat certain persons who do not seem to be able to do anything right is, if not fatal, at least paralyzing. That you are not pleased with everything I have written for some time past does not surprise me in the least. None of it could have pleased you, for it was not written for you. At most a page here and there could have misled you by a memory of our better days. I, too, was a healthy young tree, and now I am a gnarled and rotten trunk. Ah, dear friend, the play is finished. Yet I should like to talk to you once more.

Lessing died before Mendelssohn could reply. And the cryptic allusions in his letter to a divergence of view between them soon had their climax in one more controversy, the last of Mendelssohn's life. In his last days, Lessing had told a philosopher named Frederick Jacobi that he had begun to share the pantheistic views of God expressed a century before by Spinoza. He had never told Mendelssohn of this, he confessed to Jacobi, because he knew it would hurt him. Mendelssohn deeply admired Spinoza, but he himself was no pantheist and could not believe that Lessing had become one.

So, in what he regarded as a last service to his old companion, he wrote a pamphlet entitled *To the Friends of Lessing,* in which he attempted to answer Jacobi's allegations—in fact, he refuted them so thoroughly that Kant was led to remark: "It is Mendelssohn's fault that Jacobi thinks he is a philosopher." As for Spinoza himself, Mendelssohn wrote that his greatness could be measured on a personal rather than a philosophical scale: "Supposing he was a Spinozist, what have speculative doctrines got to do with the man himself? Who would not be glad to have Spinoza for a friend however much of a Spinozist he may have been?"

To the Friends of Lessing was ready for the printer on December 31, 1785. But it was Saturday, the Jewish Sabbath, so Mendelssohn arranged to deliver it after sundown. In the morning he went to the synagogue, and at nightfall he carried his manuscript to Voss, his publisher. It was a bleak and bitter day, and when he returned home he complained of chest pains and went to bed, thinking he had caught cold. On January 2, Dr. Herz was sent for, saw no cause for alarm, and prescribed rest.

Two days later, Mendelssohn's sixteen-year-old son Joseph hurried to the doctor at 7 A.M. to report that his father had taken a turn for the worse. Herz found him stretched out on the sofa in poor condition, with the family gathered anxiously about. Two busts, one of Socrates, the other of Lessing, stood nearby.

Herz had hardly begun his examination, when Mendelssohn suddenly gasped for breath and fell back dead. "He lay," wrote Herz afterward, "without motion, struggle, convulsion, or any warning of death, as if an angel had kissed his life away. The reason of his death, was that natural but not very ordinary one, an apoplexy, the result of weakness. The lamp went out for lack of oil, and no one but a man of his wisdom, self-control, moderation, and inward peacefulness could, with such a constitution as his, have kept the flame alight for fifty-seven years."

Mendelssohn's children and even grandchildren inherited from him this tendency to sudden and relatively painless deaths; it was not the least of the legacies he left them.

On receiving the news of Mendelssohn's death, the Jews of Berlin shut their shops and ceased all work, a sign of mourning usually reserved only for the death of a chief rabbi. An immense cortege accompanied his wooden coffin to the Jewish cemetery, where a simple stone was erected with the words in Hebrew: "Here rests Rabbi Moses of Dessau." Tributes came from non-Jewish thinkers, writers, and statesmen throughout Europe. There was talk of erecting a statue of Mendelssohn in Berlin's Opera Square, near that of Leibniz; but nothing came of it, which may have been just as well, since the Nazis would have torn it down 150 years later, just as they tore down that of his grandson Felix in Leipzig. At the Jewish Free School of Berlin, which had been founded at his suggestion in 1781, a marble bust was placed at the entranceway with the inscription:

> Wise as Socrates,
> True to the faith of his fathers,
> Teaching, like him, immortality
> and
> Becoming, like him, immortal.

The Jewish Free School was one of the many influences through which Moses Mendelssohn's spirit touched succeeding generations. He had insisted that it provide not only religious but secular instruction to Jewish youth, and it became the first of many such institutions that were gradually established wherever there were Jews, reaching their maximum in numbers and prestige in our own time.

A group of Mendelssohn's disciples, led by Hartwig Wessely, poet and translator, began to publish a periodical called *Ha-Me'assef* ("The Gleaner"), the first great Hebrew magazine, devoted to furthering the assimilation by Jews of western cultural values.

Only ten issues appeared, but it became the prototype for hundreds of others published down to the present day. Followers of Mendelssohn were also largely responsible for the spreading through Poland and Russia of the movement known as Haskalah, Hebrew for "enlightenment," which strove to bring the Jews of those backward lands closer to the modern world.

But the swiftest vindication of Mendelssohn's ideals came not in the east but in the west. The age of absolute monarchy was drawing to a close; Frederick the Great died in 1786, the same year as Mendelssohn. But it was in France, where the Revolution of 1789 was already seething beneath the surface, that his concept of religious tolerance and civil equality found its widest response. A few months after Mendelssohn's death, the liberal French nobleman Mirabeau visited Berlin; he had read *Nathan the Wise* and keenly regretted having missed meeting the sage about whom it was written. Mirabeau visited Mendelssohn's family; he also met a number of his followers and set out to study Mendelssohn's writings and Dohm's *Civil Amelioration.*

In 1787, Mirabeau published a treatise called *Upon Moses Mendelssohn and the Political Reform of the Jews,* in which he urged that the Jews, "so highly gifted as a nation," be freed of restrictions so as to permit their "powers to develop." Another French admirer of Mendelssohn, Abbé Gregoire, followed with a pamphlet called *Proposals in Favor of the Jews,* and on September 27, 1791, the French National Assembly formally adopted a declaration of full equality for the Jews. When the Revolutionary, and later the Napoleonic, armies marched across Europe, they carried the ideal of religious freedom with them; and in many German cities, the ghetto gates were physically dismantled, although some were restored later when the old regimes came back into power.

Perhaps Mendelssohn's influence has come down to the present day most strongly of all in a form he never intended and could hardly have envisaged—through the Reform Judaism movement. Mendelssohn himself remained an Orthodox Jew to his dying day;

for all his intellectual and philosophical probings, he practiced his religion as he found it and sought to make no changes in ritual. "The benefit arising from the many inexplicable laws of God is in their practice, and not in the understanding of their motives," he wrote in his commentary on the Book of Exodus.

Nevertheless, after his death, some of Mendelssohn's disciples, notably a young Berliner named David Friedlander, began campaigning for drastic alterations in Jewish ritual, asserting that both the rule of reason and the demands of modernity made such changes essential. Friedlander, who had, under Mendelssohn's guidance, organized the Jewish Free School, translated the Hebrew Prayer Book into German and revised the synagogue ritual, believing he was following in his master's footsteps. Through Friedlander and others who came after, a German Reform Judaism movement began, that gradually spread to other countries, including the United States. Justifiably or not, Moses Mendelssohn has been looked upon by many as its spiritual ancestor.

At that, he might have more willingly accepted the Reform movement than the complete turn away from Judaism made by many German Jews of the next generation who suddenly found themselves freed of their ancient restrictions and isolation. For they took what seemed to them the next logical step in their newly found emancipation—they underwent conversion to Christianity. Among them, Moses Mendelssohn would surely have been surprised to find his own children.

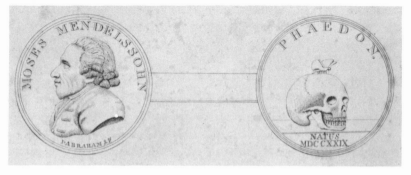

Commemorative medal struck in honor of Moses Mendelssohn's Phaedon. *Skull with butterfly over it symbolizes idea of immortality.*

Part II

ABRAHAM

Formerly I was known as the son of my father;
now I am known as the father of my son.
—ABRAHAM MENDELSSOHN
in the *Thee- und Schneezeitung*

VII *The Midianite Tent*

In 1783, three years before Moses Mendelssohn's death, the artist Daniel Chodowiecki wrote to a friend at court: "The Jews of Berlin are no longer concerned with any kind of ritual; they buy and sell on Saturdays, eat all the forbidden foods, keep no fast days. Only the lower classes are still Orthodox."

Mendelssohn had urged upon his fellow Jews a formula of believing according to reason but behaving according to the Law; but now, with the ghetto's attitudes disappearing along with its walls, many Jews opened their minds to the new ideas of religion, philosophy, and politics that were reshaping the world around them. The heady winds of emancipation blew through them. Some, regarding the term "Jew" as one of opprobrium, preferred to call themselves "Hebrews" and "Israelites," or even adopted such designations as "Deists," "Mosaists," "members of the Mosaic faith," or "Germans of the Jewish persuasion." Others chose to accept outright conversion. Between 1802 and 1810, one-tenth of all Berlin Jews underwent baptism, and among the wealthier and better-educated classes, the proportion was far higher. Conversion was encouraged by government and church officials; the Prussian ruler, Frederick William III, made acceptance of Christianity a condition for the granting of a government position or pension to a Jew.

Even more important, perhaps, was the social and intellectual acceptance which conversion brought. Although Moses Mendelssohn had succeeded in implanting, among both Christians and

Jews, the idea of equal rights for members of all religions, he had by no means eradicated all the inequalities that existed and in many cases had only made them assume more subtle forms. The young Heinrich Heine, struggling for recognition as a poet and critic against the disability of having been born Jewish, saw conversion as "the admission ticket to European culture"; and there were many, like him, ready to pay the price.

One of the first was Dorothea Mendelssohn. The philosopher's oldest child, she had from her earliest years displayed an independent spirit, dropping her original name of Brendel for the more elegant and romantic-sounding Dorothea. Ungainly and mannish-looking, she pursued eagerly the arts of reading and conversation, so that few girls in Berlin knew as much as she about the latest developments in literature and the theater. She was, in the words of one observer, "cheerful and strong, noble and mild, as passionate as a man, tender as a woman."

Dorothea's marriage to Veit turned out to be a disaster. They had four children, of whom two, Johannes and Philipp, survived, both becoming well-known painters. But Veit himself, although eminently respectable and solicitous of his wife, was uneducated, unprepossessing, and totally devoted to business. Dorothea regarded him as a bore.

To find the intellectual stimulation she needed, she took to holding regular soirees at home to which she invited close friends and members of her literary circle. Prominent among these were two other Jewish girls, Henrietta Herz and Rachel Levin, who soon established salons of their own. Thus it might be possible for a seeker after good conversation and stimulating women—then as now, they often went together—to visit a different salon each night and find the same people, a mingling of brilliant Jews enjoying their sense of "emancipation" and liberal-minded Christians, mostly young, out for a sociable and intellectual evening. Many aristocrats regularly attended the young Jewesses' soirees, for evenings at court tended to be stiff and formal by comparison. Besides, at Dorothea's or Henrietta's or Rachel's one might meet interesting people like actors or singers, who seldom were received at court by reason of their questionable professions.

Of the three girls, Henrietta was the most beautiful; Rachel, the most intellectual; Dorothea, the most romantic. Henrietta Herz, tall, radiant, and with a voluptuous figure, made it a point never to invite more than one or two other good-looking women to her salon at a time; too many besides herself, she said, distracted from the conversation. Rachel, who later married a Prussian diplomat named Varnhagen von Ense, counted among her admirers both Goethe and Beethoven; in fact, there are a few who believe she was the "Immortal Beloved" to whom Beethoven wrote his famous mysterious love letter.

At the outset, at least, Dorothea Veit's salon offered one attraction the others lacked: the presence of Moses Mendelssohn. After all, his own intellectual gatherings had provided his daughter with the model for hers, and in the few years of life that remained to him after her marriage to Veit, he took to dropping around occasionally to her "evenings." Whenever he did, he was the center of attraction, listening tolerantly to the young people around him and sometimes breaking in with the mixture of gentleness and wit for which he was noted. Once he took to teasing Henrietta Herz for something she had said, and when she became visibly upset, he said to her soothingly but pointedly: *"You* ought to be able to take such things calmly."

The customary starting time for a Berlin salon was 5 P.M.; most of the guests came by carriage, but some arrived on foot, and a few of the more dashing cavaliers on horseback. At Dorothea's the atmosphere was middle-class comfort rather than aristocratic opulence. The talk was mostly of literature, theater, music, and philosophy; politics, although sometimes discussed, seemed less predominant than at the Parisian salons of Madame de Staël and others. In this cultivated circle, it was possible to discuss Voltaire in French and Dante in Italian, although the favorite literary subject—in German, of course—was Goethe, who was adored by all.

Language itself became a cherished object at the salons: the ladies and their guests loved aphorisms, paradoxes, play with words. Occasionally, there was some sort of a philosophical demonstration or a scientific experiment; Henrietta Herz's husband Marcus was a would-be philosopher and scientist, as well as a physician, and gave talks on subjects ranging from Kant (with whom he had studied) to physics. Later in the evening refreshments were served, and about 9 P.M., the gathering broke up, with everyone feeling spiritually and intellectually refreshed. For a period of perhaps twenty years, the Jewish women's homes became the artistic and literary centers of Berlin; hardly anyone of note came to the city without seeking an invitation. Moses Mendelssohn's nightly gatherings had been for men only; now suddenly women had raised themselves to the level of men's intellectual equals and found that men adored them none the less for it. Heine called them "the Bacchantes of thought, reeling in holy intoxication after the god."

Simon Veit himself, busy in his counting house all day and hurrying home at night for Dorothea's evenings, took little part himself in the salon proceedings, staying discreetly in the background—not unlike Fromet Mendelssohn. The good-natured banker paid the bills and was content to have his brilliant wife lead the talk. So far as he was concerned, everybody came to his house merely for conversation; if there also were attractions of a more corporeal nature, he apparently was not aware of them.

Writing about the Berlin Jewesses' salons nearly one hundred years later, the meticulous and moralistic historian Heinrich Graetz seethed with indignation about what went on behind their intellectual façade. The salons, he wrote, constituted "a sort of Midianite tent" in which the Jewish girls were seduced not only of their virtue but their religion by young Christian artists and litterateurs distinguished by their "selfishness, licentiousness, vice and depravity."*

The orgiastic picture set forth by Graetz is exaggerated, but there can be little doubt that loftiness of intellect was not the only attribute admired by the salon regulars, and that many a philosophic discussion which began in the drawing room reached its climax in the boudoir. Some of the romantic attachments were even pursued on paper, for Henrietta Herz organized a *Tugenbund* ("Band of Virtue"), whose members not only engaged in romantic badinage but wrote each other letters pouring out sentimental and soulful secrets. Dorothea Veit became a member, along with her younger sister, also named Henrietta. Commented Graetz in his history: "The Jewish women felt themselves exalted and honored by their close intimacy with Christians of rank: they did not see the fanged serpent beneath the flowers."

Dorothea and her friends certainly did manage to meet some odd personages among the young Christian intellectuals of the day. Few of the leading protagonists of the German Romantic movement, just coming into flower, escaped her collection, either in Berlin or on her subsequent travels. Frederick Schleiermacher, a diminutive, hunched-over theologian with a taste for fashionable women, was a frequenter of the Jewish salons, finally attaching himself to Henrietta Herz with such persistency that people gossiped about them openly. Henrietta said she liked everything about him except his name, which she promptly shortened to "Schleier." The Humboldt brothers, William and Alexander, whom Dorothea knew from the days of Moses Mendelssohn's Morning Hours, were also in her circle. William, too, had an eye for the statuesque Henrietta Herz and corresponded with her ardently. Alexander, forced to retire for a time to the family palace in Tegel, bemoaned his inability to attend Dorothea's salon and

---

*When Nazi historians came to write about the same period, they simply reversed the charge and accused the Jewish hostesses of seducing the upstanding German lads they lured to their salons. See page 239.

wrote her letters in Hebrew datelined "Castle Ennui."

Another of Dorothea's favorites was Johann Gottlieb Fichte, a budding German philosopher and disciple of Kant, whose breadth of mind and intimacy with Jews did not prevent him from writing, in words that later impressed, among others, Adolf Hitler: "I see only one way to give them [the Jews] civil rights: to cut off their heads in one night and put others on them in which there is not so much as a single Jewish idea."

But as much as she admired these heroes of the intellect, Dorothea Veit was never really smitten until she met Frederick Schlegel in 1789. Frederick was the younger of two brothers. Literary wags of the day said the elder, William August, had talent without genius, while Frederick had genius without talent, meaning that William made the most of his abilities, while Frederick wasted his. William translated Shakespeare's plays into German so aptly that he started a craze for them; Frederick, much more impulsive and erratic, never really fulfilled his brilliant promise despite his influence as a critic and lecturer.

His love affair with Dorothea Veit, which became one of the sensations of early nineteenth-century Europe, was a strange alliance. He was twenty-five years old, unattached, and with a growing reputation. She was thirty-two, married to a respectable businessman, and had two sons. To most of her friends, she was physically unattractive. Henrietta Herz, surveying her as only one woman can survey another, wrote: "There was nothing about Dorothea to entice one to sensuality. Nothing about her was beautiful except her eyes through which, it is true, there shone the light of her lovable soul and her sparkling mind. But with the exception of that there was nothing, neither face nor figure, not even the hands and feet, which are often beautifully formed in otherwise unattractive women."

But Frederick Schlegel found her fascinating, big feet and all, and she became the great love of his life. A smallish man, he hadn't done too well with women before her, despite several attempts. Now in the daughter of Moses Mendelssohn he found a half-maternal, half-sensual kind of tenderness that seemed to fulfill all his wants. Dorothea, for her part, after fifteen years of hateful marriage to Veit, found her craving for both intellectual and physical love satisfied. Dorothea first met Schlegel at one of Henrietta Herz's soirees and forthwith invited him to her own, and before long, they were bound up with each other day and night.

Of course everybody in the world of the salons knew about their affair—except poor Simon Veit. It might have been possible to keep the affable, befuddled banker in the dark indefinitely, except that Dorothea had no wish to conduct a clandestine affair. A true Romantic, she wished to live openly with her lover.

Feeling the need for outside help, she called upon her good friend and sister Tugenbundist, Henrietta Herz. Henrietta, after consultation with her own good friend Schleiermacher, agreed to pay a call upon Veit. He was astounded by what she told him. His wife? Schlegel? Impossible! He insisted upon talking to Dorothea herself, and only when she told him the truth was he convinced. With great reluctance he consented to a separation, and with more generosity than Dorothea expected, he agreed to let her keep custody of their sons and even to send her regular sums of money for their support.

Others among Dorothea's intimates took a less tolerant view. Her brothers and sisters were outraged and, for a time at least, disowned her. Even among the salon circle, there were raised eyebrows over the curious couple and a few sympathetic words for Veit, who had never made much of an impression at the soirees but was now, everybody agreed, acting like a gentleman.

Whether because of the general disapproval or because Frederick found work as a lecturer at the university there, the couple headed for Jena, blissfully unmarried. Dorothea quickly organized a new salon. Jena, close to Weimar, where Goethe held forth, had a fine intellectual atmosphere; and this time among her satellites were the two Schlegels (William also was in Jena), Fichte, and the poet and novelist Novalis. It was a union of ecstatic contentment, for Dorothea rejoiced that she was living with the most romantic of men; and Frederick, that he had found the most intelligent of women.

In fact, so carried away was Schlegel that he impetuously decided to write a novel about the affair. Giving himself the name of "Julius" and calling Dorothea "Lucinde," he proceeded to recount the story of their romance in terms that were rather explicit for those times. A jumbled-up succession of letters, dialogues, allegories, and confessions, with an erotic touch here and there, *Lucinde* succeeded in offending and confusing most of its readers. Some were particularly outraged by a passage in which Schlegel, to demonstrate his ideal of equality between the sexes, imagines Julius and Lucinde exchanging roles while making love, so that she plays the masculine aggressor while he adopts a pose of feminine passivity. Schlegel's own brother called it a "foolish rhapsody" and tried vainly to dissuade him from publishing it. In the book Frederick praised his and Dorothea's "natural marriage," extolling it over the conventional type. Obviously alluding to Dorothea, he wrote: "I should have held it for a fairy tale that such joy exists, and such love as I now feel, and such a woman who is at the same time the most tender sweetheart and the best company, and also a perfect friend. . . . In you I have found all, and more than I could wish for."

Not to be outdone, Dorothea also decided to write a novel. But as it was considered unseemly, not to say unbelievable, for a woman to write a novel in that era in Germany, Dorothea's book *Florentin* appeared in 1801 not under her name but with the legend "A novel edited by Frederick Schlegel."

Florentin was never completed, only one of its projected two volumes being published. But most of its readers, whether or not they knew of its true authorship, regarded it as a superior work to *Lucinde*. It was better written, more closely organized, and less flowery in its language. Just as Frederick had made her the heroine of *Lucinde,* so Dorothea idealized him in *Florentin.* Frederick-Florentin was depicted not as a typical or even recognizable human being, but as a magnified romantic hero, without reproach or blemish, wandering through the world in search of his long-lost parents, tasting all the delights of the senses, worshipping beauty wherever he finds it, and finally having the wisdom to settle upon a woman not unlike Dorothea Mendelssohn.

Although *Florentin* was her only venture into the romantic novel, Dorothea proved to be a more versatile and dependable writer than her lover. Between the sums she continued to receive from the long-suffering Veit and her own literary earnings, it was Dorothea who proved the main support of the couple almost all their lives. Yet most of what she wrote appeared, by her own wish, under Schlegel's name. She said she regarded herself as merely an amateur who wished to give her consort time for repose when he needed it—to serve, as she said, "in all humility as his hand-maiden, to earn bread until he was able to do so." It may have been the ancient biblical idea of the woman as servant, or then again, the new Romantic concept of the self-sacrificing spouse; in either event, Frederick Schlegel took it as it came.

Among other works Dorothea wrote for money and signed with Frederick's name were a retelling of the tale of Joan of Arc called *The Story of the Maid of Orleans* (the title page read: "From old French sources. . . . Edited by Frederick Schlegel"); a history of Marguerite of Valois ("translated and edited by Frederick Schlegel"); and a saga called *Lother and Maller, a Tale of Chivalry* ("revised and edited by Frederick Schlegel"). The climax was the publication of a translation by Dorothea into German of Madame de Staël's *Corinne;* once again Frederick unabashedly took bows when critics praised him for his erudition and skill as a translator. Dorothea also contributed countless articles to *Athenaeum* and *Europa,* literary journals which the brothers Schlegel edited. These at least she did not credit to Frederick, signing them with the letter *D,* but few of the readers knew who the author was.

Only one cloud hung over Dorothea's stay at Jena: she was disliked heartily by Caroline Schlegel, wife of Frederick's brother. Caroline found her too abrupt and masculine and lacking in graces; probably the facts that she was Jewish, an authoress, and a little less than a certified sister-in-law did not further endear her.

In 1804, Dorothea and Frederick, along with Dorothea's children, left Jena and headed for Paris. They now had been living together for seven years, which seemed like a reasonable enough trial period. So they decided to get married. But Dorothea's Jewish faith remained a technical obstacle. She had long since ceased practicing her religion; in fact, from the moment she met Schlegel, and probably even earlier, the idea of buying the "admission ticket" by accepting baptism had entered her mind. Being Schlegel's mistress was, of course, an entry card of sorts; still, as some of her friends, including Schleiermacher, kept telling her, only full conversion would bring full privileges. She kept on pondering the situation; in one letter, she informed Schleiermacher that she was reading the Bible a good deal, in Luther's translation—surely Moses Mendelssohn must have given a twitch in his grave at *that*—and added: "I am reading both Testaments carefully, and according to my taste find the Protestant Christianity purer and much to be preferred to the Catholic. The latter bears too much resemblance to the old Judaism which I loathe. Protestantism seems to me, however, to be entirely the religion of Jesus, and the religion of culture. In my heart I am, from what I can learn from the Bible, quite Protestant."

Thus at the age of forty, she decided to adopt formally the "religion of culture." Soon after she arrived in Paris with her ménage, Dorothea ("*née* Mendelssohn and runaway Veit," as Heinrich Heine sardonically called her) was baptized and married to Frederick Schlegel. Henceforth she could officially be called Dorothea rather than the long-dropped Brendel, since it was the name she chose to be christened with.

In Paris, it was the income from Dorothea's translations that the couple subsisted on, for Frederick developed a passion for Sanskrit and Hindu philosophy and studied both assiduously, doing a minimum of editing work. Dorothea, inevitably, once again opened a salon, and with Frederick by her side, it probably was the most brilliant she had ever presided over. In Paris, salons run by women had a long and distinguished history, and Dorothea Schlegel's was welcomed warmly. Every visiting German was a caller, as were many of the French intellectuals. Dorothea's younger sister Henrietta Mendelssohn was now also a resident of Paris, and there were observers who thought they had never witnessed, even at Madame de Staël's, such a concentration of feminine wisdom as was embodied in these two daughters of Moses Mendelssohn.

Wrote a popular chronicler of the time:

> All went very pleasantly in this set. Dorothea's careful loving sense enabled her to shed a cheerful influence upon their tranquil, well-ordered life. . . . It is incomprehensible how she still found time to write. She it was who, while her quick, clever hand made and mended clothes, knitted stockings, and busied itself on the domestic hearth, was the copyist of all her husband's writings. . . . [She] carried on an extensive correspondence, found the time to see the most remarkable objects of art, read all the new books, attended concerts and the theaters, and enlivened the evenings by the charm of her social gifts or her beautiful reading aloud. . . . To very few did she ever acknowledge herself as the author of *Florentin,* her poems, and other writings. She was proud that her products should appear under Schlegel's name. . . .

In 1808, Dorothea underwent another religious convulsion. Overcoming her previous doubts about the "impure" Roman faith, and attracted by its mysticism and panoply, she persuaded the reluctant Schlegel to join her in becoming a Catholic. Journeying to Cologne, they underwent a double conversion and a remarriage in their new faith.

But if their religious progression was steady, their economic underpinning remained insecure. Income was low, and Frederick, once a romantic hero, was now turning out to be a sulky, petulant, improvident husband. From Cologne they went to Vienna, where Schlegel had managed to secure a small government post as secretary at the imperial court. In Vienna, there were once more salons to attend, for the Jewish women there had lately begun to rival those of Berlin in their zeal for conversation and conversion. Attending a Viennese salon and observing the former Jewesses with black or gold crucifixes dangling over well-exposed bosoms, the young Jewish writer Ludwig Börne maliciously remarked: "Their crosses are even longer than their noses."

But for Dorothea Schlegel, at least, much of the old spirit was gone. Her friend Henrietta Herz paid her a visit in Vienna in 1811. The entire city was filled with refugees and wounded of the Napoleonic Wars, and at the Schlegels' apartments there was little gaiety or stimulation. Dorothea had a severe cold the day her old friend called and lay shivering beneath the bedclothes. Frederick, stout, stolid, and seemingly unconcerned, sat drinking from a carafe of wine and eating oranges while the two women talked. In her mind, Henrietta could not help comparing the flabby and self-indulgent Frederick with Dorothea's first husband, old Simon Veit, who had not satisfied her intellectually but on whose generosity and forgiveness she had been able to live all her years with Schlegel.

An almost identical picture of the Schlegel ménage was given eight years later in Rome. Dorothea had gone there in 1819 to visit her sons Johannes and Philipp Veit, both active as artists. In fact, Philipp, as a member of an artistic group called the Nazarenes, had become one of the outstanding painters of New Testament scenes of the nineteenth century—another little turn for Moses Mendelssohn! Among the callers on the Schlegel ménage in Rome was Franz Grillparzer, the Austrian poet and friend of Beethoven and Schubert.

"I found him and his wife," Grillparzer wrote, "in the company of an Italian priest, who was reading to them from a prayer book or some other sort of edifying work, while the wife listened with clasped hands, whereas the husband followed the reading with rapt eyes, at the same time taking material refreshment from a dish of ham standing in front of him, and a big Chianti bottle. My worldly presence soon drove away the priest."

Frederick Schlegel died in 1829 at the age of fifty-six; according to one account, his death was due to overeating. Dorothea moved to Frankfurt, where she lived with her son Philipp Veit, and where she yet had a part to play in the life of her famous nephew Felix. Thanks to Frederick's government services, she had a small pension, and she managed to make do in the ten years of life that were left to her. She admitted to being old, weary, and ill; but some of her former spiritedness kept asserting itself in the letters she exchanged regularly with Henrietta Herz, now also a widow in the same state of near-impoverishment. "We must put up with it," Dorothea wrote to her childhood friend, "as the plants and flowers do, which . . . go on with their business of blooming as if it were the greatest pleasure." And, ruefully recalling the past as only a weary Romanticist could: "All that we children of earth used to call the Poetry of Life is far, far away! I could say, with you, that I have had enough of it. But all the same, I will not say it, and implore you not to say it again. Be brave!"

Dorothea died on August 3, 1839. In her latter days, she had written no books, done no translations, conducted no salons. Instead, she worked almost daily over her sewing and knitting. "There are," concluded Moses Mendelssohn's daughter, "too many books in the world; but I have never heard there are too many shirts."

VIII Sebastiani's Daughter

Dorothea Mendelssohn was a married woman when her father died in 1786, but her two sisters, Henrietta and Recha, were still children. They had not yet reached an age which would entitle them, for instance, to regular attendance at Moses' Morning Hours lectures. Nevertheless, they received a thorough and persistent education; Fromet Mendelssohn saw to that. For a number of years, she continued to live in her house in Berlin with all of her children except for Dorothea. Mendelssohn had left the family with a little money, and Fromet's naturally frugal tendencies enabled them to scrape by. After a time, Joseph, her oldest son, added to their income by opening a small bank employing a modest staff of two clerks. In 1804, the family moved to Hamburg, Fromet's native city, to which Joseph expanded his banking business. Moses Mendelssohn's widow died in 1812, reasonably content with all her children except Dorothea, and having survived her husband by twenty-six years.

Of her three daughters, Recha, the youngest girl, was the least vexatious. She never underwent religious conversion, and she made no objections to marrying one Mendel Meyer, the son of a banker friend of her father. However, this marriage also proved unhappy and was eventually dissolved. Recha was known as a bright and clever woman but she lived in constant poor health. Her most notable contribution to the family history was her establishment of a boarding school for girls at Altona, a town adjoining Hamburg, which had a large Jewish population. Among the tutors she recruited for her staff was her sister Henrietta, who thus gained a taste for teaching that was to shape her life into a curious course.

Like her sister Dorothea, Henrietta Mendelssohn was an independent-minded, adventurous girl. She, too, had been born with a name she didn't particularly care for, Sorel, and had taken on a more glamorous-sounding one; and just as Dorothea had become an intimate of Henrietta Herz, so did Henrietta Mendelssohn find a confidante in Rachel Levin, maintaining a lifelong correspondence with her. She was, Rachel said, "the deepest and most thoughtful" of the Mendelssohn girls. There was, however, one significant difference between Rachel and Henrietta: Rachel had a number of love affairs before she finally married, at the age of forty-three, Varnhagen von Ense; but Henrietta shied away from men all her life. Her only interest in them was intellectual.

Henrietta was no beauty; she had inherited from her father a slight deformity of the back to go along with her keenness of mind. Nevertheless, she had opportunities to marry. In 1799, she journeyed to Vienna to take a position as a tutor in a wealthy Jewish family; there she met Bernhard Eskeles, the head of a large financial firm and the descendant of a chief rabbi of Moravia— seemingly an irresistible combination. Eskeles wanted to marry her, but she refused him. Soon after, he found another wife, and eventually became an Austrian baron.

As the nineteenth century began, Henrietta moved to Paris, apparently at the invitation of her brother Abraham, who was already there. Like Joseph, who was six years older, Abraham had decided to become a banker, and he had gone for his training to Paris, where he worked in a Jewish-run establishment called Fould's.

The Foulds were one of the most prominent Jewish families in Paris; indeed they later played a considerable part in French financial and political history. Both their banking establishment and their home occupied a handsome mansion on the rue Richer.

Abraham had an apartment there, which he shared with his newly arrived sister, who kept house for him. Henrietta was in her mid-twenties and eager for new sights and people. Paris fascinated her; she remained there for twenty-five years, long after Abraham had departed.

Abraham Mendelssohn might also have stayed longer, except that Henrietta decided to play matchmaker by introducing him to his future wife. The girl, the future mother of Felix Mendelssohn, was named Leah Salomon, and she was an old friend of Henrietta's from Berlin. Henrietta knew Leah was coming to Paris for a visit; it is even possible that she suggested the trip to her. She also arranged for Abraham to escort her friend around the city, and the two young Germans, who shared an interest in music and art, were soon in love. When it came time for Leah to return to Berlin, Abraham announced that it was time for him to pay a visit home, too, and he accompanied her. Their marriage followed shortly afterward.

For Henrietta, even without her brother, it was an exciting time to be in Paris, as most times are. The Revolution was over, Napoleon was First Consul and about to become Emperor; there had been a tremendous unleashing of national vitality and intellectual ferment.

There also was a whole new class of wealthy people, and Henrietta conceived the idea of opening a school of quality for their daughters. Fould's offered an excellent location; the banker's establishment had rooms to spare and also a pleasant, shaded inner garden that could be used in fine weather. He was more than agreeable to Henrietta's suggestion that she take over part of the building for her classes, and soon her rooms were crowded with young girls whose parents were delighted to turn them over to a tutor who had the double virtues of being Moses Mendelssohn's daughter and a German schoolmistress.

Of course it was inevitable that Henrietta should have her evening salon. Despite her general plainness and slight stoop, she had an attractive manner, a gentle way of speaking, and a pair of fine, dark eyes. She was fluent in French and English and was well acquainted with the literature of both languages, not to mention her own. Nearly every German who traveled to Paris called upon her, and she had a wide circle of important Parisian acquaintances. Madame de Staël, between her periodic expulsions by Napoleon, was a regular visitor and good friend; Benjamin Constant came frequently. The composer Spontini, whose opera *La Vestale* had scored a tremendous success, liked to attend the soirees, saying little but sitting in the moonlit garden, according to one observer, "meditating on new laurels to be won."

Varnhagen von Ense, the diplomat who was later to marry Rachel Levin, left a nostalgic picture of Henrietta's gatherings on the rue Richer:

> In this garden remarkable conversations took place; the German and French views, though often seeming to admit of no possible accommodation, were reconciled through the happy translation which Fräulein Mendelssohn knew how to give them, in which it was the *words* that were least of all translated. Here the contents of Madame de Staël's book on Germany, while still in the press, were talked over, and in strict confidence I received the proofs. . . . Now and then, when the ground was safe, political opinions were uttered without reserve. . . . The real causes of Fouché's* discharge, the intrigues of the ill-famed Ouvrard,† and other matters connected with them were there detailed.
>
> In spite of the keen interest of such society, I found a greater charm in quiet domestic evenings with Fräulein Mendelssohn alone, when German subjects were discussed in the German language. Her drawing-room windows were thickly covered with a vine, which at once subdued the glare of the sun and gave shelter from the cool of the evening. In that green shade we used to sit for hours on the low window-seat, calling up the beloved images of our native country, our mutual friends and acquaintances, most of whom we constantly discovered to share our predilictions in the

*Joseph Fouché, Napoleon's minister of police.
†Gabriel-Julien Ouvrard, an unscrupulous financier and military supplier.

arts and poetry. Sometimes we discussed the highest and most sacred human interests.

One day in 1812, an unexpected visitor walked into Henrietta's establishment. He was General Horace François Sebastiani, one of the most distinguished men in the Empire by reason of his outstanding military and diplomatic career. Like his master Napoleon, Sebastiani was a Corsican, and had prospered mightily under the Empire, becoming one of the wealthiest men in Paris. His wife had died of puerperal fever in Constantinople, where she had accompanied him on a diplomatic mission, three weeks after the birth of their only child, Fanny. Now Fanny was five years old, and while her maternal grandmother, the Marquise de Coigny, was overseeing her upbringing, the time had come to find her a governess to supervise her education and otherwise look after her. General Sebastiani's proposition was simple: if Henrietta would give up her school and move into his household as Fanny Sebastiani's governess, he would see to it that she was well paid, handsomely housed, and rewarded with a generous pension once the girl was married.

After some deliberation, Henrietta accepted. She was now well into her thirties, the school was becoming taxing work, and Sebastiani was offering a higher and more dependable income for teaching one pupil than she hitherto had from a dozen. Besides, in many ways, the offer was dazzling. The Hotel Sebastiani, at 55, rue du Faubourg St. Honoré, was one of the showplaces of Paris, a lavish edifice abutting the Elysée Palace, which was then occupied by Napoleon himself, and today is the residence of the presidents of France.

Henrietta had her own suite of four rooms on the second floor of the Hotel Sebastiani, luxuriously furnished and carpeted, with a sweeping view of gardens all the way to the Champs-Elysées. She was given a cook, two lady's maids, and a manservant, and a carriage and team of horses were put at her disposal. "In short," she wrote to her brother Joseph, "it is impossible to find a more honorable and flattering position than mine. . . . I assure you it is not at all a bad thing to play the fine lady."

Only one problem nagged at Henrietta as she took over the guidance of young Fanny Sebastiani: religion. Henrietta had been disturbed by her sister Dorothea's conversion to Protestantism but had accepted it more or less resignedly and had welcomed her and Schlegel when they came to Paris. But she seethed with indignation when Dorothea and Frederick became Roman Catholics in 1811. She wrote Dorothea a nasty letter about it; in reply, Dorothea urged her to convert, also. For a time, the sisters stopped corresponding; and when Varnhagen von Ense, who knew them both well, came to Paris, Henrietta sat him down and pressed him for explanations as to why her sister and Schlegel had taken such an unaccountable step.

But now that Henrietta was rearing a Catholic child in a Catholic household, her outlook changed. The general, although he lived the life of a dashing military hero and seldom saw his daughter, would obviously be happier if her governess were a Catholic; so would Madame de Coigny, who rather liked Henrietta and was prepared to give her a free hand in raising Fanny. In the end, Henrietta told herself she was doing it for the sake of the child whom, she said, she truly loved; on a logical basis, it would be difficult to give Fanny a particular moral atmosphere without sharing it herself.

Like Moses Mendelssohn, Henrietta prided herself on obedience to reason; besides, her mother's death in 1812 removed the most reproachful voice within the family. So she, too, converted to Catholicism. For a while, she told Varnhagen, she felt a certain amount of inward doubt and discomfort. Eventually, though, she became not only an ardent Catholic but a strident one, expostulating with her brothers when they declined to join the Roman church and expressing regret, in her last will and testament, that she had not succeeded in converting the whole Mendelssohn family "to the true faith, the Roman Catholic."

For nearly twelve years, Henrietta Mendelssohn devoted herself exclusively to the care and upbringing of Fanny Sebastiani. At first she thought she had excellent material to work with. In a letter to Abraham, she described little Fanny as "inexpressively lovely . . . I have never seen a child more beautiful and with more promising gifts of heart and mind." A few years later her enthusiasm diminished, and she reported to Abraham that while Fanny "day by day gets more beautiful," she was "not keeping pace as regards information." Still later came this despairing report: "Altogether, the only excellence of the girl is in her beauty and amiability of mind and manner, but she is entirely without talent and inclination for learning. . . . Fanny has a good voice; but God knows that she sings by the sweat of *my* brow, for she is fundamentally unmusical. . . ." Clearly, Fanny, for all her governess' hard work, was turning out to be a beautiful but indolent heiress; and Henrietta went on record as fearing, with, as it proved, remarkable prescience, that her eventual entry into Parisian society would lead to some sort of disaster: "I see it coming on like a mighty avalanche, which must destroy in one moment what I have planted and tended with such care."

For the most part Fanny, such as she was, was the principal companion Henrietta had; the governess even spent her summers with the girl at the Sebastianis' country place at Viry, near Paris. The occupation of Paris by the Prussians and English after Napoleon's final defeat at Waterloo introduced crowds of foreigners, military and civilian, into the city; but Sebastiani knew how to tack with the prevailing winds, and life in his household remained serene. Like a true Parisienne, Henrietta was indignant at the pillaging by the Prussian troops; she quoted a popular saying: "The soldiers of other nations steal politely—not like the Prussians!" She even spoke sharply about it—in perfect German—to a hussar she found outside of her door; he shrugged and replied: "They hate us in France whatever we do, so it doesn't matter."

The military and political upheaval brought one benefit to Henrietta, for in 1816, her brother Abraham, now an important banker in Berlin, was sent to Paris as a member of a Prussian commission negotiating the French war indemnity. Abraham by now had four young children, and since his stay was to be protracted, he brought his family with him. Henrietta was enchanted, particularly with her brother's two oldest children, Fanny, eleven, and Felix, seven, both of them extremely talented young pianists. Felix was taken for piano lessons to a famous French pedagogue, Madame Marie Bigot; both children had a busy time in Paris and were delighted to meet their "Tante Jette," of whom their father had told them so much. They spent a good deal of their time in her apartments, and much was made of the fact that Henrietta's pupil and her niece were both named Fanny and were only a year and a half apart in age. The two little girls subsequently made a rather awkward and short-lived attempt to conduct a correspondence.

In 1819, Abraham was again back in Paris on business; this time traveling alone. Fanny Sebastiani was off on a brief trip with her father, so Henrietta was free to accept her brother's invitation to travel with him for a few days to Le Havre, where she had her first glimpse of the sea. The tide and the waves, she reported in a letter to Abraham's wife, roused her "innermost soul," but the sight of a great ship left her unmoved: "The smallest poem by Goethe touches me more, and makes me more proud of humanity."

On this trip Abraham also paid a visit to the Sebastiani summer establishment at Viry; there he and Henrietta had the pleasure of hearing Fanny Sebastiani sing a song written by Fanny Mendelssohn, who, along with young Felix, was turning out to be something of a composer. Henrietta wrote to beg both children to send more of their music so that she might listen to it at Viry. Such events, she said, afforded her far more pleasure than listening to the talk of French politicians, who now regularly thronged the Sebastiani home, or even than taking a summer trip to Provence with the general and his daughter, when the weather proved so hot as to impede her enjoyment of old Roman monuments like the Pont du Gard and the amphitheater at Nîmes.

In 1824, Fanny Sebastiani was seventeen years old, with a voluptuous figure, a complaisant temperament, and an empty head —all eminent qualifications for marriage to an eligible young French nobleman. The only question was, which nobleman? The problem was earnestly discussed by Fanny's relatives, led by the general and by her grandmother, the Marquise de Coigny. Since no fewer than ten suitors had presented themselves as candidates for the dazzling, dark-eyed heiress, considerable debate transpired. Listening to it, Henrietta said she was revolted by the crass discussions of dowry and property. "How such an affair is transacted in great French families God has mercifully spared you from knowing," she wrote to Abraham.

For herself, Henrietta realized that the marriage of Sebastiani's daughter in a sense would end her life's work. She was disturbed when friends, meaning to be sympathetic, asked her: "What are you going to do now?" She wrote to her sister-in-law Leah: "That all the devotion I have lavished upon the girl these many years was really nothing but a *role,* and that now the curtain is to fall, and Fanny, tomorrow, to act in a new piece, with no part for me to play—I ought all along to have told myself this, and perhaps I did now and then: but how different is the reality! Thank God, my dear sister, that *your* Fanny's marriage will be but new and unmixed joy to you!"

If Henrietta was upset by the mere prospect of Fanny's getting married, she was absolutely horrified when she learned who had been picked as her husband. He was the young duc de FitzJames, socially quite eligible, but in Henrietta's estimate "depraved and profligate . . . a sad choice." Even Fanny herself, as anxious as she was to satisfy the various relatives who had been plotting, intriguing, and gossiping about her future for months, got wind of the young man's reputation and called off the wedding almost at the last minute. As things turned out, she might have done better to take her chances.

Instead her choice settled on another duke, Charles-Louis-Theobald, duc de Choiseul-Praslin. He was nineteen, reasonably good-looking, not too bright, and the heir of an historic family which owned, among other property, the Chateau of Vaux-le-Vicomte, built by Fouquet in 1659. It seemed like a satisfactory match; even Henrietta acknowledged that "much good may be expected of it."

At first, the intention was that Praslin should enter the Ecole Polytechnique and complete his studies, with the marriage deferred until his graduation. However, the young man, surveying the charms of his intended, decided he couldn't wait that long; and Fanny, as eager as he, was of the same mind. So the marriage date was set for only six months in the future, and in the meantime some intellectual forced feeding was administered to the young duke. Reported Henrietta to her family in Berlin: "They have now given the young man all the teachers he ought to have had before, and he is studying, all at once and together, History, Greek, Latin, German, Law. What do you think of this? And yet the General is right in wishing to retrieve as much as possible what has been neglected."

The wedding, one of the great social events of the year, took place on October 19, 1824. With her occupation gone, Henrietta Mendelssohn prepared to go home at last and suggested to Abraham, who seemed always to be looking for an excuse to visit Paris, that he might like to come and take her back. He agreed, arriving the following March and bringing with him Felix, now sixteen and already being talked about for his early compositions. They remained two months, and on May 19, 1825, Henrietta left Paris, her home for a quarter of a century.

Only six years of life remained to her. She spent them in Berlin, residing with Abraham and Leah in their spacious house, keeping a prideful eye on the exciting achievements of her nephew Felix, and visiting frequently her friend Rachel Levin Varnhagen, who still maintained her salon. She died on November 9, 1831. Two years later, Rachel Levin died; the age of the Berlin salons was over.

In some respects, Henrietta was the most puzzling and paradoxical of all of Moses Mendelssohn's children. She had a feeling of warmth and affection for her family, yet isolated herself from them most of her life; she was a woman of philosophic breadth, yet turned into a religious fanatic; she knew dozens of Europe's brightest and most attractive men, yet shunned anything but intellectual involvement with them, and as for her own considerable talents and knowledge, she threw them away willingly on a frivolous, empty-headed girl.

What, exactly, was the relationship between Henrietta and her young ward? It was a question raised years after Henrietta's death, in the wake of the horrendous fate that overtook Fanny Sebastiani. For Fanny's marriage to Theobald de Praslin proved to be anything but the success predicted for it. By the time Fanny was thirty-two, she had borne nine children and undergone several miscarriages besides. She had grown corpulent and flabby, her once-exotic face had become coarse, and she weighed 230 pounds. Her husband apparently began to seek solace elsewhere, especially with a young governess who had been installed in the household to look after the numerous Praslin children; at least Fanny believed he was doing so. There were furious quarrels between husband and wife; suggestions were made that Fanny was going mad; the possibility of a legal separation was discussed several times.

However, the couple managed to live in the same house together until August 17, 1847. On that night the duke walked into his wife's room at the Hotel Sebastiani as she lay asleep. He carried a hunting knife, a length of rope, and a revolver. He intended to slit her throat; the rope and the gun were mere auxiliaries. Characteristically, he bungled the job. Fanny awoke when the knife touched her skin, screamed, and began struggling with him. They battled all over the room; she even succeeded in knocking the revolver from his hand. But he stabbed her repeatedly and finally finished her off by cracking her skull with a heavy brass candlestick he seized from a mantel. Servants, roused by the noises, called the police, and the duke was taken into custody. Two days later, as the preliminary legal hearings were starting, he swallowed arsenic; and on August 24, he died.

The Praslin murder-suicide was one of the sensations of nineteenth-century France; it even contributed to the fall in 1848 of King Louis-Philippe, whose government was accused of having permitted Praslin, a member of the peerage, to commit suicide in order to avoid trial and public punishment. Countless articles, pamphlets, and books about the case have appeared over the years; and in the latest one, *A Crime of Passion* by Stanley Loomis,* Henrietta Mendelssohn is practically accused of being a lesbian whose influence, continuing long after her death, helped make Fanny Sebastiani incapable of having an emotionally stable marriage. Curiously, historian Loomis gives no indication of knowing that Fanny's governess was the daughter of Moses Mendelssohn and the aunt of Felix. He never as much as mentions her first name, referring to her in such terms as "this woman, Mademoiselle Mendelssohn" and "the notorious Mademoiselle Mendelssohn." He even remarks that "time has effaced much of the outline of this person" and that "it is impossible to form any picture of her," although "Mademoiselle" Mendelssohn, in fact, was one of the best-known women in Paris, and her letters about Fanny to her family in Berlin have been published in both German and English.

What are the sources for the accusation? Loomis cites as his authority a French writer named Albert Savine, who reported, in 1903, that "Mademoiselle Mendelssohn had a bad touch. After

*Philadelphia: J. B. Lippincott Co. 1967.

Fanny Sebastiani she was to raise other young girls and wherever she went she left behind the deadly germs of vices. . . ." Actually, Henrietta raised no other girls after leaving Paris, and her "germs of vices" do not appear to have infected anybody else. Whether or not she was a lesbian would seem impossible to determine from this distance; nor does the question appear to have much bearing on the life pattern of Fanny Sebastiani who, with her constant pregnancies, her corpulence, and her fear of younger rivals had marital problems pointing in other directions.

Fanny, one suspects, would have been doomed no matter who had been her childhood governess. In any case, it was just as well for Henrietta Mendelssohn's repose that she died at the age of fifty-six without knowing what was to become of her famous pupil.

IX *Joseph and His Brothers*

Of Moses Mendelssohn's three sons, Joseph was sixteen when his father died; Abraham, ten; and Nathan, only four. Joseph, in a filial biography of his father he later wrote, records that he once heard Moses confiding to a friend that he was saddened by the thought of how his family would manage after his death "because I can leave them but little." Addressing his father sententiously on high, Joseph added: "If as an enlightened spirit you look down upon us, your children, upon earth, you will be convinced that God has taken your posterity under His care, that they all have sufficient means, and are leading an honorable life."

For all his portentousness, Joseph was speaking with considerable accuracy. All three of Moses Mendelssohn's sons were able, intelligent, and ambitious, and quick to take advantage of the new opportunities he had helped open up for Jews in Germany.

Joseph always was closest to his father, if for no other reason than his age. He was the only one of the boys old enough to be exposed to the Morning Hours lectures and to have undergone the bar-mitzvah rite while his father was still alive. Moses looked upon him with fatherly pride and affection, tinged with a little skepticism as to his ability to make his way in the world. Joseph was stubborn and lacked "gentleness," Moses wrote to one of his tutors; although he worked hard and had an active mind, his bluntness and obstinacy might hold him back in life "unless the love of some good woman may induce him to control himself."

At the age of fourteen Joseph announced, like many a Jewish

youth since, that he was giving up his Hebraic studies; Moses remonstrated with him but, again like many a subsequent Jewish father, finally gave it up as a bad job and acquiesced, telling him to study whatever he wished. To the tutor he wrote: "We have as yet no determined plans as to his future life. . . . It is, I think, too early to devote him to trade. He might scramble through life as his father has done, half-merchant, half-scholar, even if he runs the same danger of being neither one nor the other thoroughly."

Far from scrambling through life, Joseph built up a prosperous banking business that remained in existence under the name of Mendelssohn and Company until 1939. He married Henrietta Meyer, who came of a well-known German-Jewish family; they had two sons, Alexander and Benjamin. Both within and without his own family, Joseph was under constant pressure to abandon Judaism and accept conversion; his sister Henrietta in particular kept plaguing him about it. Yet Joseph, either out of loyalty to his father or because of that very stubbornness and inflexibility of which old Moses complained, refused to ride with the times and remained a Jew to the end. His son Alexander, who died in 1871, did likewise and was the last of Moses Mendelssohn's direct descendants to remain a professing Jew.

Joseph Mendelssohn made some small efforts to follow in his father's footsteps as a writer and thinker, although his clever, superior sisters were prone to poke fun at his earnest endeavors along these lines. He wrote a short book on banking that created a mild stir in business circles, but his most notable production was the first complete edition of Moses Mendelssohn's works, which he edited in 1843, prefacing it with a concise biography and memoir of his father.

In his own way, Joseph worked out his personal ideas for the practice of Judaism, for he was a long way from the Orthodoxy to which most of the unconverted still clung. With a group of young associates, he formed in 1792 an organization called "The Society of Friends," which was one of the earliest Jewish communal and fraternal organizations in Europe. It consisted entirely of unmarried men whose object was to foster social contacts and provide mutual assistance in time of need, as well as to spread culture and promote enlightenment. Their symbol was a bundle of staves, and their motto was taken from a saying of Moses Mendelssohn: "To seek truth, to love the beautiful, to desire good, to do the best." The society spread from Berlin to Königsberg, Breslau, and Vienna, and it continued as a benevolent organization for many years.

Joseph Mendelssohn, as befitted a man of the Enlightenment, maintained a strong interest in science; and if he could not contribute greatly to its advancement himself, at least he could assist those who did. Some years after he established himself solidly in the banking business, his friend Alexander von Humboldt, already famous as a scientist, came to see him in considerable alarm.

Alexander's landlord, it seemed, wished to sell his house and evict him; not only would he be without a roof over his head, he had no place to put his valuable collection of natural history specimens, which were about to be dumped into the street. Could his friend Mendelssohn at least find him storage space for his carefully catalogued specimens? Joseph pondered a moment and told Alexander he would think of something. Later that day he sent the anxious naturalist a note: "Dear Humboldt: Stay undisturbed in your house as long as you like. I am now your landlord as I have bought the house."

Joseph remained in close touch with Humboldt throughout his life. He also read all he could in science, attended lectures at the Berlin Polytechnic Institute, and even attempted to perform his own experiments. A few days before his death, he was busy studying algebra from a new textbook he had purchased. He was one of the longest-lived of the Mendelssohns, dying in 1848 at the age of seventy-eight, when he fell asleep in his armchair, without pain or premonition, and surrounded by his family.

Joseph's interest in science was basically that of a dilettante, but the youngest of the Mendelssohn brothers, Nathan, became a professional engineer. As a child, he took a keen interest in the new developments in physics and mechanics, both of which were just beginning to be formulated as scientific disciplines. The Mendelssohn children were all travelers, and Nathan went to England and France to further his studies.

He began working actively in the field in Berlin, where he helped to found the Polytechnic Society, lecturing on subjects ranging from photography to telegraphy. He invented a number of scientific instruments and began to manufacture them commercially, a project in which he was aided by a grant from the Prussian state government, which Alexander Humboldt was instrumental in arranging. Nathan, who converted to Christianity in 1823 at the age of forty, spent some years in Silesia, where he operated machinery factories; he also tried publishing a scientific journal, but only a few numbers appeared. He died in 1852. Nathan was married to Henrietta Itzig, who came of a large and distinguished family related both to the Heines and the Rothschilds. She was also related to Leah Salomon, who married the most famous of Moses Mendelssohn's sons, Abraham, father of the great composer.

X *The Human Hyphen*

Abraham Mendelssohn liked to refer to himself as a *Gedanken-strich*—a hyphen—coming between a famous father and a celebrated son. Behind the self-deprecating humor there lay a man of complexity and cultivation, proud of both father and son, and spending much of his life struggling to maintain a balance between the heritage of one and the advancement of the other.

Even if Abraham Mendelssohn had not been strongly influenced by the ideals of human equality set forth by his father, he undoubtedly would have acquired similar views during his sojourn as a young man in Paris. He was twenty-eight years old when he arrived there to begin work at Fould's banking house, and like his sister Henrietta, he planned to remain indefinitely. As a young man of democratic instincts, he was tremendously impressed by Bonaparte, who as First Consul seemed to him to be carrying out the libertarian and egalitarian concepts of the French Revolution, including civil rights for Jews.

Abraham's intention, after his marriage to Leah Salomon, was to bring her back to Paris and settle down with her there while pursuing his banking career at Fould's. But her family in Berlin objected; although they were pleased enough to have their daughter marry a son of Moses Mendelssohn, they wanted to make certain he could support her in proper style.

Abraham put up a battle, at one point telling his sister Henrietta, *"je préferais manger du pain sec à Paris"*—("I would rather eat a crust of bread in Paris"). Henrietta, sounding more like an older sister than a younger one, replied that the bread might turn bitter with the years: "At your age people. . . . always expect everything to suit their own wishes exactly, and then, while they are hesitating, their happiness is gone and lost forever. . . . Seldom, if ever, can you find a woman like her." And so Abraham reluctantly decided to give up Paris. He and Leah were married in 1804, and he went into partnership with his brother Joseph, who had just moved his banking headquarters to Hamburg. This is how Leah herself later described the circumstances: "I married my husband before he had a penny of his own. But he was earning a certain although very moderate income at Fould's in Paris, and I knew he would be able to turn my dowry to good account. My mother's ambition, however, would not allow me to be the wife of a clerk, and Mendelssohn therefore had to enter into partnership with his brother, from which period, thank God, dates the prosperity of both!"

Leah Mendelssohn was a comely and accomplished woman. She knew music, being an expert pianist and a good singer; and she spoke English, French, and Italian and had a reading acquaintance with Greek. Abraham Mendelssohn shared his wife's intellectual and artistic interests, and like her was a concertgoer and theatergoer, a frequenter of art galleries, and an avid reader. He was active in several German musical societies, and his visits to Paris, whether on banking missions or to see his sister Henrietta, always included evenings at the opera or in concert halls. In the French capital he saw Taglioni dance, heard Sontag sing and Paganini play, and sent back enthusiastic but measured opinions of all. Some music he could not tolerate; after hearing Rossini's *William Tell,* he wondered that "the author of the *Barber* and *Otello* could write music with such dissonance." Abraham also wrote home in detail about his visits to Parisian art galleries and museums; one of his letters reported on an addition to the Louvre: "In the Hall of Statues I have found nothing new but a Venus of Milo, who has lost both her arms; I know nothing further about her."

With their banking business flourishing, both Joseph and Abraham became leading citizens of Hamburg, where Abraham bought a country house named Marten's Mill. His first child, Fanny, was born on November 14, 1805. Abraham, announcing the event to his mother-in-law, wrote: "Leah says that the baby has Bach-fugue fingers"—as good a recommendation as any incipient pianist could ask.

Felix Mendelssohn, the second child and first son, was born on February 3, 1809; and another girl, Rebecca, on April 11, 1811. Paul, the youngest, was born October 30, 1813, but by that time the Mendelssohns had left Hamburg and resettled in Berlin.

The move came about because of the tightening French restrictions during their occupation of Hamburg in the course of the Napoleonic Wars. The Mendelssohn brothers both were ardent Francophiles; Abraham particularly liked to sprinkle his letters with French expressions, and he could never get Paris out of his head. "Every entrance into Paris is an important epoch in one's life," he once wrote, "and however old, cold and unstrung one may be, the remainder of the faculties must be spent in rejoicing that one is there."

But both business necessities and a growing sense of German nationalism gradually began to change the Mendelssohn brothers' attitude. Hamburg was a free Hanseatic port that sent its ships to all parts of Europe. When Napoleon, in 1806, promulgated decrees abolishing all trade with England as part of his economic blockade, Hamburg's commercial prosperity was wiped out overnight. Smuggling and other illicit activities began to flourish; evading the French regulations became a matter not only of economic necessity but of patriotic duty. As bankers and businessmen, the Mendelssohns took a leading part in illegal commerce until the French authorities began to close in on them. In 1811, they decided it was time to get out; so on a dark foggy night, Abraham, Leah, their three young children, and old Fromet Mendelssohn, now in her eighty-sixth year, all swathed and muffled to avoid recognition, got into a carriage and rode out of Hamburg. They managed to take money with them and had no difficulty in resuming and expanding the family banking business in Berlin. By 1813, in fact, Abraham had become a muncipal councillor (*Stadtrat*) of the city and had contributed large sums for the equipment of volunteers in what had now become a war of liberation against Napoleon. From a Francophile Jew, Abraham Mendelssohn had developed into a German patriot.

He also had come squarely up against the question of religious conversion. Essentially, Abraham does not seem to have been a person of very strong religious, or at least sectarian, conviction of any kind. As a rationalist, a skeptic, an intellectual, and a man of good will, he was little interested in the outward forms of ritual; there were in all religions, he insisted, "only one God, one virtue, one truth, one happiness."

A letter he wrote to his daughter Fanny, expounding his religious views, has a decidedly modern ring: "Does God exist? What is God? Is He a part of ourselves, and does He continue to live after the other part has ceased to be? And where? And how? All this I do not know, and therefore I have never taught you anything about it. But I know that there exists in me and you and all human beings an everlasting inclination towards all that is good, true, and right, and a conscience which warns and guides us when we go astray. I know it, I believe it, I live in this faith, and this is my religion."

Most of this was not in the least incompatible with the teachings of Moses Mendelssohn, and it seems altogether possible that, left to himself, Abraham would have remained at least a nominal Jew. But he was not left to himself. Both his wife Leah and her brother Jacob Bartholdy kept applying pressure on Abraham to adopt Christianity both for himself and his children.

Bartholdy was one of the most bizarre personages in the entire Mendelssohn circle. Born Jacob Levin Salomon in 1779, he began to brood about being Jewish at an early age. Since he came from a well-to-do family, he was able to travel a good deal, and he cultivated the society of as many aristocratic and wealthy gentiles as would tolerate him.

In 1805, he finally took the step of becoming a Protestant himself and going even further, dropped the annoying name of Salomon. In its place, he adopted the name Bartholdy, which he took from a piece of property he inherited, a mansion and garden on the River Spree, which had belonged in former times to a Mayor Bartholdy of the Berlin suburb of Neukoelln. The new Bartholdy lavished so much money and attention on his residence that the Mendelssohns labeled it "Little Sans Souci," after Frederick the Great's palace. Much to Jacob Bartholdy's chagrin, most other Berliners called it "the Jew-Garden."

Bartholdy did not stay long in Berlin. Attaching himself to the liberal Prussian chancellor, Prince Hardenberg, he joined the diplomatic service around 1813 and set out to make a double career for himself as a diplomat and art patron. He wound up living most of his life in Italy. He never married, preferring to surround himself with young male artists who lived with him in a Roman villa at the head of the Spanish Steps, which became known as Casa Bartholdy. Among them were Johannes and Philipp Veit, Dorothea Mendelssohn's sons. In time the Casa Bartholdy became well known for its fine frescoes. Bartholdy also was an historian, writing a book about ancient Mycenae and an account of the Tyrolese uprising against Napoleon.

Bartholdy was busy in his diplomatic endeavors; for a number of years, he was Prussia's consul general in Rome and, later, its representative in Florence. He was known particularly for the quality of his confidential reports; he had a talent for plotting, intriguing, and conniving.

Most people who knew Bartholdy disliked him. Henrietta Mendelssohn, although a Catholic convert herself, derided him as "Pope Bartholdy I" and likened him to Leo X, "who deeply loved everything beautiful but never reckoned the cost." From most of the Jewish community Bartholdy of course cut himself off, and his Christian associates, with the exception of a few like Prince Hardenberg, regarded him rather dubiously. An appraisal of him that appeared in the *Deutsche Allgemeine Zeitung* after his death would have made unpleasant reading for this clandestine diplomat and officious social climber:

> Bartholdy's head was Oriental, his Jewish looks obvious at a glance. He could stand all kinds of exertions easily, but he could not endure repose and quiet. He loved to interrupt his rest periods with gambling, sometimes for very high stakes. His memory was exemplary, his wit biting, his answers quick and sharp. He felt himself destined for bigger things than he was entitled to by his birth, or his not very attractive bearing, or his education, which had more breadth than depth. He forced old aristocrats and Christians to suffer his presence among them. He worked to make himself popular, feared or essential. He was everything to everybody, always looking upwards, to be accepted where others were accepted, and take their place.

Bartholdy's influence over Leah Mendelssohn was considerable. His sister envied him his influential friends; in fact, Abraham used to tease her for her "aristocratic inclinations." Bartholdy had a considerable fortune and had given Leah to understand that some day she would inherit it (as she actually did, although it was reduced substantially by his gambling debts), and in return he seemed to reserve the right to meddle constantly in the Mendelssohns' affairs. When young Felix began to talk about making music his career, Bartholdy rushed off some advice to the parents: "The idea of a professional musician will not go down with me. It is no career, no life, no aim. . . . Let the boy go through a regular course of schooling, and then prepare for a state career by studying law. . . . Should you prefer him to be a merchant, let him enter a counting-house early."

On matters of religion, Bartholdy was even more persistent and, as it turned out, persuasive. His own conversion had not been accomplished without some family unpleasantness. His parents, Babette and Levi Salomon, were opposed to the move; and his mother, outraged by what she regarded as her son's apostasy, cast him out of the family. Only in later years was she reconciled to him.

But Bartholdy never ceased adjuring Leah and Abraham to become Christians, if not for their own sake then for their children's. He talked to them about it while visiting in Berlin and wrote letters while he was abroad. Leah was willing enough, but Abraham, with the memory of his father on his conscience, was reluctant. Bartholdy, who knew Abraham was little attached to ritual of any kind, kept badgering him, and even added a novel suggestion by proposing that Abraham follow him in altering not only his religion but also his name:

> I was not convinced by your arguments for holding on to your name and faith. Such arguments are no longer valid in our times. . . . You say you owe it to your father's memory, but do you think it would be wrong to give your children the religion which you regard as the best one? This would be the greatest tribute you or anybody could pay to your father's efforts to spread light and knowledge; in your place he would have done exactly the same for his children, and in my place, perhaps exactly what I have done. You may remain loyal to a despised, persecuted religion and pass it on to your children along with a life of suffering, as long as you believe it to be the absolute truth. But it is barbaric to do so when you no longer so believe.
>
> I urge you to adopt the name Mendelssohn Bartholdy to mark yourself apart from the other Mendelssohns. This would please me very much, because it would be the means of preserving my memory in the family. This would enable you to accomplish your end conveniently, for in France and other places, it is customary to add the name of one's wife's family to one's own.

Bartholdy was no Lavater in the force of his arguments, but neither was Abraham a Moses Mendelssohn in his power to resist. On March 21, 1816, Abraham took his children to the New

Church in Berlin and had them baptized. Fanny was ten; Felix, seven; Rebecca, four; and Paul, two. It was all done very quietly; Abraham may have regarded the step as necessary, but he did not make—to use an expression he would have understood himself— a *tzimmes* about it. Among other things, Leah was not anxious for her mother to know about it; old Madame Salomon had cut off her son Bartholdy and might just as readily do the same to her daughter. However, six years later, on October 4, 1822, both Leah and Abraham took advantage of a trip to Frankfurt to undergo baptism themselves; to be Jewish parents of Christian children was an obvious impossibility.

Abraham Mendelssohn appears never to have been altogether comfortable about his conversion; at least he kept finding it necessary to explain to his daughter why the family had undergone a change of religion. When his daughter Fanny was confirmed in 1820, he wrote to her:

> The outward form of religion your teacher has given you is historical, and changeable like all human ordinances. Some thousands of years ago the Jewish form was the reigning one, then the heathen form, and now it is the Christian. We, your mother and I, were born and brought up by our parents as Jews, and without being obliged to change the form of our religion have been able to follow the divine instinct in us and in our conscience. We have educated you and your brothers and sister in the Christian faith, because it is the creed of most civilized people, and contains nothing that can lead you away from what is good, and much that guides you to love, obedience, tolerance and resignation, even if it offered nothing but the example of its Founder, understood by so few, and followed by still fewer.

In 1829, the hundredth anniversary of the birth of Moses Mendelssohn was observed, and the commemorations seemed to open up the old wounds and raise the old doubts in Abraham. "On September 10* is the 100th anniversary of my father's birth," he

*September 6 is the generally accepted birth date for Moses Mendelssohn.

wrote in a letter dated August 12, 1829, "and the Jewish community is building an orphan home in his name. I like the idea very much, and will do everything possible to help. But every day I hate the idea of festivals of any kind more and more. And so maybe I shall have to be grateful for the coincidence that a trip I may have to take in the near future will coincide with the ceremony."

Along with his new religious affiliation, Abraham also accepted Bartholdy's offer of his name. Henceforth, he became known as Abraham Mendelssohn Bartholdy and passed the double name along to his children, whether they wanted it or not.

Part III

FELIX

Since contented nations and contented men have
no history, one should on principle abandon the idea
of writing a life of Mendelssohn. . . .

—EMILE VUILLERMOZ,
Editions Cosmopolites

XI *Zelter and Goethe*

Although fewer than twenty-five years elapsed between the death of Moses Mendelssohn in 1786 and the birth of his grandson Felix in 1809, tremendous changes had taken place in the fabric of European life. Jewish emanicipation was only one symptom of the political, economic, social, and cultural upheavals—some of them still not terminated—that touched people of all classes and countries.

Moses had been born into a world still fairly rigid in governmental forms, class demarcations, and artistic precepts; by Felix's time, people were thinking more independently, traveling more freely, and striking out on new creative paths.

In music, the dominating figure was Beethoven, universally acknowledged as a titan, even by those who were disturbed by his force and his originality. And Beethoven, despite his *Fidelio,* was an orchestra man, not an opera composer. The symphony orchestra came to be the ultimate medium of expression for composers, especially for German composers; and local orchestras began to flourish as never before, each city and community taking pride in its own. Even that still-flourishing institution, the summer music festival, came into its glory in this period. Above all, music became more than ever before a personal vehicle of expression, a statement of a composer's credo as well as an exercise of his intellect. Classicism merged into, and sometimes was almost swallowed up by, Romanticism. Perhaps more than any other composer of his time, Felix Mendelssohn felt the pull of both the old world and the new.

However, he certainly had few artistic problems in his childhood. He was born at the Mendelssohn home in Hamburg at 14 Grosse Michaelisstrasse, but spent much of his time at Marten's Mill, their summer house. In later years, when Felix was already famous, Abraham Mendelssohn wrote to Leah: "Dear Wife, we have a certain amount of joy in this young man, and I often think: 'Hurrah for Marten's Mill!' "

An aura of contentment with the progress of all the Mendelssohn children was prevalent in the family from the start, particularly in music. Both parents were excellent musical amateurs and intended to make their children the same, and Leah herself began giving Felix his first piano lessons when he was four, starting with sessions five minutes long and gradually extending them. For years, neither Felix nor Fanny practiced without their mother sitting in the same room, knitting in hand.

As for Abraham, he was never happier than when he saw his children working hard at their music. The remarkable and repeated parallels between the musical lives of Felix Mendelssohn and Wolfgang Amadeus Mozart begin with their fathers. The traditional image of Leopold Mozart is that of a martinet and disciplinarian who exploited his son's talents; whereas Abraham Mendelssohn has often been depicted as a kindly and cultivated man who merely let his son's musicianship develop along its natural course.

Neither picture is wholly justified. Leopold Mozart was himself an accomplished musician who was keenly appreciative of his son's unique genius and was determined to make the world aware of it, too; Abraham Mendelssohn had an amateur's love and knowledge but was limited in his musical insight (he did not care much for Beethoven, for example), and he pushed Felix toward the composition of dramatic vocal music, such as opera and oratorio, which despite the later success of *Elijah,* were not forms altogether congenial to him.

A stern and self-made man, Abraham was consumed with ambition for his children in whatever field they entered. In the Mendelssohn household, the children were awakened at 5 A.M. to begin their morning's lessons. Felix told a friend in later years that he used to long for Sundays to come so that he might sleep later, and that his father's regimen had been "too strenuous" for him. In his childhood, he developed an ability, which astonished his friends, to fall asleep instantly upon lying down, sometimes in midday; and it often became a prodigious job to arouse him from his deep slumber. Henrietta Mendelssohn used to scold Abraham for treating his children too strictly and irascibly, and Felix's friend Eduard Devrient reported that Leah had a habit of interrupting her son's conversations in his room with a friend by calling out: "Felix, are you doing nothing?" Concluded Devrient: "His brain from childhood had been taxed excessively."

Abraham Mendelssohn engaged even a wider variety of tutors in his household than had his father Moses. Felix even had a personal teacher for landscape painting. His principal music tutor, hand-picked by Abraham, was Carl Friedrich Zelter, rough-tongued and somewhat coarse, but a musically shrewd composer and pedagogue.

Zelter was fifty-nine years old when he began to teach the eight-year-old Felix; among his other distinctions, he was director of the Berlin Singakadamie, the city's foremost institution for choral music. In musical matters he was a conservative, but that did not prevent him from leading a full and varied social life. He was one of the frequenters of Henrietta Herz's salon, had had a love affair with a young Jewess he met there, and had been acquainted with Moses Mendelssohn.

It was through Zelter that Felix had a memorable first meeting with Johann Wolfgang von Goethe, the sage of Weimar. Goethe's position in Germany at this time is hard to visualize today, for few literary men have ever attained such all-encompassing eminence. His writings almost defied count and classification. He had witnessed the onset of the French Revolution, lived through the rise and fall of Napoleon, helped create the spirit of the new Germany, whose literature, philosophy, science, and art he ruled as from Olympus. He knew everything and everybody; among his acquaintances were both Dorothea and Abraham Mendelssohn.

Zelter was one of his intimates. Goethe, who was by no means free of vanity or unaware of his own position, had liked the old musician ever since he had set some of his poems to music. The settings were not very distinguished, but then, Goethe's musical tastes were rather limited. He never really understood Beethoven, who was still alive and flourishing, and he had rebuffed an effort by Schubert to submit some compositions to him.

Now the poet was seventy-two years old, and his home had become a shrine. Visitors stood outside, hoping for a glimpse of the old man strolling in the gardens; and to be invited within was considered almost a mystic and ennobling experience.

Zelter proposed not only that he be allowed to bring the precocious Felix to see Goethe but that they spend some time as houseguests. With characteristic crudity, he wrote to the poet describing Felix as his "best pupil," then adding, "To be sure, he is the son of a Jew, but no Jew himself. The father, with remarkable self-denial, has let his sons learn something, and educates them properly. It would really be *eppes rores** if the son of a Jew turned out to be an artist." One wonders what the twelve-year-old Felix or his father might have felt had they seen Zelter's genial letter.

In any event, Felix's visit to Weimar was an exhilarating experience. "Now listen, all of you," he wrote to his family enthusiastically in a letter dated November 10, 1820. "Today is Tuesday. On Sunday the Sun of Weimar—Goethe—arrived. In the morning we went to church and they gave us half of Handel's 100th Psalm. Afterwards I went to the Elephant [a hotel] where I

---

*Yiddish-German for "something rare." Zelter was familiar with the dialect and apparently thought Goethe was, too.

sketched the house of Lucas Cranach. Two hours afterwards Professor Zelter came and said, 'Goethe has come; the old gentleman has come,' and in a minute we were down the steps and in Goethe's house. . . . He is very friendly, but I find all his pictures unlike him. . . . One would never take him for seventy-three, but for fifty."

Later that day Felix played for Goethe for two hours: mostly Bach, which the old man loved, but also several of his own compositions and some improvisations that were so wild that even Zelter, who knew his pupil's capacity, asked him in surprise what "goblins and dragons" were chasing him. There was Mozart, too, in the form of the *Marriage of Figaro* Overture, and soon Goethe began to make the comparisons—by now familiar to Felix's ears—of his own youthful accomplishments as a pianist and those of the earlier prodigy.

Felix in the meanwhile was receiving all sorts of adjurations in letters from his anxious family. His father warned him "to sit properly and behave nicely, especially at dinner"; his mother wished she could be "a little mouse so as to watch my dear Felix while he is away and see how he comports himself as an independent young man"; his sister Fanny told him to keep his eyes and ears open in Goethe's presence and warned that "after you come home, if you can't repeat every word that fell from his mouth, I'll have nothing more to do with you."

While on his visit, Felix displayed a precocious interest in other than musical spheres. Among the houseguests was a handsome girl named Ulrike von Pogwisch, the sister of Goethe's daughter-in-law. She took a good deal of interest in Felix's playing and, for his part, he found her very decorative. "Fräulein Ulrike also threw herself on his [Goethe's] neck," he reported home, "and as he is making love to her, and she is very pretty, it all adds to the general effect."

So pleased was everybody with Felix's visit that Goethe insisted it be prolonged to a total of sixteen days. The poet kept him busy at the piano, playfully remarking to him: "I have not heard you yet today—make a little noise for me." When Felix was finally permitted to depart, it was with a generous supply of gifts, including some verse specially written for him by Goethe; even more important, the poet wrote to a number of friends describing to them the young musical marvel from Berlin.

Others besides Goethe were impressed with the young Felix Mendelssohn—and not merely with his music, but with his good looks, bright demeanor, animation, and intelligence. Eduard Devrient, who was seven years older, first saw Felix when he was a boy of thirteen, playing marbles with other boys outside of his house or running along the street with them in big shoes, long brown curls flying. Devrient also recalled him at the Singakademie, which he had entered as a boy alto at the age of eleven, singing without self-consciousness among grownups, his hands thrust in his pockets, swaying from one foot to the other in time to the music. Judging by his contemporaries' accounts, Mendelssohn was one of the most attractive and agreeable, as well as talented, children who ever lived.

Curiously, although he grew up in a milieu far different, there were resemblances between his childhood and that of Moses Mendelssohn. Moses seems to have bequeathed certain physical characteristics to his grandchildren: Fanny Mendelssohn had a trace of spinal curvature, and Felix had a slight speech defect (described variously as a lisp or a drawl) and bore a strong facial resemblance to him.

But the principal link between Moses and Felix was their inquisitive intellectual spirit. As children, both were bright, precocious, and avid for knowledge. However, whereas Moses received his first tutoring and guidance from the local rabbi in Dessau, Felix as a youngster had access to the latest thought of all Europe in music, art, and literature.

It was more than a matter of hobnobbing with Goethe, or studying with Zelter, or traveling to Paris *en famille* at the age of seven. To Felix, as to Moses before him, learning was something to be pursued with zest and enthusiasm. His interests, like his grandfather's, were unbounded, so that he became an accomplished linguist, artist, and letter writer, as well as a musician. His sketches and watercolors, many of which have been preserved, show life and charm as well as pictorial accuracy; his correspondence, beginning with childhood, is in the great tradition of nineteenth-century travel writing. He spoke English virtually without an accent and French fluently. He knew Italian well enough to translate some sonnets by Dante into German for his uncle Joseph, who was contemplating writing a book about the Florentine poet; he studied both Greek and Latin, and his matriculation project for the University of Berlin, which he entered at sixteen, was a translation from Terence (which he also gave his mother as a birthday present, conveniently killing two birds with one stone).

Even the childhood entertainment he enjoyed was unusual. He and his sister Fanny, four years his senior, put on a series of Shakespearean performances at home in which the younger children, Rebecca and Paul, also took part. In 1825, the family moved to a new and larger house—in fact, it was an estate—at 3 Leipzigerstrasse, near the Potsdam Gate, in what was then a remote, almost rural area of Berlin. Among the amenities of this luxurious establishment, which covered some ten acres, was a vast private park abounding in lofty trees, beautiful gardens, and subsidiary buildings of various sorts and sizes in addition to the dignified and spacious main house.

The first summer at 3 Leipzigerstrasse, the Mendelssohn children turned the park into a setting for outdoor Shakespeare, going enthusiastically about the business of distributing the parts to themselves and their friends. It would be pleasant to think that they made use of the translations into German made by their grandfather Moses, but this does not seem to have been the case. Instead, they depended upon the popular new version of William August Schlegel—something of a family connection at that, since he was the brother-in-law of their Aunt Dorothea. Their favorite play was *A Midsummer Night's Dream,* and Fanny remembered in afteryears how they each took turns at all the roles. Indeed, performing under illumination at night amid their stately trees and fragrant lilacs, they might well have applied to themselves the words of Peter Quince: "Pat, pat; and here's a marvellous convenient place for our rehearsal. This green plot shall be our stage, this hawthorne brake our tiring house. . . ."

In one of the summer houses in the park the children also began to publish a "newspaper," a journal to which all visitors were invited to contribute, and which was later read aloud. It took the form of several pens, ink, and a stack of paper neatly arranged on a table; among the contributors were Alexander Humboldt, Frederick Hegel, and Heinrich Heine. In the summer, the journal was called *The Garden Times;* in the winter, *The Tea- and-Snow Times.** It was in this "publication" that Abraham Mendelssohn first inscribed the comment: "Formerly I was known as the son of my father; now I am known as the father of my son." Later he so fancied his bon mot that he repeated it elsewhere.

As avidly as Felix plunged into theatricals, writing, and painting, all these activities were made insignificant by his tremendous activity as a musician. No child since Mozart had composed more prolifically. In 1820, when he was eleven years old, he began keeping a record of his compositions, writing them down with the date and place of completion, in a series of notebooks that eventually reached a total of forty-four, all in a hand so distinctively neat and precise that it resembled printed music. By the age of eleven, he had completed sixty works, ranging from songs to a three-movement trio for piano, violin, and cello. At twelve, he composed five string quartets, a motet, and two one-act operas; at thirteen, six symphonies, five concertos, and a three-act opera entitled *The Uncle from Boston.* This tremendous mass of music,

---

* *Thee- und Schneezeitung.*

most of it still in manuscript, is mainly of academic interest today; but it is marked with the finish, polish, and impeccable regard for form that were the characteristics of all Mendelssohn's music.

As with Mozart, everything Mendelssohn saw or touched turned to music. When he went as a boy on a trip to Switzerland, his letters were full of the awe induced by the great snowy mountains, but he also analyzed Swiss yodeling for the benefit of Zelter: "It consists of notes which are produced from the throat and generally are ascending sixths. . . . Certainly this kind of singing sounds harsh and unpleasant when it is heard near by or in a room. But it sounds beautiful when you hear it with mingling or answering echoes, in the valleys, on the mountains, or in the woods. . . ."

As a performer, too, Felix was a precocious child. He made his first public appearance at the age of nine, playing the piano part in a trio for two horns and piano composed by Josef Woelfl, a Viennese pianist who had died a few years before; four years later, in 1822, he joined the well-known pianist Aloys Schmitt in a two-piano recital, playing a duet by Dussek. Unlike young Mozart, whose father worked hard for a living, Felix didn't play for money, gold watches, snuffboxes, or other princely remunerations. Abraham Mendelssohn was a wealthy man and at the time had no thought that his son might make a career as a musician. As a child, Felix was considered strictly a gifted amateur. Later in life, he was surprised to find that other, less independently situated muscians regarded him as unfair competition because he was willing to accept engagements for token fees, or none at all.

Mendelssohn's most important and enjoyable musical performances took place in his own home. Even before the family moved to 3 Leipzigerstrasse, they had turned their first Berlin home, on the New Promenade, into a center of musical and cultural activity. It was Moses Mendelssohn's open house all over again, although this time more elegant and lavish. Leah Mendelssohn sent out handwritten notes to musicians and other prominent people, inviting them to the Mendelssohn musicales, which were held on alternate Sunday mornings. The attractions included luncheon (far more elaborate than Moses' and Fromet's raisins and almonds!) and performances by all her children, for Fanny played the piano, Rebecca sang, and Paul was a budding cellist.

But the big attraction was Felix; travelers to Berlin in the 1820s were as eager to hear the amazing young musical genius as those in the 1770s and 1780s had been to hear the old philosopher. There was nothing casual or haphazard about these musicales; after the move to 3 Leipzigerstrasse, they were held in a spacious summerhouse whose hall could accommodate an audience of several hundred. A small orchestra or chorus, engaged for the day, was on hand, and everything revolved around Felix. He selected the programs, held the rehearsals, appeared as piano soloist, and also conducted, even when he was so small that he had to stand on a stool to be seen. Few musicians have been introduced at so early an age to the concert business, not to mention the exigencies of performing before an audience, and few composers have had the opportunity of trying out so young the actual sound of their music.

Ignaz Moscheles, the famous pianist and pedagogue, then thirty years old, was among the luminaries Leah Mendelssohn invited to her parties. At her behest, he gave Felix, then fifteen, a few lessons, then declared good-humoredly that he had nothing more to teach him. Moscheles, fascinated by the Mendelssohns and their music, preserved a record of two of the programs he heard in 1824:

> *Nov. 28. Morning music at the Mendelssohns':*—Felix's C minor Quartet; his D Major Symphony; Concerto by Bach (Fanny); Duet for two pianos in D minor, Arnold.

> *Dec. 12, Sunday music at the Mendelssohns':*—Felix's F minor Quartet. I played my Duet in G for two pianos. Little Schilling played Hummel's Trio in G.

In that same year Zelter, particularly moved by a composition of his young pupil, arranged a little mock ceremony in which he told Felix, half-humorously, half-solemnly: "From this day forth you are no longer an apprentice but a member of the brotherhood of musicians. I proclaim you independent, in the name of Mozart, Haydn, and old father Bach."

But there were things in the back of Felix's mind that never troubled old father Bach or his other illustrious predecessors. Although his outward life was that of a solid, if not particularly ardent Lutheran, and he eventually married the daughter of a Calvinist pastor, he was constantly aware of his Jewish descent— indeed, if he had not been, there were always those to remind him of it.

Many nineteenth-century biographers of Mendelssohn either touched lightly upon or totally ignored his Hebraic origins; a standard German biography by W. A. Lampidius, published in 1865, has almost an entire chapter devoted to "his Christian character." But recent research, notably by the musicologist Eric Werner, and the opening of hitherto unavailable family letters and documents, indicate that Mendelssohn accepted his childhood change of religion less lightly than his Aunts Dorothea and Henrietta and that, had he been left to himself, he conceivably would never have taken the step—even though, once it had been done for him, he never attempted to reverse it.

Felix's first recorded encounter with overt anti-Semitism came in 1819, the year of the *Judensturm* in Germany, a widespread wave of looting and violence aimed at the newly "emancipated" Jewish citizenry and a distant forerunner of the Nazis' *Kristallnacht* of 1938. The war cry for the *Judensturm* outbursts was "hep, hep!" —an exclamation concocted by university students from the initials of the Latin words *Hierosolyma est perdita* ("Jerusalem is destroyed"). While the demonstrations were going on, Felix happened to meet in the street one of the Prussian royal princes with whom he had a slight acquaintance; the boy marched up to him, spat at his feet, and exclaimed: "Hep, hep, *Judenjung.*"

Considering the physical violence inflicted on many Jews that year, Felix got off easily, but the experience was one he remembered. Five years later another occurred, this time in Rostock on the Baltic, where the family was vacationing. A group of toughs threw stones at Felix and Fanny and called them names; when they returned home, Felix broke down in tears of rage and humiliation.

Such incidents seemed to nurture Felix's feelings for his Judaic origins. A strong streak of stubbornness was one of his characteristics; so was his innate feeling of respect for and obedience to his parents. That there should be a conflict within him over the Jewish question was inevitable, and it came out openly during the trip he made to Paris with his father to fetch his Aunt Henrietta back to Berlin after the marriage of General Sebastiani's daughter. Felix was sixteen years old at the time, and his reputation had already spread to France; so Abraham, for the first time thinking in terms of a professional career for his son, wished to present him to some of the leading musicians of Paris.

Now that his son was about to step into the world, Abraham had a set of calling cards engraved for him. Deliberately, he had them printed: "Felix M. Bartholdy." Equally deliberately, Felix refused to accept them. His name, he said, was not Bartholdy but Mendelssohn, although if his father insisted, out of respect for him he would agree to be called Felix Mendelssohn Bartholdy.*

They argued the matter out during a wild carriage ride on the last stage of their journey from Berlin to Paris. In the jolting vehicle, Felix asked his father pointedly why he had changed the family name, and Abraham, distressed at the question, attempted to justify his action by pointing out that his father, whose original

---

*Felix never used a hyphen between the two names. The form Mendelssohn-Bartholdy was adopted by his younger brother Paul and belongs to his line. Although the point is a small one, it seems to be another indication that Felix wished to keep his name clear of direct linkage with his uncle's.

name in the Jewish style was Moses ben Mendel, had changed it to Moses Mendelssohn and "by that name identified himself with a different group." In the same way, he contended, he, too, was making a new identification with his times by adopting the name Bartholdy. To continue to use the name Mendelssohn, he said, was almost an affront to old Moses, who had made it famous in Jewry: "A Christian Mendelssohn is an impossibility. There can no more be a Christian Mendelssohn than a Jewish Confucius. If Mendelssohn is your name, you are *ipso facto* a Jew."

The dispute—rare in the well-ordered Mendelssohn family—was renewed four years later when the young composer, then on his first visit to London, had his name listed on the programs, as well as in newspaper announcements, as Felix Mendelssohn. His father wrote to him angrily from Berlin, repeating his arguments of the 1825 carriage ride and telling him bluntly: "You cannot, you must not carry the name Mendelssohn. Felix Mendelssohn Bartholdy is too long; it is unsuited for daily use. You must go by the name Felix Bartholdy."

Nevertheless, Felix continued to use the name Mendelssohn throughout his life. Only in Germany has the composer invariably been listed as Mendelssohn Bartholdy, except of course in the Nazi era, when his name was banned altogether because he was born a Jew.

XII *A Dream and a Nightmare*

To the generations that followed, Felix Mendelssohn has been primarily famous as the composer of such works as the *Midsummer Night's Dream* incidental music, the *Scotch* and *Italian* Symphonies, and the Violin Concerto in E Minor, all solidly and, one assumes, imperishably established in the orchestral repertory. In his own time, too, he was well known for his compositions, but he was equally celebrated as a pianist, an organist, a conductor, and a musical organizer and administrator. He became, during his short lifetime, probably the foremost musical authority of his day; no German until Herbert von Karajan in our time exerted so much influence over European orchestral playing and programing. Mendelssohn was the hub of musical activity in Germany and in England. He had his enemies, rivals, and detractors; but it was always to him that other young musicians of the time, from Schumann to Chopin, turned for advice, encouragement, and leadership. And he achieved his pre-eminence both as a musical creator and as an organizer by the time he was twenty.

It was his visit to Paris in the spring of 1825 that set Felix on the road to musical professionalism. Abraham Mendelssohn took him to call on Luigi Cherubini, the celebrated Italian-born composer who headed the Paris Conservatoire. Cherubini was sixty-five, had a reputation for irascibility, and was near the end of his career—Felix called him "an extinct volcano"—but his word carried weight, and after listening to Felix participate in a performance of his Piano Quartet in B Minor op. 3, he declared: "This

boy is rich; he will do well; he is already doing well." Both Felix
and his father went away pleased with Cherubini's verdict, and
from then on he was bent on a musical career, even though he
pursued some academic studies for a time at the University of
Berlin.

Other aspects of Paris were less to Felix's liking, and he wrote
about them acerbically to his sister Fanny: "You say I should try
and convert the people here, and teach Onslow and Reicha to love
Beethoven and Sebastian Bach. That is just what I am trying to do.
But remember, my dear child, that these people do not know a
single note of *Fidelio,* and believe Bach to be a mere old-fashioned
wig stuffed with learning. . . . The other day, at the request of
Kalkbrenner, I played the organ preludes in E minor and B minor.
My audience pronounced them both 'wonderfully pretty', and
one of them remarked that the beginning of the prelude in A
minor was very much like a favorite duet in an opera by Monsigny.
You could have knocked me over with a feather."

Beethoven at this time was fifty-five years old and had two years
more to live. Mendelssohn never met or corresponded with him
but had a profound admiration for his works, particularly the later
ones that many of his contemporaries found "difficult." Beethoven, along with religion, was a point of contention between Felix
and his father; Abraham regarded late Beethoven as incompre-
hensible and could not fathom his son's excitement over such
fractious music. Felix met much the same reaction from Goethe.

Nevertheless, he played Beethoven wherever he went, memo-
rizing such difficult works as the Sonata in B-flat op. 106 and a
piano reduction of the Ninth Symphony. For Goethe, who had
actually met Beethoven in 1812, Felix played a piano version of
the Fifth Symphony. The old poet found it exciting but erratic, "as
if the house were caving in."

Felix's music, though, followed its own course. There is little
reminiscent of Beethoven in those smooth and sparkling early
symphonies, operas, quartets, concertos, and shorter works that

flowed from him with such seeming ease and which were performed under his direction at the Sunday musicales. But gradually, signs of individuality began appearing—a touch of gentle melancholy in a song, a brilliant but orderly virtuoso passage in a piano work, or even an entire movement imbued with a spirit of enchantment such as had rarely been heard in music before.

The first of these was the scherzo of the B Minor Piano Quartet with which Felix had won over Cherubini: an inventive, impulsive movement that was the first of a family of scherzos uniquely Mendelssohnian in their lightness and grace. Mendelssohn himself must have recognized it as something special, for he dedicated the quartet to Goethe, on whom he paid another, friendly visit at Weimar, on the way home from Paris. Here Mendelssohn began a strange practice that he continued throughout his life: on the top of each completed score, he wrote the cryptic letters *L.e.g.G.* or *H.d.m.* He never told anybody what they meant, nor has the mystery been solved to this day.*

In 1825, Felix took what Sir George Grove, the first editor of *Grove's Dictionary of Music and Musicians,* called "a wonderful leap into maturity." He composed, for performance at the Sunday musicales, the Octet in E-flat, which remains his first enduring masterpiece. A work for double string quartet, it is music of such radiance and vitality that it remains an incredible achievement for a boy of sixteen. Not even Mozart wrote anything like it at the same age. Of the Octet's scherzo movement, Fanny wrote proudly: "To me alone he told his idea: the whole piece is to be played staccato and pianissimo, the tremolandos coming in now and then, the trills passing away with the quickness of lightning; everything new and strange and at the same time most insinuating and pleasing. One feels so near the world of spirits, carried away in the air, half inclined to snatch up a broomstick and follow the

---

*Suggestions made over the years include *Lobt einen guten Gott*—("Praise a Good God") and, *Hilf du mir* ("Help Thou Me"). But these are only guesses.

aerial procession. At the end the first violin takes flight with a feathery lightness—and all has vanished." Felix himself said years later that the Octet remained his favorite work and added: "I had a beautiful time writing it."

The following year came an even more perfect achievement, the Overture to *A Midsummer Night's Dream,* a unique piece of musical sorcery beginning with four suspended wind chords which when they are played perfectly—as sometimes they are not —open up a whole moonlit universe. Bernard Shaw described the D Minor chords of the statue music in *Don Giovanni* as "a sound of dreadful joy to all musicians"; similarly, the E Major opening chords of the *Midsummer Night's Dream* distill the essence of musical romanticism.*

The *Midsummer Night's Dream* Overture created a sensation among the first audience that heard it at a Sunday musicale in the garden house, and soon invitations began arriving for the young composer to conduct it elsewhere, its first public performance being at Stettin on February 20, 1827, with Mendelssohn journeying to the Pomeranian city in bitter winter weather.† He also made a version of it for piano duet, which he and Fanny often played.

So talked about was the Overture that all sorts of stories and legends sprang up about it. According to one account, Mendelssohn extemporized it at the piano seated beside a young neighbor girl of whom he was temporarily enamored. Another story said that he composed it at a little table in the family garden, where the evening breezes wafted past him, each bringing to him one of the opening chords. Still a third version had him working it out on music paper while attending dull lectures at the University of Berlin. At least one other person even claimed to have had a hand

---

*The third chord unexpectedly changes to A Minor, heightening the magical effect.
†The musical director there was Carl Loewe, later to become well known as a composer of ballads for voice. At the same concert, Loewe and Mendelssohn joined in playing Felix's Concerto for Two Pianos in A-flat.

in bringing the Overture to its final shape. He was Adolph Bern-
hardt Marx, a musical editor and writer ten years older than Felix,
who was a frequent caller at the house. Marx said afterward that
he had told Felix the Overture didn't reflect the action of Shakespeare's play, and that the composer, though initially upset, had
reworked the entire piece according to his advice. Marx and Mendelssohn later had a falling-out; in any case, Marx is chiefly remembered for his prophetic words after the first performance of the
Overture: "Here begins a new music."

With all these successes went a failure. All his life, Felix Mendelssohn wanted to write a stageworthy opera, and he never did.
His most serious attempt came when he was sixteen, with a three-
act opera buffa entitled *The Wedding of Camacho.* Based on an
episode in Cervantes's *Don Quixote,* which was then enjoying a
revival of interest in Germany thanks to a new translation, it dealt
mainly with the unsuccessful effort of a rich landowner named
Camacho* to thwart the marriage of a poor peasant lad to a pretty
young girl he craves for himself. Both the plot and, occasionally,
the music are vaguely reminiscent of Mozart's *Marriage of Figaro.*
Don Quixote, although not the principal character, has a scene for
himself in which, in a fit of madness, he mistakes the bride, Quit-
eria, for his own Dulcinea.

Mendelssohn, despite his youth—or because of it—thought his
opera should be produced at the Royal Theater of Berlin, whose
musical director was Gasparo Spontini, the famous composer of
La Vestale. Spontini, then fifty-two, was, like Cherubini, one of
those itinerant Italians who had wandered far from their native
land to take important musical posts abroad. He had come to
Berlin by way of Paris, and although he was a composer of sub-
stance, he also was a vain, foppish man continually involved in
administrative intriguing and conniving, so that he had a reputation for undependability.

---

*Gamacho in Cervantes.

In Paris he had been one of the frequenters of Henrietta Mendelssohn's salon, and he was well acquainted with the Mendelssohns of Berlin, too, so there seemed reason to hope he would look kindly upon the performance of the new opera by the banker's son. However, such proved not to be the case. Spontini delayed and temporized over the score for a year, while the Mendelssohns became increasingly fretful and exerted as much pressure as they dared through their court connections to get the opera produced. Finally Spontini sent for Felix and received him in his office, wearing a frock coat covered with decorations and holding a lorgnette in front of his eyes. The full score, 371 pages long, lay on his desk, and Spontini condescendingly explained its shortcomings to the boy. Then, pointing out of his window to the dome of the main Berlin synagogue, which happened to be visible, he said in French: "My friend, you must have great ideas, as great as that dome." Whether his choice of a synagogue dome was a studied reference to Felix's Jewish ancestry is not clear, but the incident so angered Abraham Mendelssohn that he never forgave Spontini.

Oddly, after all this, Spontini allowed the performance to go forward, and *Die Hochzeit des Camacho* had its première on April 29, 1827, not in the main hall of the Berlin Opera House but in its smaller chamber theater. A distinguished audience turned out, among them the Sunday afternoon "regulars" from the Leipzigerstrasse musicales. Many were old family friends, going back to the days of Moses Mendelssohn. Henrietta Herz, still beautiful despite her sixty years, was there; she had lost most of her money and now supported herself as a language teacher. With her was her friend Schleiermacher, still active as a preacher and proselytizer.

Despite the sympathies of the audience (the applause after the first act was hearty), it gradually became evident that the opera was failing to have its effect. The applause dwindled; the house became restless; Felix himself sensed that his music wasn't working as well on stage as on paper. Before the final curtain came down, he left the theater and walked out into the night. The applause at the end was polite, and there were a few calls for the composer, which quickly died out when it developed he was no longer on the premises. The following day the singer who took the role of Don Quixote became conveniently ill, and further performances were canceled. *The Wedding of Camacho* was never given again, and is unlikely to be attempted until some enterprising operatic group or record company becomes curious to see whether an opera by the composer of the *Midsummer Night's Dream* can be as bad as all that.

Camacho was neither Mendelssohn's first nor last exposure to adverse criticism. Even at the Sunday musicales, there were listeners who found things to cavil at, and sometimes their comments made their way into the press. Zelter wrote to Goethe complaining about the Berlin critics' reaction to Felix: "They have reviewed his quartets and symphonies somewhat coldly in the musical papers. . . . Things that are completely above the heads of these gentlemen they cut up as coolly as possible, and fancy they can judge the whole house by one brick." Reading his critics, Felix himself was stirred to compose a bit of verse in reply, although he intended it for no wider circulation than that of *The Garden Times:*

> If the artist gravely writes,
>   To sleep it will beguile.
> If the artist gaily writes,
>   It is a vulgar style.
>
> If the artist writes at length,
>   How sad his hearer's lot!
> If the artist briefly writes,
>   No man will care one jot.
>
> If an artist simply writes,
>   A fool he's said to be,
> If an artist deeply writes,
>   He's mad, 'tis plain to see.

> In whatsoever way he writes
> He can't please every man;
> Therefore let an artist write
> How he likes and can.

The failure of *Camacho* upset Mendelssohn for a time, and the death of a friend of his own age named August Hanstein deepened his melancholy. But he had too much music in his head and vigor in his heart to remain depressed for long, and a summer trip to the Harz mountains with two young friends, Eduard Rietz, a violinist, and Gustav Magnus, a physician, restored him quickly. After one particularly exhilarating excursion near the town of Erbich ("a poor little place"), he wrote home:

> If three of the most remarkable families of Berlin knew that three of their most remarkable sons are roving the roads at night with carriers, peasants and tramps, and exchanging biographies with them, they would be dreadfully distracted. . . . In all the towns, hamlets and villages we go through with our pilgrim-staffs we cause great excitement; the girls come to the windows, and the street-boys follow us laughing for three streets at the least—a proof of popularity and clean linen! We get on together quite well as we enjoy ourselves, and this is saying a great deal. Our talk is alternately of musicians, fevers, and home, so each has his own topic, and in a student song and refrain we all join as one. . . .

One consequence of the triumph of the *Midsummer Night's Dream* Overture was a parting of the ways, as pupil and teacher, of Mendelssohn and Zelter. Although it was not put into so many words, the feeling in the family now was that Felix had outgrown the crusty old pedagogue, and could operate musically entirely on his own. The affair must have been handled by Abraham with considerable finesse, for Zelter remained on more or less agreeable terms with the family and, as a matter of fact, spent the remaining eight years of his life taking bows for Felix's achievements. "The old man has seen the fish swim," commented A. B. Marx sarcastically, "and imagines he has taught him how."

XIII The Great Bach Revival

Even with his favorite pupil gone, Zelter, of course, remained as head of the Berlin Singakademie and a leading figure in the city's musical activities. As things turned out, he still had a part to play, both in life and in death, in two of the most momentous events of Felix Mendelssohn's career.

The first occurred in 1829, the hundredth anniversary year of the composition of Johann Sebastian Bach's *Passion According to St. Matthew*. Today it seems incredible that this masterful work should have gone unperformed for a full century, but this was the case when Mendelssohn, at the age of twenty, decided to restore it to life. The problem with Bach's music in those days was not that it was unknown, but that it was unplayed. Whatever his reputation among musicians, his works, especially his great choral master-piece, were virtually unknown to the public at large.

Mendelssohn knew that Zelter had a copy of the *St. Matthew* score in the archives of the Singakademie. One legend, popularized some years ago in a novel called *Beyond Desire* by Pierre La Mure, is that Zelter possessed the original manuscript and that it had once been used as wrapping paper by a cheesemonger. Actually, Zelter's was only a copy of the original, but it was complete and faithful and a rare-enough document at that. Mendelssohn had known about Zelter's score even as a child, and now his maternal grandmother, old Madame Salomon, engaged his friend Eduard Rietz to copy it out for him, with Zelter's permission, as a gift. Mendelssohn was ecstatic and immediately began assembling a

126

small choir to try out passages from it in his house.

The results were overwhelming. Everyone who participated even in those fragmentary performances was carried away by the beauty and grandeur of the music. Felix almost immediately began dreaming of a public performance of the *Passion,* and the obvious year was its centenary, 1829— a year that, as he was well aware, also marked the hundredth anniversary of the birth of Moses Mendelssohn.

Felix's main ally in planning the performance was his friend Eduard Devrient, twenty-eight years old, who at the time was pursuing a double career as a singer and an actor. He eventually concentrated on the latter, becoming director of the court theaters in Dresden and Karlsruhe. At the time, however, he was the possessor of a sturdy bass voice and wanted to undertake the role of Jesus in the *Passion.*

Mendelssohn made several attempts to interest Zelter in the idea of having the Singakademie put on an actual performance of the *Passion.* But the old man kept reiterating the difficulties of the work, the lack of public interest, the inability of the academy's forces to cope with its complexities, the numbers of performers required, and all the dozens of other reasons that had prevented it from being given anywhere for an entire century. And, although he did not go into them, he also knew of other reasons: that there was a certain amount of hostility in Berlin musical circles toward the overeager young composer, the wealthy amateur who didn't care whether or not he was properly paid, the son of the Jewish banker who could hire his own orchestra and now, evidently, was trying to buy the Singakademie, too.

Finally, Devrient, who was a leading member of the Singakademie, decided to make one final attempt by going with Felix to see Zelter. Later on the actor described this supreme effort:

> One evening in January, 1829 we sang the entire first part of the work for a small group. I spent a sleepless night afterwards, during

which I hatched my plan for putting across a public performance. Felix, the old man's favorite pupil, must win the old man over. Impatiently, I waited for the late winter dawn, and then set out for the Mendelssohn house. Felix was still asleep. I thought I should leave, but his younger brother Paul* volunteered to wake him, and began the operation. Felix lay in his well-known death-like slumber. Paul took him under the arms, then around the waist, and sat him up. 'Felix, wake up, it's eight o'clock.' He rocked the upper part of his body back and forth, but it was a long time before Felix, who was apparently dreaming of music, murmured: 'Oh, stop it, I always said so, it's sheer squawking.' His brother, however, did not stop shaking and calling him by name, until he had at least roused him a little. Then he allowed him to lie back on the pillow. At this point Felix opened his eyes wide, and seeing me by his bed exclaimed in Berlin dialect: 'Hey, Eduard, what are you doing here?' I told him that I had something I wanted to talk over with him. Paul led me into the low-ceilinged study where Felix's breakfast was waiting on the big white desk, and his coffee on the stove.

At breakfast, Devrient told Mendelssohn that he had resolved that the *St. Matthew Passion* must be given at the Akademie within a matter of months, that Mendelssohn would conduct and he would sing Jesus, and that Zelter should be made to give them use of the concert hall. He suggested that they propose to Zelter that the proceeds go to charity, thus making it difficult for the board of trustees to refuse. Moreover, he and Felix should go to see Zelter immediately.

Felix reluctantly consented but said that he would leave if Zelter got nasty and began to quarrel. "He'll certainly get nasty," replied Devrient, "but leave the quarreling to me."

At the Singakademie, they went into Zelter's office. Remembered Devrient: "We found the old giant sitting at his grand piano with its double keyboards, a long pipe in his mouth, and a dense cloud of tobacco smoke surrounding him. . . . He was wearing his usual short, snuff-colored, beribboned and betasseled Polish

*Paul was then sixteen.

jacket and knee breeches, stockings of coarse wool and embroidered shoes. . . . He peered at us through his spectacles, and when he saw who it was he called out good-naturedly: 'What do two such handsome lads want with me so early in the day? To what am I indebted for this honor? Here, sit down. . . .' "

Devrient then launched into his well-studied speech about how they admired Sebastian Bach, dreamed about performing his *Passion,* had already begun working on it, and now wished his permission to use the Akademie for this noble purpose.

Zelter listened gloomily and replied: "Oh yes, that is all very well, but nowadays things like that can't be done so easily." He enumerated the obstacles: the need for extra musicians, the difficulties of the music, the inadequacies of the choristers, problems, problems. . . . Mendelssohn, who had heard it all before, edged toward the door, but Devrient persisted. He told Zelter that under his wise guidance the Singakademie chorus had reached such a pinnacle of excellence that it could meet the challenge, and that the orchestra, too, would rise to the occasion. Zelter replied impatiently that "much better people than you two" had talked of putting on the *Passion* and never done so. "Why should a couple of snot-noses like you succeed?" he asked.

Mendelssohn was standing with his hand on the doorknob by now, but Devrient kept arguing: "We may be young but we're not so immature. After all, young people are supposed to have a certain amount of courage and enterprise, and a teacher should be pleased if two of his pupils want to attempt something so important." Zelter answered that the women on the board of trustees would oppose the plan, but Devrient told him that some had actually joined in the choral rehearsals at the Mendelssohn home. "Women!" Zelter exclaimed scornfully. "Today ten of them come to rehearsals and tomorrow twenty stay away!" For an hour they kept wrangling, until Zelter finally weakened to the extent of promising to lay the question before the board. "I won't oppose you," he said, "and will put in a good word for you if I can. Good luck to you, and we will see what comes of it all."

Devrient and Mendelssohn rushed out into the street exulting and shaking hands with each other. "To think," Felix exclaimed, "that an actor and a Jew should give back to the people the greatest Christian music in the world." It was the only time, Devrient later wrote, that Mendelssohn ever alluded in his hearing to his Jewish origin.

A hectic period of organization and preparation followed, with Felix and Devrient compiling a list of singers, mostly from the opera, they wished to appear as principals and then seeking them out. None had ever sung the music before, which meant they would have to learn it and then participate in numerous rehearsals. But everybody joined eagerly in the project, and since the work was to be performed for charity, most of the singers even offered to pay their way into the concert. In the end, only six free tickets were issued, and two of these were for Spontini, who disapproved of the whole business. Rietz copied out the orchestral parts for the players and refused compensation. The only reluctance came, as Zelter had foretold, from the directors of the Akademie. Mendelssohn paid a call on them, purchasing a pair of yellow kid gloves ("very important in their eyes," his sister Fanny noted ironically) for the purpose. He proposed that, since this was to be a charitable affair, the directors waive the customary fifty-thaler fee for the use of the main Singakademie hall. If the *Passion* were successful, he proposed to give a second performance, with all proceeds going to the Akademie. The directors politely declined, insisting on payment in advance for the hall. Mendelssohn paid the fifty thalers himself.

Mendelssohn made certain cuts and alterations in the *St. Matthew Passion* and has been much criticized for it ever since. But his object was not to present a scholarly replica of the manuscript but to make the work seem alive and vivid to an audience of his own time. At that, the extent of his editing has been exaggerated: he eliminated some of the solo arias and duets out of fear that the public of 1829 wouldn't last through four hours of Bach, and he orchestrated one recitative passage, "And behold, the veil of the temple was rent in twain." Everything else was untouched; Bach would have had no trouble recognizing his work.

The first performance in one hundred years of the *St. Matthew Passion* was given at the Berlin Singakademie on March 11, 1829. The hall was sold out weeks in advance; more than a thousand people were turned away at the door. However long the work had lain neglected, it can at least be said for the audience of Mendelssohn's day that when they heard it, they responded with excitement and wonder.

Fanny Mendelssohn, who sang in the chorus, wrote to a friend about the event three days afterward: "As soon as the doors were opened, the people, who had already been waiting long outside, rushed into the hall, which was quite full in less than fifteen minutes. I sat at the corner, where I could see Felix very well, and had gathered the strongest alto voices around me. The choruses were sung with a fire, a striking power, and also with a touching delicacy and softness such as I have never heard. . . . The room had all the air of a church: the deepest quiet and most solemn devotion pervaded the whole, only now and then involuntary utterances of intense emotion were heard."

So overwhelming was the reception that the *Passion* had to be repeated ten days later, which happened to be the date of Bach's birth; this time extra seats were put up in the lobby and a small rehearsal room that opened onto the main hall, so the crowd was even larger than at the first performance. Afterward all the main participants went to Zelter's home for a party, with Felix and Devrient seated at the head of the table and the conviviality and congratulations lasting far into the night.

Mendelssohn's Berlin revival of the *St. Matthew Passion* was followed by performances in Königsberg, Stettin, and other cities and by the publication of the music, in a piano reduction, by the house of Schlesinger. It also fostered renewed interest in other

works by Bach, with Mendelssohn himself cataloguing manuscripts, directing performances, and sponsoring publications
throughout his life. The universal understanding and appreciation
of Bach begins with the great revival of 1829.

For Mendelssohn himself, his contact at twenty with the *St.
Matthew Passion* had significant artistic consequences. For he paid
to Bach that most sincere, but also most insidious, of all compliments: imitation. Until now, he had written little religious music
himself, but having felt so personally the force and fervor of
Bach's great setting of the Gospel, he began thinking along the
same lines and planning out his own oratorios, which were to
become a principal source of his acclaim during his lifetime, and
of his denigration afterward.

XIV *The Grand Tour*

Three Germanic composers dominated British musical life for two hundred years. Handel settled in London in 1712 and set its musical style until his death in 1759. Haydn made two extended visits in the 1790s, writing his greatest symphonies there and being lionized by the London public. The last of this triumvirate was Felix Mendelssohn. He first arrived in England in April, 1829; he made nine subsequent visits in the course of the next seventeen years and, after his death, left an influence and impression on British musical life that persisted for almost a century.

Mendelssohn's first visit was no casual affair, but part of a master travel plan devised by his father and himself. Mendelssohn never much liked Berlin. For all his outward success there, he felt an undercurrent of resentment and hostility stemming from his Jewish birth, his father's wealth, and his own precocity, none of which sat well with the old-line musical establishment. The Royal Orchestra actually rebuffed a suggestion that he conduct them in a public concert. Henry F. Chorley, the British musical traveler, reported encountering the attitude in Berlin: "Mendelssohn? Ah, he had talent as a boy." Obviously there was little to be lost by spending a few years visiting the rest of the world.

Felix was already well traveled for a young man of twenty; he had been to Paris twice and Switzerland once, as well as visiting wide areas of Germany. But the itinerary laid out by himself and Abraham was to constitute a grand tour in the grandest sense. For the next three years, Felix pursued an unhurried series of journeys across the Continent, stopping off from time to time at his home in Berlin. From 1829 to 1832, he visited England twice, enjoyed prolonged stays in Paris and Vienna, and spent an entire year wandering through the Italian peninsula. As he went, he sketched pictures, wrote letters, and composed music. It was on this journey that he first set down the ideas for the *Hebrides* Overture, the *Italian* Symphony, and the *Scotch* Symphony, although he did not complete them all at once. He now worked more deliberately and carefully than before; the years of speedy, effortless composition were over.

To send him off to England for the first time with a proper show of family affection, Felix's father and younger sister Rebecca accompanied him to Hamburg, where he boarded a steamer called the *Attwood* for the passage to London. Felix had just completed an overture entitled *Calm Sea and Prosperous Voyage,* and he wrote home later that he repented it bitterly the next few days, for the three-day crossing was a nasty one, and he was seasick until the final night.

He had a friend in London, a young German diplomat from Hanover named Karl Klingemann, who had been a bosom companion in the old days and who now took charge of him. Klingemann found him lodgings with a German irondealer at 103 Great Portland Street; on his first night in town steered him to the King's Theater, where Maria Malibran was singing in Rossini's *Otello;* and subsequently introduced him, as one young bachelor being helpful to another, to some of the local girls. He was also welcomed by Ignaz Moscheles, who had once given him piano lessons and, now a Londoner himself, was glad to show him around the town's musical circles.

Mendelssohn was fascinated by London from the moment he got there. Berlin by comparison was a poky, hidebound, provincial capital; London was the center of a vast industrial and commercial power beginning the climb toward its zenith. Everywhere were factories, railways, bustling business establishments; and if the English were not producing much noteworthy music of their own, at least they knew how to play and appreciate that of others. In his letters home he could hardly contain his exuberance and delight:

> London is the grandest and most complicated monster on the face of the earth. . . . Not in the last six months at Berlin have I seen so many contrasts and such variety as in these last three days. Could you but once, turning to the right from my lodging, walk down Regent Street and see the wide bright street with its arches (alas! it is enveloped in a thick fog today!). . . . There are beggars, negroes, and those fat John Bulls with their slender, beautiful daughters in pairs on their arms. Ah, those daughters! . . . Last but not least, to see the masts from the West India docks stretching their heads over the housetops, and to see a harbor as big as the Hamburg one treated like a mere pond, with sluices, and the ships arranged not singly but in rows, like regiments—to see all that makes one's heart rejoice at the greatness of the world.

Under the tutelage of his friend Klingemann, Mendelssohn quickly became at least a temporary Londoner. He began dressing in the latest mode, and there is a charming aquarelle by the artist James Warren Childe showing him holding a top hat and garbed with the elegance of an English dandy. He led a vivacious and convivial social life, with Klingemann taking him to the diplomatic gatherings and Moscheles to the musical affairs. He even developed a taste for English cookery, sending home redolent descriptions of plum pudding and cherry pie enjoyed at friends in Kensington, "German sausages" purchased and devoured in the street by himself and Klingemann, and a succulent dish of crabs consumed on a visit to Ramsgate.

Mendelssohn also developed an eye for the English girls and according to his letters met nothing but one ravishing beauty after another. He kept writing of being seated alongside "two very wonderful brown eyes" at dinner, or of watching a "beautiful young English lady" at a phrenology exhibition undo her "long fair hair" so that the doctor could feel the bumps upon her head upon which "I gave three cheers for phrenology and warmly praised everything concerning it."

Musically, Mendelssohn found himself in almost constant demand. To an extent, his reputation had preceded him. The "Diary of a Dilettante" column in a musical publication called *Harmonicum* reported: "Another arrival in London is the young M. Mendelssohn, son of the rich banker of Berlin, and I believe, grandson of the celebrated Jewish philosopher and elegant writer. He is one of the finest piano-forte players in London, and is supposed to be better acquainted with music than most professors of the art." The Philharmonic Society, founded in 1813 and the city's most prestigious orchestra, invited him to conduct a concert on May 25, 1829, at the Argyll Rooms on Regent Street—his formal debut in London. Featured on the program was his Symphony No. 1 in C Minor, actually his thirteenth symphony, and composed five years previously. A large-scale work clearly modeled on Mozart's famous G Minor Symphony, it has a drive and freshness of its own and is still occasionally performed today. For the London performance, Felix scrapped the original third movement, a minuet, and substituted an orchestral version of the quicksilvery scherzo from his Octet in E-flat. The scherzo had to be repeated and the ovation was unending. Five days later, he appeared in another concert in the same hall, as piano soloist in Weber's *Concertstück;* and shortly afterward, he completed his conquest of London by playing for the first time in England the *Midsummer Night's Dream* Overture.

It is almost impossible to overstate the impact that the twenty-year-old Mendelssohn made on London. One modern parallel might be the sensation created overnight in New York in 1943, when Leonard Bernstein conducted the New York Philharmonic as a last-minute replacement for Bruno Walter and was launched on a brilliant career that has never abated. But Bernstein was five years older at the time and, for all his gifts, had no *Midsummer*

Night's Dream music of his own to play. The British audiences of Mendelssohn's day simply couldn't do enough for him: he was given honorary membership in the Philharmonic Society; he was invited to dinners and galas and balls; he even received an offer from the governor of Ceylon, who happened to be in London at the time, to compose a festival song celebrating the anniversary of the island's freedom. The incident vastly amused Felix, who promptly signed himself in his letters "Composer to the Island of Ceylon."

Mendelssohn to musical Londoners was more than just a brilliant newcomer; he arrived as a veritable demigod, one of the race of master musicians. Recalled Sir Julius Benedict, a prominent figure in British music at the time: "The effect of the first performance of this [*Midsummer Night's Dream*] Overture was electrical. All at once, and perhaps when least expected, the great gap left by the death of Beethoven* seemed likely to be filled up."

It was not only as a prospective replacement for Beethoven that Mendelssohn overwhelmed London; it was also as a brilliant pianist and, especially, as an innovative and daring conductor. The art of conducting was just coming into flower, and Mendelssohn was one of its earliest practitioners, establishing a brisk, direct "classical" style that had a direct line to twentieth-century conductors like Arturo Toscanini and George Szell.

In his first stay in England and those that followed, Mendelssohn made the British public aware of conductorial methods and approaches that many of them had never encountered. He used a baton—an instrument that had been introduced to England only ten years previously by Ludwig Spohr. Prior to that, directions had been given to the orchestra either by a rolled-up paper held in the hand or by a violin bow. Sometimes there were several "conductors" operating simultaneously, to the confusion of the players and the detriment of the music—a pianist seated at his

---

*Two years earlier, in 1827.

keyboard, nodding and gesticulating to the other musicians; the first violinist trying to play and beat time at once; perhaps the composer himself trying to give signals. Mendelssohn from the start was for a single conductor—himself—and although divided control persisted for some time, his idea generally prevailed in England and elsewhere.

Mendelssohn had an elegant white baton made especially for himself in England. The British wood carver he engaged for the job couldn't imagine what it was for and engraved a little crown on it in the belief that Mendelssohn was an alderman of some sort. Mendelssohn also caused murmurs by conducting without a score. His musical memory was prodigious; in his teens he could play all the Beethoven symphonies at the piano by heart. When he found that it disturbed audiences to watch him conduct without music, he took to leaving the score on the stand in front of him and turning pages as he went along without looking at them. He also had a way of becoming so absorbed in the music he was leading that having established his tempo, he reduced his beat to the merest minimum while he listened intently to the sounds rising around him. He knew how to get the effects he wanted with a flick of the finger or a nod of the head; for all his slim stature (Mendelssohn was about 5 feet 6 inches tall and very slender) and refined bearing, he obviously was a commanding, magnetic figure on the podium. Wrote Benedict: "Nobody, certainly, ever knew better how to communicate—as if by electric fluid—his own conception of a work to a large body of performers." British audiences, especially women, adored him; and the London musicians, unlike their Berlin counterparts, found him amiable and understanding. Not that he couldn't be sarcastic when he felt the occasion demanded it, as in another instance recounted by Benedict:

> Once, while conducting a rehearsal of Beethoven's Eighth Symphony, the admirable allegretto in B-flat not going at first to his liking, he remarked smilingly that "he knew every one of the gentlemen engaged was capable of performing, and even of com-

posing, a scherzo of his own; but that *just now* he wanted to hear Beethoven's, which he thought had some merits." It was cheerfully repeated. "Beautiful, charming," cried Mendelssohn, "but still too loud in two or three instances. Let us take it again, from the middle."—"No, no," was the general reply of the band: "the whole piece over again, for our own satisfaction;" and then they played it with the utmost delicacy and finish, Mendelssohn laying aside his baton, and listening with evident delight to the more perfect execution. "What would I have given," he exclaimed, "if Beethoven could have heard his own composition so well understood, and so magnificently performed!"

On another occasion Mendelssohn told a women's chorus he was rehearsing: "Really very good, for the first time, exceedingly good; but because it *is* the first time, let us try it again."

Mendelssohn did more than exude personal charm as a conductor; he also got musical results that apparently were unlike his contemporaries'. The choral dynamic shadings noted by his sister Fanny in the *St. Matthew Passion* were carried over into his instrumental performances; his strong sense of rhythm and accent were noted approvingly. But it was his fast tempos that created most comment, and also provoked the greatest criticism. Of course, we cannot be certain today of exactly how fast Mendelssohn did conduct; Wagner, who was his bitterest enemy and who denounced him after his death in a scurrilous anti-Semitic tract, accused him of superficiality and of racing through the very same movement of Beethoven's Eighth that Julius Benedict praised.

But Wagner cannot be trusted on Mendelssohn (or on a good many other musicians), and Felix's tremendous success on the podium not only in Britain but in later years in Düsseldorf, Leipzig, and elsewhere indicates that for all his elegance, he was a conductor of force and fire. Joseph Joachim, the great violinist, who played with all the European orchestras, in later years called Mendelssohn the greatest conductor he had ever seen and referred, as so many other musicians did, to his "indescribable electrifying influence."

Eventually the Mendelssohn tradition of conducting was countered by a more romantic and personalized one, in which tempos were less rigorous and the musical pulse more variable. In the twentieth century, the latter approach found its most notable exponent in Wilhelm Furtwängler; whereas the Mendelssohn style was embodied and probably intensified by Arturo Toscanini, who, it may be remembered, was also accused of conducting too fast and too literally.

In addition to performing himself, Mendelssohn eagerly attended musical events in London, which were far more diversified and brilliant than those in Berlin. Not everything he heard was to his liking. Of a Mozart night at the Italian opera, he wrote home: "The other night I heard *Don Giovanni* given by the Italians; it was funny. Pellegrini sang Leporello, and acted like an ape; at the end of his first song he introduced a string of cadences out of any half a dozen Rossinian operas; the mandolin part in 'Deh vieni' was played very delicately on the bow of a violin. . . . The Commendatore had on a dressing gown. Malibran gave a mad version of Zerlina; she made her a wild, flirting Spanish country romp. She has an extraordinary talent. How Sontag sings Donna Anna, you know. . . ."

On a less-elevated plane, he was driven almost out of his mind by a group of street musicians, known as the Marylebone Band, who had a way of appearing outside of his lodgings daily just as he was beginning his piano practice. A friend arriving one day just as the morning session started found him standing at the top of the stairs and crying "in tones of anguish" to his landlord's son: "Henry, Henry! Send them away! Here is a shilling!" Folk music of any kind never appealed much to Mendelssohn; he impartially denounced "Scotch bagpipes, Swiss cow-horns, Welsh harps" and said he couldn't even bear Beethoven's national songs.

Mendelssohn wound up his first trip to Britain by taking a pleasure jaunt through Scotland and Wales with Klingemann. The two friends had an exuberant time, wandering through the highlands, catching a touristic glimpse of Sir Walter Scott at his estate, visiting Edinburgh and Glasgow, lodging for a while with a friendly family that included three pretty girls whose charms were fully described by Felix in a letter addressed to, of all people, his two sisters. His impressions of Scotland permeated not only his letters but his music as well. Climbing through Holyrood Castle in Edinburgh, he entered the ruined chapel where Mary, Queen of Scots had worshipped: "Everything around is broken and mouldering, and the bright sky shines in. I believe I found today in that old chapel the beginning of my Scotch Symphony." Actually, it took him twelve more years to put the *Scotch* Symphony in a form that satisfied him. He worked more quickly on his *Hebrides,* or *Fingal's Cave,* Overture, his most magnificent achievement since the *Midsummer Night's Dream.* This music, one of the greatest seascapes ever written, was the outcome of a visit to the famous basalt cavern on the tiny island of Staffa in the Hebrides. In a small ship, Mendelssohn underwent another bout with his old enemy, seasickness, to get there; but on his return to the mainland, he triumphantly sent to Fanny, scrawled in a letter, the opening twenty measures of the Overture.

XV *Son and Stranger*

Felix's first visit to England lasted six months, two months longer than planned. The extension was necessitated by an injury to his knee, suffered when a small carriage in which he was a passenger overturned in a London street. For weeks he lay in bed while his English admirers plied him with books, fruit, flowers, and conversation. Because of the delay, he was unable to attend the marriage of his sister Fanny to the painter Wilhelm Hensel. When he finally returned to Berlin in December, 1829, it was with a slight limp that soon passed and a new set of side whiskers that remained.

He also brought home a silver anniversary present for his parents in the form of an operetta called *The Return from Abroad,* designed for performance at a Mendelssohn matinee. Klingemann had written the libretto for it, revolving about a mistaken identity; and although it was intended mostly as a lark, it turned out to be a lively, tuneful, and well-constructed little work. One of the characters, named Schulz, is required to sing only one note throughout the work; this part was intended for Hensel, Fanny's new husband, who was absolutely tone-deaf. Hensel managed to spoil the part in spite of the fact that his one note was "blown and whistled to him on every side." The opera might make a pleasant subject for revival today; as it is, it survives chiefly through its occasionally played overture, usually called *Son and Stranger.*

"Son and stranger" represents an apt description of Felix Mendelssohn himself at this stage of his life. He still was a loyal member of the close-knit family, and would be to the end of his days, but he was increasingly pursuing an independent artistic and personal course and beginning to think of eventually settling elsewhere than Berlin.

Three months after his return from England, Felix was back on the road again. This time he began with two sentimental pilgrimages. The first, on which his father accompanied him, was to Dessau, the childhood town of Moses Mendelssohn, who had been born just one hundred years before. Felix and Abraham visited the house where Moses had lived, now deserted, and also the little synagogue where he had studied, but neither of them recorded any emotions they may have felt. After a few days' stay, Abraham went home to Berlin, and Felix continued alone to Weimar to pay a final visit to Goethe, now in his eightieth year.

The old sage once more made a fuss over Felix, throwing his arms around him on his arrival, commissioning an artist to paint his portrait during his stay—Felix thought the resultant picture made him look "sulky"—quizzing him eagerly about his travels, inviting the belles of Weimar to a dance in his honor, and above all, making him play the piano. It always is difficult for us to picture a past in which the only way to hear music was to have it actually performed in one's presence. Goethe was avid for it, and kept Felix at the keyboard hour after hour. He wanted mostly to hear Mendelssohn's music, but Mendelssohn played him mostly Beethoven's. Several times Goethe induced his visitor to prolong his stay beyond scheduled departure dates, and when Felix finally told him gently that he must be on his way, the poet presented him with a sheet of the manuscript of *Faust* inscribed: "To my dear young friend F.M.B., powerfully tender master of the piano—a friendly souvenir of happy May days in 1830. J. W. von Goethe." With it went a parting embrace. The two never met again; two years later, Goethe was dead.

From his last visit to Goethe, Mendelssohn carried away the idea of setting to music one of his old friend's longer poems. He selected a work entitled *Die erste Walpurgisnacht* ("The First Walpurgis Night"), so called to distinguish it from Goethe's later treatment of similar material in *Faust.* Goethe heartily approved of the young composer's proposal to set his dramatic ballad of witches, demons, and Druids sporting about the Brocken, that mysterious, fog-shrouded peak in the Harz Mountains; in fact, he told Felix that he had vainly tried in the past to persuade other composers to write music for it.

Now, after leaving Goethe and traveling south into Italy, Felix began working on it earnestly, eventually producing an hour-long cantata for orchestra, chorus, and four vocal soloists. In his verses, Goethe had wanted to rationalize the old legends about wild doings on the Brocken, so he had turned them into a drama of pagan Druids frightening off Christian interlopers by staging terrifying revels. Mendelssohn, utilizing every instrument from the big drum to the piccolo, wrote a score full of (for him) extravagant sounds and strange dissonances, but setting things right at the end with a concluding C Major chorus in praise of the powers of light. It took years before the *Walpurgis Night* was completed, for its final version was not presented until 1843; and in the intervening years, Mendelssohn, evidently uncertain of its effect, made a practice of trying it out on his friends.

Mendelssohn kept his eyes open and his pen busy during his journey south. Wherever he went, he inspected the scenery, made the musical rounds, worked on his compositions, and sent off a barrage of letters to his family. After leaving Weimar in June of 1830, he stopped off in Munich, Salzburg, and Vienna. In the latter city, he was distressed to find the music of Haydn, Mozart, and Beethoven ignored in favor of that by Hummel, Field, and Kalkbrenner. Vienna, he wrote, was "a frivolous dump"—not that that prevented him from having a good time there.

From October, 1830, to July, 1831, Mendelssohn was in Italy. He haunted the art galleries of Florence, Venice, and Rome; made touristic excursions to Naples and Pompeii; met all the other musicians he could find. He discovered, to his surprise, that he was well known almost everywhere. "My looking-glass is stuck full of visiting cards, and I spend every evening with a fresh acquaintance," he wrote from Rome.

One of these was Hector Berlioz. The French composer was five years older than Mendelssohn and wrote music that was far less fettered in form and feeling than his younger colleague; yet like so many of the contemporary musicians of his day, he looked on Felix as a leader and counselor. Felix, for his part, was anxious to have Berlioz's opinion of his works; he played him both the *Walpurgis Night* and *Hebrides* Overtures at the piano, and Berlioz was filled with admiration both for the music and for Felix's pianism. Like many others, he marveled at Mendelssohn's ability to achieve orchestral effects upon a keyboard. Although Berlioz, in a famous phrase, once said of Mendelssohn that he "was a little too fond of the dead"—an allusion to his love of classical forms and of composers like Bach—he always retained his affection and regard for him.

Mendelssohn's attitude toward his friend was much more equivocal, for although he admired and liked Berlioz as a person, he never really understood his tempestuous and free-ranging music. Berlioz was in Italy because, after two failures, he had finally won the Prix de Rome, France's most coveted musical award, by writing a rather conventional work, *Sardanapalus*. Berlioz himself did not care much for parts of it, including the first allegro, and frankly admitted as much to Mendelssohn. Whereupon, as Berlioz wrote in his memoirs years later, Felix rather disingenuously said: "Ah, good! I congratulate you on your taste! I was afraid that you were pleased with that allegro, and honestly it is wretched!"

Privately, in a letter to his mother, Mendelssohn expressed the opinion that Berlioz's music was full of "atrocities," that his instrumentation was "a confused smear," and that the over-all effect of a typical work was "boring" and "absurd." On another occasion, he said that Berlioz "with all his efforts to go stark mad, never once succeeds." But he was careful to confine his views to his intimate family circle; he never once spoke a word of criticism of his friend in public and did as much as he could to help him. In Rome, Berlioz took to lounging around Felix's workroom, and the two went for long walks together through the Roman ruins, discussing youth, art, and religion as ardently as only young men can. Recalled Berlioz afterward: "Mendelssohn believed firmly in his Lutheran religion and I sometimes shocked him profoundly by laughing at the Bible."

Mendelssohn spent New Year's Day of 1831 in Rome, and, his Lutheranism notwithstanding, the revelry of the holiday seemed to depress him and awaken remembrances of his Jewish background, for he wrote to his friend Klingemann in England that he thought both New Year's Eve and New Year's Day should be celebrated solemnly: "The two days are *real days* of atonement, and one should experience them all alone with oneself and not be afraid of grave thoughts. . . ."

In June of 1831, Mendelssohn turned northward from Rome and began his return journey. He had disliked most of the Italian music, both sacred and secular, that he had heard for nearly a year and was steadily working on his own, including the buoyant piece which he himself called his *Italian* Symphony and which took him two years to complete. On his way back, he stopped several weeks in Milan, where he visited Baroness Dorothea von Ertmann, a woman in her fifties who had once been Beethoven's pupil, and to whom he had dedicated one of his piano sonatas. In fact, the Baroness' name has always been included along with Rachel Levin Varnhagen, on the long list of candidates for Beethoven's "Immortal Beloved." The Baroness was now married to the military commandant of Milan, and Felix's intention in calling on her was to hear some stories of Beethoven's life from one who had known him so well. But the Baroness and her husband were so delighted to meet the young and celebrated Mr. Mendelssohn that they immediately took him under their wing, gave parties for him, introduced him to their friends, and conducted him around Milan. More interesting to Felix were the hours he spent at the Ertmann home, where Dorothea played Beethoven sonatas to him as Beethoven had taught them to her, and he played them back to her in his own way.

Another sentimental call Mendelssohn made was upon Karl Mozart, eldest son of the great Wolfgang Amadeus, who was a minor Austrian consular official in Milan. Felix, deeply moved at meeting Mozart's son, played for him the *Don Giovanni* and *Magic Flute* Overtures at the piano, as well as his own *Walpurgis* music.

Felix lingered even longer in Munich, for the simple reason that for the first time in his life, he had fallen in love. The girl was a seventeen-year-old pianist named Delphine von Schauroth, whom he had met briefly while passing through the city the previous year. Now, on his return trip, he spent more and more time with her. Besides being an excellent musician, she was beautiful and came of a substantial family, and people who watched the two of them dancing at social gatherings or strolling through the parks together thought they made an uncommonly handsome couple. Felix even reported to his father in a letter that the king of Bavaria, who happened to be attending a ball with them, had suggested "that I should marry Fräulein von Schauroth: that would be an excellent match." Felix professed to have been slightly annoyed by the royal suggestion, but perhaps he was floating a trial balloon in the direction of his family. If so, the answer was negative. For although Felix and Delphine played four-handed sonatas together and he helped her with one particularly difficult note, an A-flat ("my little hand cannot reach it," she archly told him), their romance died with his departure from Munich, and she eventually married someone else.

The most significant encounter of the affair, if it may be called that, was Mendelssohn's Piano Concerto No. 1 in G Minor, which he wrote in Munich and dedicated to Delphine. Mendelssohn himself gave it its first performance in Munich, at a concert at which he also conducted his Symphony No. 1 in C Minor and his *Midsummer Night's Dream* Overture and improvised at the piano on Mozart's "Non più andrai" at the suggestion of the king of Bavaria, who was in the audience. Mendelssohn described his piano concerto as "a thing rapidly thrown off," but it became one of the most popular concertos of the day, widely admired for its agreeable melodies, its brilliant solo part, and for its tight, inter-locking construction. Although less frequently played than in for-mer years, it remains in the repertory of a good many of today's great pianists, notably Rudolf Serkin. Among the pianists in Men-delssohn's time who played it was Delphine von Schauroth her-self. The last time she did so was at a Mendelssohn Festival in Leipzig in 1870, when she was fifty-six and the handsome young genius who had once held down the A-flat for her had been dead for twenty years.

In December of 1831, Felix reached Paris on his travels and settled down for the winter. He never really cared for the French capital: London was his city. Mendelssohn had a strong puritanical streak; unabashed frivolity and free thought were not for him, however much they might appeal to that other converted Jew, Heinrich Heine, who was living in the city at the time.

His disdain also extended to Parisian musical life, which the opera composer Giacomo Meyerbeer was just beginning to domi-nate. There may have been an element of jealousy in this; Meyer-beer, like Mendelssohn, was a Berliner and also the son of a Jewish banker. But unlike the Mendelssohns, the Meyerbeers never con-verted. Meyerbeer himself remained Jewish to the end of his life, and his father became a leading figure in the new "Reform" movement and even operated a synagogue in his own home along the liberalized lines supposedly stemming from the teachings of Moses Mendelssohn.

In 1831, Meyerbeer was forty years old and had just produced his first great success at the Paris Opéra, *Robert le Diable.* Mendels-sohn went to see it and disliked it, saying it had "something for everybody—but no heart in it." Mostly he objected to what he considered the vulgarity of some of the scenes. In a letter to his father he wrote: "We must take our stand against immorality. When in *Robert le Diable* the nuns come one after the other and try and seduce the hero, until the abbess at last succeeds. . . . the Parisian public applauds. . . . When in another opera the girl undresses, meanwhile singing an aria about how she will be married by this time the next day—it made a sensation, but I would not have that kind of thing in an opera of mine. . . . If things like that spell success these days, I prefer to write church music."

In effect, that is just what happened, although Felix kept on insisting he was looking for a good operatic subject. So strongly did Mendelssohn feel about Meyerbeer that when a friend told him he thought there was a physical resemblance between them, Felix promptly went to a barber and had his hair cropped short so as to look different.

Although Mendelssohn's life is often depicted, as in the quotation from Emile Vuillermoz that precedes this section of this book, as a series of unbroken triumphs and unalloyed successes, it actually was no such thing. He had his share of disappointments, and a major setback occurred during his stay in Paris. The year before, Felix had composed a work he called the *Reformation* Symphony to commemorate the tercentenary of the Augsburg Confession, the statement of beliefs and doctrines of the Lutheran Church. But the Augsburg celebration was called off, and Mendelssohn had an unplayed symphony on his hands.* He wished to have the Conservatoire Orchestra, famous throughout Europe for its Beethoven interpretations, take it up; and François-Antoine Habaneck, the conductor, apparently agreed. Habaneck liked Mendelssohn and engaged him as soloist in Beethoven's Piano Concerto No. 4 in G Major on a program that also included the *Midsummer Night's*

---

*Since it was the last published of Mendelssohn's symphonies, it has become designated the Symphony No. 5, although it was actually completed before the *Scotch*, No. 3, and the *Italian*, No. 4.

Dream Overture. But the men of the orchestra balked at the *Reformation* Symphony, rejecting it as "much too learned, too much *fugato,* too little melody." Perhaps they were referring to Mendelssohn's quotation in the opening andante of the "Dresden Amen," the theme in rising sixths that Wagner later used in *Parsifal;* in any event, the *Reformation* Symphony had to wait for another time to find its audience.

What really made his Parisian stay memorable to Mendelssohn were the young musicians he met there. His friend Ferdinand Hiller, also a Jewish-born musical prodigy, has left an account of what was surely one of the most distinguished musical foursomes ever to gather around a café table on the Boulevard des Italiens at any epoch: Hiller, Mendelssohn, Chopin, and Liszt. All were barely into their twenties, filled with exuberance and the sure instinct of their craft. They happened to see Friedrich Wilhelm Kalkbrenner walk by, a man much older and the most fashionable pianist of the day. Friedrich Wilhelm was dignified, vain, and pompous, so the young men beckoned him over, made him sit down among them, and—in Hiller's words—"assailed him with such a volley of talk that he was nearly driven to despair."

Kalkbrenner it was who attempted to take Chopin in hand when the young Pole came to Paris, provincial in his outlook and uncertain of his talent. Mendelssohn urged Chopin not to take piano lessons with Kalkbrenner on the grounds that he already played better than the pedant. Chopin followed this advice, permitting his unique talent to develop along its natural course. He gave a concert at the Salle Pleyel, playing his E Minor Concerto and several mazurkas and nocturnes. The audience was taken by storm, with Mendelssohn leading the applause. Thus Chopin became another of the young European musicians who regarded Mendelssohn as their leader and spokesman, and they were to have further meetings over the years.

In April, 1832, Felix left Paris for his second visit to London, "that great smoky nest." This time the city's welcome to him was even more ardent than before. He himself reported the reaction when he walked into a rehearsal of the Philharmonic: "One of the orchestra called out 'there is Mendelssohn,' on which they all began shouting, and clapping their hands to such a degree that for a time I really did not know what to do; and when this was over, another called out 'Welcome to him,' on which the same uproar recommenced, and I was obliged to cross the room, and to clamber into the orchestra, and return thanks."

Triumph followed triumph throughout the spring. The Philharmonic Society played his *Hebrides* Overture to tremendous acclaim, and when he presented them with the manuscript score, they responded by giving him an engraved silver plate. His G Minor Piano Concerto was a huge success at two concerts. Novello published the first volume of his *Songs Without Words*, little "album leaf" piano pieces that he had been writing over the years and that now, to his astonishment, were greeted with wild enthusiasm and became the favorite drawing-room fare of English maidens.* He and Moscheles played Mozart's two-piano Concerto in E-flat, for which he composed new cadenzas: another triumph. Critics and other musicians could hardly find words to praise his piano playing. It was more than a matter of technique. "His fingers *sang* as they rippled over the keyboard," wrote Charles Salaman, a veteran pianist. Another musical observer, John Edmund Cox, emphasized the impression Mendelssohn made as a personality: "Scarcely had he touched the keyboard than something that can only be described as similar to a pleasurable electric shock passed through his hearers and held them spell-

---

*Mendelssohn always declined to discuss the "meanings" of his *Songs Without Words*, most of which he left without titles. To someone who importuned him for information he wrote: "People often complain that music is ambiguous. . . . whereas everyone understands words; with me it is exactly the reverse—not merely with regard to entire sentences, but also to individual words; these, too, seem to me so ambiguous, so vague, so unintelligible when compared with genuine music, which fills the soul with a thousand things better than words. What the music I love expresses to me not too *indefinite* to be put into words, but on the contrary, too *definite*. . . . If you ask me what *my* idea is, I say—just the song as it stands. . . ."

bound." Much the same effect was produced when he played the organ in St. Paul's Cathedral before a huge audience and astonished his hearers with his ability not only to play music as written but to improvise in double and triple counterpoint.

Once again Mendelssohn made dozens of new friends in London. His favorites this time were a family called the Horsleys, who lived in the country in Kensington. Felix liked the father, William Horsley, an eminent choral writer and an authority on English glees, but he was particularly charmed with the three Horsley daughters, who were young, vivacious, and musical. Apparently Mendelssohn could be something of a nuisance, or at least a very demanding person at times, because one of the Horsley girls wrote: "Mamma and Mary think Mendelssohn will never marry. I do, that is, if he does not plague his mistress to death before the day arrives." Another close friend was the composer Thomas Attwood, who had been a pupil of Mozart's and who now held an influential position in British musical life.

Never has a foreigner felt more at home in Britain, and in the early summer of 1832, he apparently was in no hurry to leave. But the family, led by Fanny, urgently summoned him home in a flood of letters. A new situation had arisen in Berlin. Felix's old teacher Zelter had died, and his job as head of the Singakademie was open. The entire Mendelssohn clan had decided that Felix should apply for the post, and they wanted him to return for a family council on strategy. The grand tour was over.

XVI *Felix and Fanny*

Johannes Brahms once remarked jokingly that a Jewish composer whom he knew had wished to make a change in one of his scores, but "the whole family was against it," so the passage remained unaltered. Brahms, who had few domestic ties himself, knew of the Jewish reputation for strong family life and found it amusing but not astonishing that an entire household should participate in artistic decisions.

Certainly that was the way things worked in the Mendelssohn circle. Felix was quick to try out his scores, projects, and ideas on his parents, sisters, and brother. Music was one of the bonds that linked them, for all were proficient in the art. Paul, Felix's younger brother, was an expert cellist; it was for him that Felix wrote his Cello Sonata in B-flat op. 45, and also a set of *Variations concertantes.* Paul married Albertine Heine, a cousin of the poet, and had two sons and three daughters. He went into the Mendelssohn banking business, and although he was the last-born, soon became regarded as the head of the family whenever practical business affairs were concerned. He became, in effect, Felix's business manager, supervising his finances and often acting as an intermediary in the arrangement of musical engagements and commissions.

Rebecca, the younger of Felix's sisters, was a sprightly, pretty girl with a good singing voice. Felix adored her; when, in his youth, he decided to study Greek for a time, he insisted that she take lessons with him, and she obligingly did so. He postponed one of his trips because she came down with measles the night before he was to leave, and according to his own account, he was delighted when he broke out with the disease a few days later so they could spend their convalescence together.

Rebecca shared Felix's views on a number of matters; for example, on his opposition to the name Bartholdy when their father wanted to add it to their own. For a time she even signed her letters Rebecca Mendelssohn-*meden*-Bartholdy, *meden* being Greek for "never." On another occasion, though, Felix chided her for a letter in which she wrote rather crossly about how embarrassed she had been when a relative of Moses Mendelssohn, an untutored man named Dessauer, was introduced into Berlin society. "I am not a Jew-hater," she wrote to Felix, "but this has been too much." Felix indignantly replied from London: "What do you mean you are not a Jew hater? . . . It is really very sweet of you not to look down on your whole family. I am looking forward to a fuller explanation of the Dessauer affair in your next letter."

Rebecca Mendelssohn had no lack of male admirers, Jewish and non-Jewish; among them was Heine, who said later that he called at the house only because she was there. But at the age of twenty-one, she married a mathematics professor named Gustav Peter Lejeune Dirichlet, a gentle, bearded man who taught at the University of Berlin.

Dirichlet, who was twenty-eight when he married Rebecca, was to become one of the most famous European mathematicians of the nineteenth century. Although he came from a completely different background, his career had curiously Mendelssohnian overtones. One of eleven children born to a post-office director at Düren, a small town near Cologne, he began studying mathematics as assiduously as Moses Mendelssohn had studied Maimonides. When someone told him that no child could possibly understand such books he replied: "I read them *until* I understand them." At a Jesuit college in Cologne he worked under the renowned physicist Georg Simon Ohm, but decided to go to Paris, then the center of mathematical study. Here, like Henrietta Mendelssohn, he obtained a position as a tutor in the family of a French general, Maximilien-Sébastien Foy; the general's wife remembered him, a tall, thin youth, sitting atop a small iron stove "the whole day long, teaching the children and doing his own work at the same time."

In Paris Dirichlet absorbed not only mathematical knowledge but the political ideals of the French Revolution, so that he became known as the ultra-liberal of the Mendelssohn clan, which in general was known for its progressive outlook. Dirichlet's mathematical specialty was in the theory of numbers, and he became the first to lecture on this subject at a German university. His work is commemorated in the "Dirichlet integral" and "Dirichlet's problem," both well-known to mathematicians.

Dirichlet was introduced to the Mendelssohns by Alexander Humboldt, whom he had met in Paris, and although Rebecca's parents at first resisted the marriage (Dirichlet was a Roman Catholic; they wanted a Lutheran), they ultimately consented. Rather than going off on their own, Dirichlet and Rebecca took over one of the small houses scattered through the Mendelssohn gardens at 3 Leipzigerstrasse. Eventually they had five children. Felix and Rebecca remained on affectionate terms until his death.

But it was his elder sister Fanny to whom Felix was closest—so close, indeed, that their relationship has engaged the attention of more than one amateur psychoanalyst over the years. Even in their own times, there were jests upon the subject, with several family friends jovially asking the Mendelssohns when Fanny's marriage to Felix would take place. Abraham, one imagines, was not amused.

Although she led an outwardly happy life and became both a wife and a mother, Fanny Mendelssohn was in some ways a tragic figure, one who never saw her great talent come to fruition. A true descendant of Moses Mendelssohn in her inquiring mind and sensitive nature, she also inherited a trace of his physical deformity, for one of her shoulders was higher than the other; and aside from her luminous black eyes, she was rather a plain girl. She was a remarkable musician; Felix himself stoutly insisted she was his superior as a pianist. "But you should hear my sister Fanny!" he kept telling people who admired his playing in London. It is tempting to ascribe such praise to brotherly affection, but false modesty was not one of Felix's characteristics. Besides, there is plenty of corroborative evidence. Henry F. Chorley, the critic of the London *Athenaeum,* who heard her in a family matinee in Berlin, said that if only she had been born poor and had to earn her way in the world, she would have become as great a pianist as Clara Wieck Schumann. When she was thirteen years old, she gave her father a gift no other girl would have thought of: she played him twenty-four Bach preludes by heart.

Once again there are parallels between Felix Mendelssohn and Wolfgang Mozart, who also had a sister four years older than himself who was an excellent pianist. But although Mozart was extremely close to his Nannerl in childhood, their paths diverged, and they all but passed out of each other's lives with the advancing years. Felix and Fanny, on the contrary, remained inextricably linked throughout their lives, and even in their deaths.

Abraham Mendelssohn, unlike Leopold Mozart, had an almost pathological aversion to seeing his daughter perform in public. "Only that which is feminine befits a woman," he told her; and Felix, to his discredit, in this case took his father's part rather than his sister's. There must have been prolonged family discussion, for Abraham reverted to the matter sternly in a number of letters. On the occasion of Fanny's birthday in 1828, he wrote her a series of admonitions such as Polonius might have sent to Ophelia had he been a letter-writing man: "You must become more steady and collected, and prepare more earnestly and eagerly for your real calling, the *only* calling of a young woman—I mean the state of a housewife. True economy is true liberality. He who throws away money must become either a miser or an impostor. Women have a difficult task; the constant occupation with apparent trifles . . . the unremitting attention to every detail, the appreciation of every moment and its improvement for some benefit or other— all these and more (you will think of many more) are the weighty duties of a woman."

A fine way to talk to a twenty-three-year-old woman, Fanny may well have reflected. And yet she accepted her father's counsel meekly; it was only in later years that she made an attempt to bring her musical activities before the public.

Whether by way of sublimating her own talent, or out of sheer sisterly love—probably a combination of both—Fanny devoted herself from the start to the furtherance of Felix's musical career. She watched over him with a fierce jealousy, and he, for his part, took her into his confidence as he took no one else, showing her almost every note as he wrote it. He shared with her his ideas for the Octet, for the *Midsummer Night's Dream,* for practically every piece he wrote in that enchanted garden in the days of his youth. When she was seventeen and Felix thirteen, Fanny proudly wrote: "I have watched his progress step by step, and may say I have contributed to his development. I have always been his only musical adviser, and he never writes down a thought before submitting it to my judgment. For instance, I have known his operas by heart before a note was written. . . ."

Fanny in the meantime was composing music herself—short piano pieces and songs, which she and her brother tried over together, giving each other the benefit of their criticism. "They are really vain and proud of each other," their mother remarked.

Although he supported his father in opposing public appearances for Fanny, Felix had a high opinion of her compositions; he jokingly called her "the Cantor," and imitated her habit of making little coughing noises when she disliked something he had written. He sought her opinion eagerly on his *Walpurgis Night,* saying "I feel she would say 'Yes,' and yet I feel doubtful." He sent home a new *Song Without Words* unfinished and noted: "Fanny may add the second part." Receiving some of her works, he wrote: "I have just played your Caprices. . . . all was unmixed delight." And although he would not agree that she have her songs printed, he had six of them published along with his own under his name. Then, when—as sometimes happened—one drew praise, he would say: "It is by my sister Fanny."*

Throughout the letters exchanged by Fanny and Felix in their youthful years, one glimpses the extent of the possessiveness she felt for him. At times Felix even reproved her, as when at the age of eighteen he found cause to write: "You must get a rap on the knuckles. . . . You were in my room? Prying into my things? . . . Take care, fair flower, take care!" Felix also loved to tease her by allusions to the attractive girls he met on his travels in England and elsewhere; most of his descriptions of feminine pulchritude occur in his letters to her and Rebecca, rather than to his parents or his brother.

Felix's penchant for simultaneously arousing and assuaging his sister's jealousy is shown in a half-bantering letter he wrote to her while he was paying court to Delphine von Schauroth in Munich. It was almost as if he wanted to let her know that the situation was a bit more serious than similar episodes in the past, but not important enough to give her real cause for alarm:

> *My darling little sister:* One thing is certain: that you are a capital creature and know something of music. I felt the truth of that last night while flirting very considerably. For your brother is as foolish as you are wise, and last night he was trying to be very sweet. . . . the girl plays very well. . . . But yesterday morning, when I heard her alone, and again admired her very much, it came into my mind that we have a young lady in our garden-house whose ideas of music are somehow of a different kind, and that she knows

*Songs published under Felix's name that are actually by Fanny are "The Homespell," "Italy," and "Suleika and Hatem," Op. 8 Nos. 2, 3, and 12, respectively; and "Sleepless," "Forsaken," and "The Nun," Op. 9 Nos. 7, 10, and 12. "Suleika and Hatem" is a duet.

more music than many ladies together, and I thought I would write
to her and send her my best love. It is clear that you are this young
lady, and I tell you, Fanny, that there are some of your pieces the
mere thought of which makes me quite tender and sincere.
. . . you know really and truly why God has created music, and that
makes me happy.

With all this, it might have seemed dubious that either Fanny
or Felix would ever take the first step toward marriage. But in
point of fact, Fanny did get married in 1829 at the age of twenty-
four, although the break with Felix that it necessitated represented
a tremendous emotional wrench for her.

She had met her husband-to-be, Wilhelm Hensel, six years
previously and, had it not been for the peculiar behavior of her
parents, might have married him sooner. Hensel was a skilled if
not inspired artist who had had the good fortune to catch the eye
of King Frederick William III of Prussia with some paintings he
had made for a theatrical spectacle called *Lalla Rookh,* based on
a romantic poem of Thomas Moore. Fanny, along with Felix, went
to see the paintings at an exhibition in Berlin, and there she met
the artist. She was seventeen; Hensel, twenty-five. He proposed
almost immediately that they become engaged, and Fanny was
eager to consent. But Fanny's mother had doubts. Leah Mendelssohn suspected that Hensel was after Fanny's fortune; she thought
he was too old for her; and she didn't much care for his being an
artist, a shiftless and unreliable métier.

Fanny was not one to argue with her parents, so the engagement
idea was dropped. Leah went even further, however. As a result
of his success with *Lalla Rookh,* Hensel received a state stipend for
protracted studies in Rome, and while he was there, Leah forbade
him even to correspond with her daughter. "I will not have you,"
she informed him, "by love-letters transport her for years into a
state of consuming passion and a yearning frame of mind quite
strange to her character, when I see her now before me blooming,
healthy, happy and free." If Hensel insisted on writing, the

mother said, let him write to her, and she would respond.

And that is exactly what happened. For five years Hensel remained in Rome, corresponding regularly with the mother of his intended, keeping her advised of his artistic activities and receiving in return the latest news of Fanny and the family. He also astutely eroded Leah's resistance by using his art as a weapon. Before he left for Rome, he painted the entire family, and while he was away, continued to send back drawings of them, usually idealized in the style of Raphael. Leah, who knew art, was highly flattered and began to consider him more favorably as a son-in-law in prospect. Of one drawing she wrote: "I cannot tell you how much its exquisite beauty of execution and fine delicate idea has surprised and touched us. The spiritualized, *à la Hensel* idealized likeness of the four children has not escaped our eyes. . . . I have never seen anything of the kind more elegant, neat, lovely and perfect in execution, either by yourself or any other artist. . . ." Eventually Leah broke down to the extent of actually reading Hensel's letters aloud to Fanny and showing her the pictures. She also asked her brother Jacob Bartholdy, who lived in Rome, to keep an eye on the young man. Bartholdy ended by inviting Hensel to join the corps of young artists who were painting frescoes for him at his palace, the Casa Bartholdy. When Bartholdy died in 1828, leaving his fortune to Leah, Hensel was appointed executor for his art collection, bringing him one step closer to the family. When he returned to Berlin, his engagement to Fanny was at last announced.

The wedding took place on October 3, 1829, and as fond and respectful as she was of Hensel, it was a fearful time for Fanny. Felix was in London on his first visit, and his carriage accident there prevented him from returning in time for the wedding, as he had planned. Fanny's letters to him during her engagement became almost hysterical: "I play your *Hora est,* stop before your portrait and kiss it every five minutes. . . . I love you, adore you immensely." Her sister Rebecca, with a touch of jovial malice, wrote to Felix: "Last night during charming conversation by the side of the most ardent beloved, Fanny fell asleep. . . . Why? Because you are not here."

From London Felix wrote: "This is the last letter that will reach you before the wedding and for the last time I address you as Miss Fanny Mendelssohn Bartholdy. . . . Live and prosper, get married and be happy, shape your life so that I shall find it beautiful and homelike when I come to you (that will not be long), and remain yourselves, you two, whatever storms may rage outside. . . . Whether I address my sister henceforth as Mademoiselle or Madame means little."

On her wedding day, Fanny broke down completely and wrote piteously to Felix: "I have your portrait before me, and ever repeating your dear name, and thinking of you as if you stood at my side, I weep! . . . every morning and every moment of my life I shall love you from the bottom of my heart, and I am sure that in so doing I shall not wrong Hensel."

Poor Hensel was almost the forgotten man in all these emotional displays; in fact, he found the Mendelssohns' "coterie language" a bit puzzling until he, too, was drawn into the tight family circle. In any case, the wedding, even without Felix, was a gala event. Abraham came back from a business trip to Hamburg and Holland laden with gifts for his daughter, and, looking them over, she told him that "Nathan the Wise could not have brought home anything more exquisite." She was pleased most of all with a delicate veil, "especially suitable on account of my red neck." She had wished Felix to write a wedding anthem for the occasion; but since he had not sent one, she composed her own, and it was played on the church organ.

However restrictive Leah Mendelssohn's attitude toward courtship and romance may seem, this marriage, like all her children's, worked out well. The newly married couple moved into the 3 Leipzigerstrasse establishment, where Abraham Mendelssohn had a studio built in the garden so that his new son-in-law could work at his art. Besides painting, he took in advanced pupils, adding a new crowd of lively visitors to the Mendelssohn grounds. In his day he was one of the most fashionable artists in Berlin. He developed rather a peculiar specialty of painting portraits of famous people "from the death"—as they lay in their last repose. Among those he thus was required to memorialize, sad to say, were Fanny and Felix Mendelssohn. The Hensels had one child, Sebastian, who in 1879 wrote a history of the Mendelssohn family that has served as a basic source for all subsequent biographies.

Fanny's marriage to Hensel did not end her musical activities; on the contrary, he encouraged her to expand them. With Felix away most of the time, it was Fanny who took over the Sunday musicales, embellishing them with a small choral group of her own, which she rehearsed on Friday afternoons. Her son Sebastian remembered: "On a beautiful summer morning nothing prettier could be seen than the Garden Hall, opening onto the beautiful trees and shrubs, filled with a crowd of gay, elegantly dressed people, and Fanny at her piano, surrounded by her choir, performing some ancient or modern masterpiece."

With Hensel's support, Fanny was at last permitted to appear in public as a pianist in Berlin in 1838 playing Felix's G Minor Piano Concerto at a charity concert—"one of those amateur affairs," she wrote, "where the tickets are twice the usual price, and the chorus is composed of countesses, ambassadresses, and officers." She was thirty-three years old. About the same time, Hensel also persuaded her to let her songs be published, and eventually two books of them came out. Felix had one of Fanny's newly published songs performed at a concert he was putting on in Leipzig and wrote her a warm letter of congratulations:

> How beautiful it was! You know what my opinion of it has always been, but I was curious to see whether my old favorite, which I had hitherto only heard sung by Rebecca to your accompaniment in the gray room with the engravings, would have the same effect here in the crowded hall, with the glare of the lamps and after listening

to noisy orchestral music. I felt so strange when I began your soft, pretty accompaniment imitating the waves, with all the people listening in perfect silence; but never did the song please me better. The people understood it, too, for there was a hum of approbation each time the refrain returned. . . . and much applause when it was over. . . . I thank you in the name of the public of Leipzig and elsewhere for publishing it against my wish.

Nevertheless, Felix kept arguing against Fanny's publishing any additional songs, even though by now Leah favored the idea; he kept insisting he didn't want her to get mixed up with the sordid commercial world. But Fanny, at last beginning to assert her own independence, complained there was no point to writing songs if they went unsung. Rebecca, she pointed out, had given up singing; Felix, "who alone is sufficient public for me," was no longer at home, and nobody else "takes the slightest interest." When several more of her works were published in 1846, Felix, after receiving his copies, finally dropped his opposition altogether and wrote: "May you have much happiness in giving pleasure to others; may you taste only the sweets and none of the bitterness of authorship; may the public pelt you with roses and never with stones; and may the printer's ink never draw black lines upon your soul—all of which I devoutly believe will be the case, so what is the use of my wishing it!"

Altogether about a dozen of Fanny Mendelssohn's compositions, including a Trio for Piano and Strings in D Major, were published before and after her death. But most of her music lies today in manuscript form in the Mendelssohn Archive of the Prussian State Library in Berlin. In death as in life, she continues to be known only as the sister of Felix Mendelssohn. Perhaps she would have wished for no greater distinction.

XVII The First Battle of Berlin

Fanny Mendelssohn and her parents always wanted to keep Felix close by their sides in Berlin, which was one reason they were so insistent that he apply for the post of Zelter's successor as director of the Singakademie in 1832. Felix wasn't so sure that the Singakademie wanted him. He was twenty-three years old and interested in new ideas; most of the Akademie's officials were double that age and devoted to the past. Besides, they had a perfect candidate of their own, Zelter's assistant of many years, one Karl Friedrich Rungenhagen, conservative, experienced, and safe.

Against his better judgment, Felix permitted himself to be talked into presenting himself as a candidate by his parents, sisters, and old friend Devrient, who had been called into the family council. While awaiting the outcome, and perhaps to further his candidacy a bit, Felix engaged the Singakademie concert hall for three concerts, at which he brought forth his *Walpurgis Night* and *Reformation* Symphony in addition to his *Midsummer Night's Dream, Calm Sea and Prosperous Voyage,* and *Hebrides* Overtures.

But the events that followed were disastrous. Opposition to Mendelssohn developed quickly; his age, inexperience, and long absence from Berlin were all raised as points against him. It was pointed out that despite his years of singing as a boy alto in the choir and his historic *St. Matthew Passion* revival, he had never been as intricately bound up with the Singakademie's affairs as had Rungenhagen. On top of everything else, his Jewish birth came into the discussions. Devrient reported hearing one member say during the debate that "the Vocal Academy was a Christian institution and that on this account it was an unheard-of thing to try and force a Jewish lad upon them as a conductor." For months the argument went on in Berlin musical circles, with much maneuvering and intriguing, and the Mendelssohn family doing its best to persuade Singakademie members to support Felix. Mendelssohn himself watched the proceedings rather sardonically and, more aware than his parents of the opposition to him, did no campaigning himself. Finally, on a January night in 1833, more than two hundred members of the Singakademie gathered for the decisive meeting. After a tense final discussion, the question was put; and as each individual called out his vote, it slowly became apparent that Felix was falling behind. The final tally was Rungenhagen 144, Mendelssohn 88. As a consolation, Felix was offered the vice-directorship, which he declined. The entire Mendelssohn family, which had been among the Akademie's most active and generous supporters, resigned en masse, and the institution itself suffered a steady decline under Rungenhagen's plodding leadership. On Felix himself the effect was drastic, for he came to the conclusion that Berlin had no place for him and immediately began looking around for a musical position elsewhere.

Fortunately, two excellent offers reached him just as his rejection in Berlin was coming about. The city of Düsseldorf was to be the scene of the annual Lower Rhine Music Festival and wished him to take charge of planning and directing this event and to remain there afterward in charge of its year-round musical activities. And from London came a commission to write for the Philharmonic Society "a symphony, an overture and a vocal composition." For these he would be paid the equivalent of $2,000, with performance rights for the three works belonging to the society exclusively for two years.

Felix made a quick trip to London in April, bringing with him his *Italian* Symphony, which he had been revising ever since his trip to Rome and which he now felt was at last ready for performance. Also on the program was Mozart's Piano Concerto No. 20 in D Minor, with Felix as soloist. The *Italian* Symphony received instant acclaim, with one critic calling it "a composition that will endure for ages, if we may presume to judge such a work on a single performance." Mendelssohn himself regarded it as "the most mature thing I have ever done," and it has indeed proved the most durable of his symphonies—a warm, brilliant, vigorous work that never grows stale. Among its first hearers and admirers was the great violinist Niccolò Paganini, who had often been a guest at the Mendelssohns' Berlin musicales; now, listening to Felix as a pianist, he forthwith invited him to play Beethoven violin sonatas with him, a suggestion that unfortunately never came to fruition.

The Düsseldorf Festival was held in May, with people from a wide area journeying to the city on the Rhine, crowding its streets and shops, and sleeping eight and ten in a room in hotels and inns. One of the guests was Abraham Mendelssohn, invited by his son to attend the festivities as an antidote to the bitter experience of the Berlin fiasco. In his letters home, Abraham reveled in what he saw and heard. "I have never yet seen anyone carried around on a silken cushion as Felix is here," he wrote to his wife. The Düsseldorf Festival itself lasted only three days, but it was a delightful affair. The concerts were held in a hall that seated 1,300, about a mile from the city itself. People either came out on foot or arrived in carriages or farm wagons. Great trees stood all around, and during intermissions, which were very long, the audience sat at tables consuming "masses of sandwiches and May wine," to quote Abraham. There was a great deal of informality among both the musicians and the audience; the former taking an inordinate time to tune their instruments and the latter chattering a great deal during some of the numbers. Felix spoke sharply to the instrumentalists and the audience alike, with the result that both promptly reformed. Abraham, who had never seen his son in action before as such a large-scale organizer, was impressed. To him it appeared "like a miracle that 400 persons of all sexes, classes and ages, blown together like snow before the wind, should let themselves be conducted and governed like children by the youngest of them all, too young almost to be a friend to any of them, and with no title or dignity whatever."

The principal work presented at Düsseldorf was Handel's *Israel in Egypt,* in its original form and instrumentation—the first time it had been performed complete since Handel's own time. Also on the schedule were Beethoven's *Pastoral* Symphony, still a relative novelty, and Mendelssohn's martial-sounding "Trumpet" Overture in C Major op. 101. During the opening concert, the ladies of the choir kept roses and carnations hidden beneath their scarves and music sheets all through the performance and then at the end began pelting the astonished Felix with a shower of flowers. One young woman rushed up to him bearing on a velvet cushion a laurel wreath which she fastened on his head. He quickly took it off and just as quickly she replaced it, until finally he gave up and took his bows wearing the crown. Abraham, beaming in the audience, was reminded of an old legend that his family possessed royal blood as descendants of Saul Wahl, the fabled one-night king of Poland.*

Mendelssohn was due to return to Düsseldorf in October to assume the general directorship of the town's musical life. Preferring not to remain in Berlin during the intervening months, he decided to spend the summer in London, and this time persuaded his father to accompany him there. Abraham was now fifty-seven

---

*None of the Mendelssohns took the legend seriously, but all, including Felix, enjoyed talking about it and referred to it in letters. According to the tale, a dispute between two Polish factions after the death of King Bathory in 1586 prevented the throne from being filled. Since there was a law that it might not remain empty for any period of time, a young Jewish scholar named Saul Wahl was installed as temporary king. Some traditions say he reigned only overnight; others, that he occupied the throne for a few days. According to one version, he was executed the moment his "rule" ended. No historical foundation has been found for the story, but it persists both in Polish and Jewish folklore. Moses Mendelssohn's father, Mendel Dessau, was said to have claimed descent from Saul Wahl.

years old and troubled by failing eyesight and other health problems. But Felix assured him that London was like no other city on earth, that he had wonderful friends there, and that the two of them could have a fine time going to concerts, visiting art galleries, and sightseeing in general. Abraham, after some hesitation, consented and was rewarded by seeing first-hand the adulation with which his son was treated in London. But he cannot be said to have enjoyed the city as much as Felix; in one letter he wrote of awakening on a mist-shrouded July day and being told by his barber that it was a fine morning. " 'Is it?' I asked. 'Yes, a very fine morning,' and so I learned what a fine summer morning is like here." He also injured his leg when he slipped during a tour of Portsmouth Dockyard, delaying their homeward journey a full month.

Among the sightseeing visits made by the two Mendelssohns was one to the Houses of Parliament. By coincidence, Commons was debating a measure designed to remove the lingering legal restrictions on the Jews of Britain. Felix eagerly sat in on the deliberations and was almost incoherently exultant in a letter home on July 23, 1833: "This morning the Jews were emancipated. This makes me proud, especially since a few days ago your lousy Edicts of Posen* were criticized here, as was only right and proper. The Times felt noble and said that it is much better for us† in England. After many Jew-haters. . . . had blathered, Robert Grant, who had originally introduced the bill, concluded the question by asking whether they were there to fulfill the prophecies of Scripture as they claimed to do, whereas he himself wanted to stick to the words: 'Glory to God and good will to men,' and then followed 187 ayes and 52 noes. This is noble and beautiful and fills me with gratitude to the Heavens."

In the fall, Mendelssohn moved into his new post in Düsseldorf,

---

*The Edicts of Posen sharply limited Jewish emancipation to a small upper class.
†That is, the Jews. Mendelssohn's use of "us" is striking.

the most important he had yet held in a German city. He remained in the Rhenish town for two years, with his contract providing him with three months' leave of absence each year, enabling him to plan annual visits to England. He took over the entire musical life of the town, symphonic, operatic, and even ecclesiastical.

He was disturbed, however, that his advent should mean the displacement of the former director of church music, with whom the town authorities had long been unhappy. This is his own description of the demission of the old man:

> A very crabbed old musician in a threadbare coat was summoned. When he came and they attacked him, he declared that he neither could nor would have better music; if any improvement was required, someone else must be employed; that he knew perfectly well what vast pretensions some people made nowadays, everything was expected to sound so beautiful—this had not been the case in his day, and he played just as well now as formerly. I was really very reluctant to take the affair out of his hands, though there could be no doubt that others would do infinitely better; and I could not help thinking how I should myself feel were *I* to be summoned some fifty years hence to a town-hall, and spoken to in this strain, and a young greenhorn snubbed me, and my coat were seedy, and I had not the most remote idea why the music should be better; and I felt rather uncomfortable.

To give Düsseldorf the kind of church music he thought it should have, Mendelssohn traveled by coach to Bonn, Cologne, and other cities to purchase copies of scores by de Lassus, Palestrina, and Pergolesi. Many of the church scores he performed in Düsseldorf were Catholic, but to Mendelssohn, half-Lutheran, half-Jew, music was music, to be evaluated only by its intrinsic quality. He decided to stage opera in the city, which had seen little of it before; and to begin, he chose Mozart's *Don Giovanni,* engaging the singers, directing the rehearsals, conducting the performances himself—the first time he ever conducted opera in public. Not everybody in Düsseldorf cared for *Don Giovanni* or, for that matter, for Felix Mendelssohn; at the first performances, for which prices had been increased steeply, a few members of the audience created a brief disturbance as the second act started. Eventually, they apologized to Mendelssohn, and the opera was a success. Nevertheless, the incident rankled, and Mendelssohn gradually concluded that he simply was not cut out for the special kind of administrative delicacy needed to run an opera theater, with its rivalries and intrigues. Besides, his operatic management problems were interfering with his own music. "When I sat down to my composing in the morning," he wrote to Leah, "every hour was punctuated with a ringing of the bell; there were grumbling choristers to be soothed, stupid singers to be taught, seedy musicians to be engaged: this went on all day. . . ." The upshot was that he abruptly walked out of his opera-theater duties in Düsseldorf, accepting a salary reduction to do so. Some people in the town were scandalized, and even Abraham thought he was lacking in tact.

Mendelssohn, in truth, was not a very sweet-tempered individual; during a rehearsal of Beethoven's *Egmont* music, which was to be performed with Goethe's play, he indulged in Toscanini-like tantrums with the orchestra, once tearing up a full orchestral score in front of them. He reported the episode quite proudly in a letter: "They love to beat each other up in the orchestra—but with me they are not allowed to do that, and so from time to time I must stage a furious scene. . . . Today for the first time I tore a score in two; and thereupon they immediately played with more expression."

All in all, Mendelssohn was beginning to realize the limitations of Düsseldorf, which, despite the opportunities it offered him, remained essentially a provincial town. But he managed to do a fair share of composing there, including such works as the *Fair Melusine* Overture and the *Rondo brillant* for Piano and Orchestra op. 29. A Düsseldorf friend, the poet Karl Immerman, with whom he had a falling-out over his abrupt dropping of his theatrical duties, had urged him to write an opera on Shakespeare's *The*

Tempest and even presented him with a libretto for it. But Mendelssohn found it unsatisfactory and instead began working on a massive oratorio called *St. Paul,* which he had had on his mind almost since the days of his *St. Matthew Passion* revival.

The Lower Rhine Festival, which alternated among several cities, was held in Aix-la-Chapelle in 1834; Mendelssohn went there as a guest and met his old Paris friends Chopin and Hiller. Delighted with the unexpected reunion, he took them back to Düsseldorf with him, and they spent hours playing and talking music. Mendelssohn found that Chopin had advanced greatly even over his marvelous playing in Paris: "He produces new effects, like Paganini on his violin, and accomplishes wonderful passages, such as no one could formerly have thought practicable." Mendelssohn was thought by many to be the finest pianist of his day, but certainly there is nothing in the least begrudging or half-hearted in his praise for his contemporary and, in a sense, rival. Mendelssohn later played parts of his *St. Paul* for Chopin, who responded by performing several of his newest études and his latest concerto. Neither in the least understood the other's music; it was, Mendelssohn himself said ruefully, "just as if a Cherokee and a Kaffir had met to converse."

It seems unlikely that Mendelssohn would have remained long in Düsseldorf no matter what happened; but in point of fact, he had only been there a little more than a year when the city of Leipzig began putting out feelers in his direction. Negotiations went on for more than six months, but it was only a matter of working out the terms. The specific post offered to Mendelssohn was the directorship of the Leipzig Gewandhaus Orchestra, but he knew this meant he would actually be taking charge of virtually all the musical activity in one of Germany's most important cities. When friends asked him what he expected to do in Leipzig, he replied: "Everything."

XVIII The Leipzig Years

Mendelssohn came to Leipzig at just the right time for the city and himself. At twenty-six, he might have been considered young for so important a position, but he was better traveled and more widely experienced than most musicians twice his age. Leipzig, a thriving business center, had a rich musical tradition; it was the city of Johann Sebastian Bach, who lay buried in the churchyard of its Johanneskirche; its orchestra and its choirs had been famous throughout Europe.

Yet the town had been in a period of some decline just before Mendelssohn's arrival and was only just beginning to emerge, thanks to the accession of Saxony to the German Customs Union in 1834. Commerce was the lifeblood of Leipzig; the word *Gewandhaus* itself literally means "clothing hall," for the orchestra had begun by playing in the ancient market hall of the city's linen merchants. When Mendelssohn came to Leipzig, its narrow, twisting streets, lined by houses with high pitched roofs, and its great central market square were crowded with merchants and travelers, particularly during its great commercial fairs. Then as now it was a center for book publishing, and its university was one of the most respected and influential of the nineteenth century. Goethe had described it as "a little Paris," and one of its most distinguished resident musicians, Robert Schumann, told that Franz Liszt had spoken slightingly of the city's lack of "countesses and princesses," replied: "Let him take care! We have our own aristocracy: 150 bookshops, fifty printing plants, and thirty periodicals."

Schumann himself, twenty-five years old, had first come to Leipzig seven years before to study law at the university, but turned to music instead. He studied piano with Friedrich Wieck, a celebrated pedagogue, lived at his house, and fell in love with his daughter Clara, the first of the great woman pianists. Eventually he married her, over her father's violent objections. Schumann, who had yet to win fame as a composer, was waging a youthful, vigorous battle against the musical mediocrities and reactionaries of the day. His weapon was a journal called the *Neue Zeitschrift für Musik* (the "New Periodical for Music"). He saw himself as the head of a League of David sworn to do battle against the cultural Philistines, and he eagerly welcomed Felix Mendelssohn, one year older than himself, not only as a companion-in-arms but also as a leader in the struggle. In fact, he inscribed Mendelssohn on the roster of this fanciful organization, assigning to him the pseudonym "Felix Meritis."

Mendelssohn fell in eagerly with Schumann, Clara Wieck, and the other young musicians of Leipzig; furthermore, he found that the civic authorities really meant to keep their promise of giving him a free hand in re-energizing the city's musical life. He was sustained in Leipzig by the same kind of affection from the musical public that Mozart had encountered from the citizens of Prague, who had admired the composer of *Don Giovanni* and *Figaro* with far more warmth than he ever met in his own city of Vienna. But unlike Mozart, who kept returning to his indifferent Viennese, Mendelssohn turned his back on his home town of Berlin and planted new roots in Leipzig. And, in return for its hospitality, he made it the musical capital of Germany, creating a tradition of great conductors at the Gewandhaus that reached down through Arthur Nikisch to Wilhelm Furtwängler in our own century.

Among his actions was a campaign for higher salaries for the members of the Gewandhaus Orchestra—surely the quickest way to a musician's heart. In a letter to his friend Moscheles, he explained his refusal, for the moment, to assist a campaign to erect a statue of Bach:

> I declined to give anything. . . . nor would you have done so, had you known all their doings and dealings in Germany with regard to monuments. They speculate with the names of great men in order to give themselves great names; they do a great deal of trumpeting in the papers, and treat us to ever so much bad music with real trumpets. If they wish to honor Handel in Halle, Mozart in Salzburg, and Beethoven in Bonn by founding good orchestras and performing their works properly and intelligently, I am their man. But I do not care for their stones and blocks as long as their orchestras are only stumbling-blocks, nor for their conservatories in which there is nothing worth conserving. My present hobby is the improvement of our poor orchestra. After no end of letter-writing, soliciting and importuning, I have succeeded in getting the salaries raised by 500 thalers; and before I leave them I mean to get them double that amount. If that is granted, I will not mind their setting up a monument in front of the St. Thomas school; but first, mind you, the grant!

He was as good as his word, for once his men got their money, he entered wholeheartedly the Bach statue campaign, giving an all-Bach organ concert himself at St. Thomas's for its benefit.

At the Gewandhaus, Mendelssohn presented to the avid Leipzigers a dazzling array of programs, studded with works new to their ears—obscure Mozart symphonies, neglected Bach concertos, unplayed works by Beethoven. Though there was a constant demand for his own music, lists of composers played during his Leipzig years show Felix Mendelssohn only in tenth place, well behind Mozart, Beethoven, Haydn, Bach, Handel, and others. His opening program of October 4, 1835, consisted of his own *Calm Sea and Prosperous Voyage* Overture; an aria from Weber's *Freischütz;* Spohr's Violin Concerto No. 8 in A Minor, the *Gesangsszene;* Cherubini's Overture and Introduction to *Ali Baba,* with the Leipzig Singakademie and St. Thomas Choir participating; and finally, Beethoven's Symphony No. 4 in B-flat, then a decided novelty. Afterward he wrote home that he had been satisfied only with the performances of his own Overture and the Beethoven symphony; there had been too little rehearsal time for the other works. Among those who praised his first concert was Schumann, who wrote in his *Neue Zeitschrift:* "F. Meritis stepped out. A hundred eyes flew towards him in the first moment. . . . That a change of administration had taken place, everyone could recognize in the choice of pieces." Schumann was a bit disturbed by Mendelssohn's use of a baton, arguing that "the symphony orchestra should be like a republic"; but in time he and the rest of Leipzig came to accept Mendelssohn's insistence that a conductor had to run an orchestra more or less like a dictator.

So great were the crowds that came out to see the new conductor that people began to complain about the size of the Gewandhaus auditorium. Its acoustics were remarkably good, but in seating arrangement it was a most unusual structure, with the audience seated not facing the stage but at right angles to it, so they had to twist their necks to see the performers. Henry Chorley gave this description: "The Gewandhaus, a moderately-sized room, was in 1839–40, infinitely too small for the audience who crowded it, paying their sixteen *groschen* (two shillings) for entrance. . . . The ladies of the place occupied the center of the room, sitting in two *vis-a-vis* divisions—that is, sideways to the orchestra. Behind them crowded gentlemen so thickly that anyone going as late as half an hour before the music struck up, ran no small chance of being kneaded into the wall. . . ." A lady observer compared the arrangement of benches to that on an omnibus and said that the women stared at each other's dresses while the men stared at the women. Over the proscenium were engraved the words: *Res severa verum gaudium* ("Seriousness alone is true amusement").

As the Leipzig seasons unfolded, Mendelssohn conducted a variety of works such as no other European city offered. He put his friend Schumann solidly before the public, premièring two of his symphonies and an extraordinary vocal work called *Le Paradis et le Peri.* He introduced Bach's *St. Matthew Passion* to Leipzig. He played Beethoven's four overtures to *Fidelio* on a single program, apparently the first time that this had ever been done. He gave a hearing to young symphonic composers, many of them since forgotten—Adolf Fredrik Lindblad, Johann Wenzel Kalliwoda, Johann Friedrich Kittl. For his own B Minor *Capriccio,* he engaged Clara Wieck as a soloist and wrote admiringly afterward that she had played it "like a witch." Mendelssohn himself played the Mozart D Minor Concerto "as written"—apparently it was then usually heard in an adulterated version. Beethoven's Ninth Symphony and Bach's Triple Concerto in D Minor, both rarities in those days, were given, the latter with Mendelssohn, Moscheles, and Clara Wieck as the three soloists. The British composer Sterndale Bennett was engaged to play his own Piano Concerto in C Minor. Mendelssohn, who always eagerly welcomed a visiting Englishman, made a big fuss over Bennett, introducing him to all the musical and social leaders in town. Bennett wrote home that he was pleased with his reception and that he had met "a very nice fellow who is named Schumann and whom I like very much—he composes a great deal, although his music is rather too eccentric."

It was through Schumann that Mendelssohn was able to give the first performance anywhere on March 21, 1839, of Franz Schubert's great Symphony in C Major, a discovery on a level with his revival of the *St. Matthew Passion* in Berlin. Schumann, on a visit to Vienna, had come upon the manuscript of the work, never played during the composer's lifetime, in the hands of Schubert's brother, who had held it since his death in 1828. It is significant that instead of seeking a performance from the musical authorities in Vienna, Schumann sent the music on to Mendelssohn in Leipzig, who recognized its stature immediately. For accomplishments like these, the University of Leipzig conferred an honorary doctor of philosophy degree upon Felix less than a year after his arrival.

In addition to obtaining more pay and later a pension system for his musicians, Mendelssohn increased his orchestra's permanent personnel until it numbered fifty, large for the time, and of course a figure that could be augmented for special performances. He also brought in a new concertmaster, the great violinist Ferdinand David, twenty-six years old, who forthwith became his close friend, assistant, and adviser. Mendelssohn and David organized a series of Gewandhaus Chamber Music Concerts, opening up a whole new area to the Leipzigers who, if they wished to hear chamber music previously, had to play it in their own homes. At one of these concerts, Mendelssohn's youthful Octet, with its marvelous scherzo, was performed, with himself and Kalliwoda playing the two viola parts. As part of a Bach-Handel "historical concert," David played Bach's Chaconne for Violin, then unknown to the public, with Mendelssohn extemporizing an accompaniment at the piano.

Through Mendelssohn, Leipzig became a major attraction for visiting musicians. Chopin came and was made the center of a festival devoted to his compositions. Liszt's arrival was cause for even greater excitement; by now he was regarded by almost everybody (especially himself) as supreme among the world's pianists and comported himself accordingly. When he turned up dressed in the utmost elegance, lithe, slender, and exuding self-assurance, Mendelssohn, who rather preferred Liszt's great rival Thalberg, nudged Hiller who was standing nearby and said: "There's a new phenomenon, the virtuoso of the nineteenth century." When Liszt claimed that he could achieve virtually all the orchestral effects of Beethoven's nine symphonies upon a modern piano, Mendelssohn commented drily to Hiller: "I'd believe it if I could only hear the first eight bars of Mozart's G Minor Symphony, with that delicate figure in the violas, sound on the piano as they do in the orchestra."

Liszt's appearance created a tumult in Leipzig because his manager demanded, and got, steeply increased admission prices. To still the consequent ill feeling, Mendelssohn had the idea of staging a special soiree for Liszt at the Gewandhaus, to which 350 prominent Leipzigers were invited without charge. Punch and pastry were served, and the musical program, in Mendelssohn's own words, consisted of: "Orchestra, chorus, bishop, cake, *Calm Sea and Prosperous Voyage,* Psalm, Bach's Triple Concerto (Liszt, Hiller and me), choruses from *St. Paul,* fantasy on *Lucia di Lammermoor, Erlkönig,* the devil and his grandmother!" Both Liszt and the audience went away happy.

A spectacular visit to Leipzig also was made by Berlioz, who had not seen Mendelssohn since their encounter in Rome a dozen years previously. Berlioz walked into the Gewandhaus one afternoon as Mendelssohn was rehearsing his *Walpurgis Night,* and the two fell into each other's arms.

As Berlioz set it down later, the conversation went like this:

MENDELSSOHN: And is it twelve years? Twelve years since we dreamed on the plains of Rome?

BERLIOZ: Yes, and in the baths of Caracalla.

MENDELSSOHN: Ah! Always joking! Always ready to laugh at me!

BERLIOZ: No, no; I hardly ever jest now; it was only to test your memory, and see if you had forgotten all my impieties. I jest so little, that our very first interview I am going seriously to ask you to make me a present, to which I shall attach the highest value.

MENDELSSOHN: What is that?

BERLIOZ: Give me your baton with which you have just conducted the rehearsal of your new work.

MENDELSSOHN: Willingly, on condition that you send me yours.

BERLIOZ: I shall be giving copper for gold, but never mind, I consent.

Thus the two men solemnly exchanged batons, Mendelssohn giving up his elegant, light stick, made of whalebone covered in white leather, and receiving in return what Berlioz himself described as "my heavy oaken staff." Berlioz, who had been reading James Fenimore Cooper, enclosed the following effusive note:

To the Chief Mendelssohn!
Great chief! We have promised to exchange tomahawks. Mine
is a rough one—yours is plain. Only squaws and pale-faces are fond
of ornate weapons. Be my brother! and when the Great Spirit shall
have sent us to hunt in the land of souls, may our warriors hang
up our tomahawks together at the door of the council chamber.

Mendelssohn, one imagines, must have taken some time to
digest *that.* But he put on two magnificent Berlioz concerts, including such works as the *King Lear* and *Francs-Juges* Overtures,
the *Fantastic* Symphony, and excerpts from *Romeo and Juliet* and
the Requiem. Mendelssohn went to great lengths to obtain the
extra performers and instruments necessary for these works, and
Berlioz was overwhelmed by the ability and responsiveness of
the Leipzig musicians. He also was surprised to see how carefully
Mendelssohn himself worked with the choristers who were learning the new and difficult music, writing: "It grieved me to see a
great master and virtuoso like Mendelssohn engaged in such a
menial task, although it must be said he fulfilled it with unwearied
patience, all his remarks being made with perfect sweetness and
courtesy, the more gratifying from their rarity in like cases."
Berlioz would have been all the more astonished at this consider-
ateness had he known how little Mendelssohn cared personally for
his music. Berlioz himself appears to have had a fine time in
Leipzig. Many of the public made clear that they disliked his
scores, but when he fell ill there, the physician attending him
refused a cash fee and asked instead for a few measures scrawled
from the Requiem with the composer's signature.

Mendelssohn's most durable contribution to Leipzig's musical
life was the founding in 1843 of a conservatory which became one
of Europe's foremost educational institutions. For its faculty he
enlisted the most eminent men he could find, including Schumann
for piano and composition, David for violin, and Moritz Haupt-
mann, the eminent theorist and cantor of the Thomas School, for
counterpoint. Later additions were Moscheles for master classes in

piano and Niels Gade for composition. Mendelssohn himself taught piano and composition classes and administered the school. He saw to it that full scholarships were available for many who needed them, writing to the king of Saxony (who gave the new institution a grant): "Scholars desirous of enjoying fuller instruction almost invariably consist of those who propose devoting themselves to art, but who rarely possess the means of paying for good private lessons." One such student was a twelve-year-old boy named Joseph Joachim, who came from Vienna, attracted by the fame and liberality of the new school, and who, under the tutelage of Mendelssohn and David, developed into one of the favorites of the Gewandhaus and one of the foremost violinists of the century.

Meanwhile the Leipzig years were bringing profound changes in Mendelssohn's personal life. In November, 1835, his father died. Abraham Mendelssohn's sight had grown steadily worse and now, at the age of fifty-nine, he was almost blind. Felix came up from Leipzig to pay him a visit in October, bringing Moscheles with him. Since the entire family was at home, once more the house at 3 Leipzigerstrasse rang with piano improvisations and other musical entertainments. Felix, who had concerts to prepare in Leipzig, departed after a few days, promising to return for Christmas. But within a month, Abraham died, much in the same manner as his father, suffering a slight cold and then, without warning, passing away in his sleep.

There was another curious reminder of Moses Mendelssohn in his last days. The final controversy of Moses' life had involved a defense of Lessing over what he considered the unjust accusations of Frederick Jacobi. In like manner, Abraham Mendelssohn had a dispute about Lessing a few days before his own death. His old friend Varnhagen von Ense paid him a social call one afternoon, and the two men sat in a darkened room discussing literature. The conversation turned to several writers who were friends of Varnhagen, and the diplomat rather undiplomatically remarked that he preferred them to Lessing. Abraham became indignant; one word led to another; and the two friends started quarreling bitterly. Finally Varnhagen called for his cloak and left abruptly.

Abraham was troubled by the dispute, and the next morning began a letter of explanation to Varnhagen. Fanny found it unfinished on his desk after his death three days later:

> November 16, 1835
>
> *Honored Sir and Friend,*—If you consider that Lessing during a great part of his life was my father's most intimate friend, deeply loved and esteemed by him; that Lessing has written *Nathan, Emilia Galotti, The Education of Mankind, Laakoon.* . . . that he was incontestably a profound scholar; and that almost every line of his displays the clearest understanding united to the deepest feeling—you will kindly excuse me for speaking rather too warmly yesterday in his defense. I cannot deny that I was surprised at finding you, who I have so often heard speak with the warmest admiration of Lessing and his works, *Nathan* especially, and the views therein expressed —at now finding you place this man, who thought so highly of truth as to believe that it belonged to God alone and that he himself could only strive after it, in short, this sun in which dark spots may be seen through smoked glasses, on a level with men who as yet have only shown spots, behind which we are allowed to suppose a sun. . . .

Thus, nearly fifty years after Moses Mendelssohn's death, and only a few days before his own, Abraham Mendelssohn performed an act of homage to his father's memory. In his fashion, he had been faithful to it, for despite the doubts that sometimes assailed him, he believed he was adapting ancient ideals to a new way of life. He had received not only religion from his father; from his hands he had also inherited honesty, fidelity, respect for scholarship, and love of family; and these, at least, he passed on to his children. Unlike Moses, he never rose above his own times, but he may surely be written down among the upright men of his generation.

XIX *Felix and Cecile*

Abraham Mendelssohn's death had the effect of spurring Felix on to the completion of his oratorio *St. Paul.* Abraham had taken a particular interest in the work, apparently seeing in it a religious utterance that could bridge the gap between Judaism and Lutheranism and being convinced that his son could produce a choral masterpiece. It was given in May, 1836, at that year's Lower Rhine Festival, held in Düsseldorf, with Felix conducting. *St. Paul* had a profound effect upon its first listeners (including Schumann) and attained widespread popularity on the Continent and in England for many years. It is an act of homage to Bach, following the scheme of the *St. Matthew Passion* in its succession of chorales, arias, and recitatives. But it is Bach toned down and made easier to take, with the drama diluted and the ruggedness smoothed away. Neverthless, *St. Paul* has passages of character and nobility and deserves something better than the total obscurity into which it has been cast.

The Mendelssohn clan was well represented at Düsseldorf for the première of the oratorio. Felix's brother Paul, now the business head of the family, traveled down, bringing with him his wife Albertine and Fanny. It was just as well Fanny was there, for she averted a disaster at the première. She had decided to join in the chorus for the performance, singing with the altos, and observed that one of the solo performers, appropriately singing the role of a False Witness, had missed his entrance. Quickly she hissed out his cue to him and got things going again.

Not unexpectedly, Felix felt Abraham's loss more keenly than did his brother or sisters. Father and son had traveled much together; between them existed a mutual respect; Felix had often told his father that for a layman, he had an astonishing grasp of the musical art. But even more pertinent was the fact that Fanny, Rebecca, and Paul were all married, with families of their own; whereas he was living by himself in austere bachelor quarters in Leipzig. Fanny, who in her six years of marriage, had conquered her overemotional feelings toward Felix and matured into a sympathetic and discerning older sister, sat down with him quietly and told him that at the age of twenty-seven, he must think seriously about marriage. She recalled that their father had once told Devrient, in connection with Felix's finicky requirements for an operatic poem: "I am afraid that Felix with his fault-finding will no more obtain an opera libretto than he will a wife." Now Fanny kept urging him to make a more concentrated effort, as the two of them continued to exchange letters during that sad winter of 1835.

One of the subjects they corresponded about was a curious musician who passed through Leipzig on an extensive concert tour of Europe. His name was Mikhail Gusikow, and he was a Jew from Poland who made a point of traveling in Orthodox garb, wearing a long black coat, a skullcap, and a full beard. His instrument was a kind of homemade xylophone, consisting of a row of wooden sticks laid upon a bedding of straw, and upon this he produced surprisingly beautiful musical effects. Mendelssohn, who was always quite open about his interest in anything Jewish, was fascinated by Gusikow. He called him "a real phenomenon . . . a true genius . . . who is inferior to no player on earth in style and execution, and delights me more on his odd instrument than many do on their pianos, just because it is so thankless. . . . I have not enjoyed a concert so much for a long time."

Mendelssohn sent Gusikow on to see his family in Berlin; the itinerant musician called on Leah, who thought he had an "interesting physiognomy." She and Fanny agreed that Abraham would have been keenly interested in meeting him. Gusikow impressed a great many other musicians in addition to Mendelssohn and might have gone on to a notable virtuoso career had he not died of tuberculosis at the age of thirty-one.

Fanny's insistence that Felix find himself a wife, seconded by his mother's urgings along the same line, had their effect upon him. Or perhaps he would have married without their importuning. He was, after all, still younger than either his father or grandfather had been when they married; he simply had not experienced until now any great need to found a family of his own. It was as much a matter of awaiting the right time as the right girl.

Mendelssohn's sex life affords little opportunity for speculation, from which most observers have come to the possibly erroneous conclusion that it did not exist. Certainly he was in this matter, as in many others, the very soul of circumspection. He did not, like Mozart, write bawdy letters to a cousin; nor, like Beethoven, leave an impression of hidden and unidentifiable loves; nor, like Schubert, contract syphilis; nor, like his contemporaries Liszt and Chopin, create scandals with his *amours*. Whatever he did, he did discreetly. After his marriage, he and his wife even agreed to burn their love letters, which, to them at least, must have seemed reasonably combustible.

Yet there are indications that for a man of breeding, respectability, and a strict upbringing, Mendelssohn got around. As already noted, from his earliest days as a visitor to Goethe, he was highly susceptible to pretty girls and accepted their attentions with eagerness. In England he was regarded as a prime escort and dancing partner for society girls, and he cast an appraising eye from time to time on less-fashionable young women as well. Delphine von Schauroth undoubtedly was his first serious love; two years after their meeting, when she had already married, he was still bemoaning her loss to his friend Klingemann.

Among the most intriguing of Mendelssohn's female acquaintances prior to his marriage was Maria Malibran, the most beautiful and spectacular opera singer of the day. Felix had heard her perform in Rossini's *Otello* on the first night of his first visit to London and found her "a young woman, beautiful and splendidly made, her hair *en toupet,* full of fire and power, very coquettish. . . . I shall constantly go to hear her."

Five years later Mendelssohn, again in London, actually met Malibran at a party given by his Kensington friends, the Horsleys. He was twenty-five, and the singer, twenty-six. She had had a tempestuous career, running away from an aged, wealthy husband to whom her father, the singer Manuel Garcia, had married her off at the age of eighteen; singing in London, Paris, and New York; and finally taking up with a Belgian violinist named Charles de Beriot. There were all kinds of stories about Malibran; it was variously said that she liked to drink, play with dolls, wear male clothes. These attributes, added to her sparkling voice and a figure which one observer described as "rounded to a becoming degree of embonpoint," made her an intriguing personality to Felix as to everyone else in the musical world.

Apparently Malibran took a fancy to young Mendelssohn that night at the Horsleys. She sang for the assembled guests, beginning with a Spanish song, and Felix, who could not take his eyes off her, promptly requested two more. She gracefully complied, and followed them with an English sea chanty and a French troubador song. Aware of the effect she was having on Felix, she asked him to play the piano, but he suddenly became reticent and, murmuring that he couldn't think of trying to follow her as a performer, tried to slip into another room. Malibran went right in after him and, while the guests looked on amused, emerged a moment or two later clutching him by the arm. Felix sat down at the piano, but instead of playing his own music, performed a series of improvisations on the Spanish songs Malibran had sung—and which he had never previously heard. The evening ended with Malibran singing more Spanish and French music and Felix accompanying her. They had a few more meetings in London, but Mendelssohn left for home soon afterward. When she died three years later from injuries suffered in a fall from a horse, Mendelssohn talked for a time of writing a Requiem for her. He never did so, but neither did he ever forget their encounter in London.

As much as Mendelssohn admired and valued women professional musicians, he apparently had no thought of ever marrying one. In 1836, during the illness of a friend, Mendelssohn was invited to take over for six weeks the direction of a series of choral concerts by the St. Cecilia Society of Frankfurt. It turned out to be an eventful trip both musically and personally, for there he met both the famous composer Gioacchino Rossini and, singing among the choristers, a girl named Cecile Jeanrenaud, whom he was to marry.

Rossini, the celebrated composer of *The Barber of Seville* and *William Tell,* was only forty-four years old but had all but retired as an active musician and settled down to enjoy the life of a wit, sage, and *bon vivant.* He was in Frankfurt as the guest of the banker Lionel de Rothschild, who had returned to his ancestral city from Paris to marry his cousin Charlotte Rothschild and had taken the composer along in his train of distinguished wedding guests. Rossini, fat and amiable, spent a week in Frankfurt, being lavishly feted and graciously receiving the local musicians who came in awe to call upon him.

Mendelssohn was among those receiving invitations to the various galas arranged by the Rothschilds. The families were well acquainted, and Felix wrote his mother that he admired the Rothschilds very much: "Their splendor and luxury, and the way they compel the philistines to regard them with the utmost respect (though these would gladly give them a sound thrashing if they were let loose!) is a source of exultation to me, because they owe all this entirely to their own industry, good fortune and abilities."

Mendelssohn and Rossini had a private meeting at the home of his friend Hiller, who was a native of Frankfurt. The older musician listened intently as the younger played through some of his early piano pieces. "That smells a bit of Scarlatti's sonatas," muttered Rossini after listening to the *Capriccio* in F-sharp Minor, op. 5. Felix afterward expressed irritation to Hiller over the remark, but his friend asked him, "Well, what's so bad about that?" Actually, Rossini had a point, for Scarlatti did have an influence on Mendelssohn's early piano writing. Rossini later told Hiller that he admired Mendelssohn's Octet and *Italian* Symphony greatly and that he wished he would try his hand at an opera. When Hiller replied that German composers usually preferred instrumental to vocal music, Rossini said: "They usually begin with instrumental music and that may make it difficult for them later on to accept the restrictions imposed by vocal music. It is hard for them to become simple, whereas it is hard for Italians not to become trivial."

Mendelssohn told Rossini that among other works, he would conduct Bach's B Minor Mass for him during his stay in Frankfurt. "It will be quite fun to see Rossini obliged to admire Sebastian Bach," he wrote with a hint of malice to his mother. During his six weeks with the Cecilia Society, Mendelssohn played Bach's funeral cantata *Gottes Zeit,* which he dedicated to the memory of Abraham Mendelssohn, and Handel's *Samson.*

The Cecilia Society was a local choral group, largely amateur, which included in its membership a goodly number of the daughters of the town's best families. One of these was a beautiful, blue-eyed, eighteen-year-old soprano named Cecile Jeanrenaud. Felix observed her singing in the choir during rehearsals, but he was actually introduced to her by a member of his own family—although one who might have seemed the least likely to be cast in the role of matchmaker. It was none other than his Aunt Dorothea von Schlegel, for years the pariah of the clan, who brought Felix and Cecile together.

Dorothea had moved to Frankfurt with her son Philipp Veit after the death of Frederick von Schlegel seven years previously. Felix visited Dorothea soon after his arrival in Frankfurt. Now seventy-one years old, she was as sprightly and opinionated as ever, if not quite the fire breather of her earlier years. She and Veit, who had become a prominent artistic figure in Frankfurt, gave Felix a cordial welcome; and he called on them frequently, delighted to further his acquaintanceship with a brilliant if slightly disreputable branch of the family. Leah Mendelssohn was none too happy about Felix's rediscovery of his Aunt Dorothea and wrote to him to warn against his falling under the influence of "that Schlegel woman."

Both Dorothea and Philipp Veit knew Cecile Jeanrenaud well. Philipp had made her portrait and was acquainted with her family, so it seemed perfectly natural for him to present her to his distinguished cousin, Felix Mendelssohn, while Dorothea looked on, beaming in approval.

The Jeanrenauds were of Swiss origin, coming from Neuchâtel, but had lived in Frankfurt many years. Cecile's father, a clergyman of the French Reformed Church, had died when she was two, leaving her mother a widow—and a rather attractive widow at that, for when Felix began calling at their home, the neighbors were not quite sure whether it was the mother or the daughter he was courting.

An intimate bond between Felix and Cecile was quickly established. Felix talked about her to Hiller for hours on end and began to drop hints in letters to his mother and sisters that he had met a girl whose "presence has given me very happy days in Frankfurt, at a time when I badly needed them." So guarded were his references that for a long time he never mentioned her name or indicated that he was considering marriage; in fact, to settle the matter in his own mind, he took the unusual step of absenting himself from Frankfurt for a month to go to the seashore and think things over quietly and in solitude. When he returned in September, 1836, he was resolved to marry her. "All I ask," he wrote to his mother, "is that you will give me your consent; for though I suppose my age no longer makes it legally necessary, I will not act without it."

In some ways, Felix Mendelssohn's selection of a wife had its resemblances to Moses Mendelssohn's seventy-five years before. He was not looking for a musician any more than Moses was seeking a philosopher; like his grandfather, he fell in love with a girl some ten years younger than himself, of moderate intellectual attainments, attractive appearance, settled family background, and strongly domestic inclinations. True, Cecile Jeanrenaud was not a Jewess, either converted or unconverted; but it may be significant that her Huguenot background made her a member of a minority sect that participated fully in the life around them but still preserved their own practices and viewpoint, as did the emancipated Jews of Germany.

Much like Fromet Gugenheim, Cecile was at first a little overawed by her famous suitor. She had heard of Mendelssohn as a young girl and, as she later told a friend, pictured him as a morose old gentleman, wearing a satin skullcap, playing interminable fugues at the piano. The reality was quite different: a slender, elegant, if somewhat smallish young man, whose dark, curly hair was beginning to recede from the high forehead; olive-complexioned, with deep, dark eyes; sideburns that ran down past the angle of his jaw—altogether a captivating figure to a romantic young girl. Furthermore, Mendelssohn pursued his courtship in rather original ways. He took her for the customary strolls and carriage rides of young couples through the old town on the River Main; but he also played the piano for the family on his visits to their home, and he made drawings of the local scenery as seen through their windows. When he finally asked her to marry him, it was under a cluster of beech trees on an afternoon's excursion to the town of Kronenthal in the wooded Taunus region near Frankfurt.

Felix and Cecile were married on March 28, 1837, in the Wal-

loon French Reformed Church of Frankfurt; the service was performed in French. Hiller was present and, as a surprise, composed
a wedding chorus for women's voices that was sung at a reception
held after the ceremony. Felix's family, though not actively opposing the marriage, was unenthusiastic about it to the extent of not
coming to the ceremony. The only Mendelssohn on hand in the
Huguenot congregation that day was old Dorothea, and she, poor
lady, had been through so many churches in her life that one more
or less could make but little difference.

The reasons for the rest of the family's absence were never
explained, or at least never preserved on paper. Cecile's mother
belonged to the Souchays, one of the leading families of Frankfurt;
Felix was certainly not marrying "down" in the world. It may be
that the Mendelssohns would have preferred his finding a wife
within their own Berlin circle; it is also possible that Felix's moth-
ers and sisters, who were used to being courted, did not like
having someone in the family whom they had to consider as an
equal power—a description which, by all accounts, fitted Cecile's
rather strong-willed mother.

Whatever the causes, a certain reserve was noticeable at the
outset between the two families of Mendelssohns and Jeanrenauds. Fanny and Rebecca in Berlin seemed particularly put out
that the happy couple had not traveled from Leipzig for a visit to
the family homestead; nevertheless, they maintained a correspondence of sorts with their new sister-in-law. Wrote Fanny to Cecile
with a touch of testiness on October 5, 1837:

> I am eagerly looking forward to Felix's concerto. Will it be
> printed soon, so that we may have it? When I see Felix's works for
> the first time in print, I look at them with the eyes of a stranger,
> *i.e.,* criticize them without partiality; but it always makes me sadly
> recall the time when I used to know his music from birth. It is so
> different now, and what a pity it is that fate should have decreed
> that we are to live so far apart, and that he should have had a wife
> these eight months whom I have never seen. I tell you candidly that
> by this time, when anybody comes to talk to me about your beauty

and your eyes, it makes me quite cross. I have had enough of
hearsay, and beautiful eyes were not made to be heard.

Finally, a month after writing this letter, Fanny found an excuse
to travel to Leipzig, and there for the first time she met Cecile. All
things considered, the meeting went well, for Fanny wrote to
Mendelssohn's old friend in England, Karl Klingemann: "At
last I know my sister-in-law, and I feel as if a load were off my
mind, for I cannot deny that I was very uncomfortable and out of
sorts at never having seen her. She is amiable, childlike, fresh,
bright and even-tempered, and I consider Felix most fortunate; for
though inexpressibly fond of him, she does not spoil him.
. . . Her presence produces the effect of a fresh breeze, so light
and bright and natural is she."

A correspondence between the two girls ensued, bringing with
it a friendlier spirit. The following spring, a son, named Carl
Wolfgang Paul, was born, but only after Cecile had undergone a
difficult and dangerous confinement. Felix's brother Paul and his
wife Albertine journeyed to Leipzig for the christening, further
strengthening the ties between Cecile and her in-laws. Felix, Cecile, and their infant son spent the summer of 1838 in Berlin,
moving their ménage into the seemingly inexhaustible confines of
3 Leipzigerstrasse. There Cecile entered into the close life of the
clan, with three separate families, Hensels, Dirichlets, and Mendelssohns, sharing the premises. For the Swiss pastor's daughter
from Frankfurt, it must have been quite a revelation, for whatever
their nominal religion, this was a family that in many ways displayed the characteristics and followed the conventions of upper-
class German Jews. Felix, as we have seen, usually took the lead
in such matters. His bride even discovered that he had a particular
taste for *kuchen,* a Jewish-style butter cake. "Moses must have
been a great lawgiver," he told her while stuffing himself with it
for a whole evening. Later he remarked to Rebecca: "Cecile insists
on knowing if such a cake can be baked only by Jews, and why?"

Domesticity is not a state associated with most of the great

composers, but it was one that Felix Mendelssohn ardently
yearned for and quickly attained. Five children were born to him
and Cecile within eight years: Carl in 1838, Marie in 1839, Paul
in 1841, Felix in 1843, and Lili in 1845. Mendelssohn continued
to work unrelentingly at his composing as well as his conducting and administrative duties; he traveled on musical business
throughout Germany and to England; he was in constant communication with musicians and musical leaders everywhere in
Europe. But he always remained the center of his household, and
he resented the time spent away from it.

On a trip to England a few months after his marriage, he complained bitterly of having to leave Cecile behind—"all for the sake
of a music festival!" His letters to Fanny, once so largely devoted
to musical matters, now began to brim over with domestic details
—how he had been stricken with remorse after slapping his eldest
son and was relieved to find that the boy had seemingly forgotten
all about it the next day; the kind of Christmas decorations being
put up in the house and a list of his holiday gifts; the fun of
teaching his daughter to play the piano ("Marie is learning the
scale of C and even that I partially forgot, for I made her turn her
thumb under after the third finger, till Cecile came in upon us and
was amazed"); the general family horseplay ("Here come Cecile
and Carl, the latter with a live crayfish, which he sets crawling on
the floor, while Marie and Paul scream with delight. . . . even the
baby looks about quite intelligently with his blue eyes"). To
Rebecca he wrote: "We are leading a very quiet life, for my
horror of aristocratic acquaintances has if possible increased
. . . we stay home in our family circle, and that is much the best."
Even the sketches and drawings he continued to make for his own
relaxation were largely those of his wife and children at home or
on a holiday. Like his grandfather Moses, he had work to do in
this world, but his deepest pleasure in life was his own family.

XX The Second Battle of Berlin

While it was now Felix who preferred to remain homebound, his sisters at last had their chance to travel. Fanny and Rebecca each set out in turn for leisurely sojourns in Italy, their families going with them. First Fanny and Hensel, with their son Sebastian, set out, beginning the journey with a visit to Felix and Cecile in Leipzig. Thence they traveled southward, stopping briefly at Munich, where Fanny cast a curious eye on the now-married Delphine von Schauroth, who had so smitten Felix a few years before, and pronounced her "a charming person" who played the G Minor Piano Concerto better than anyone save Felix himself.

Fanny and her family passed the entire winter of 1839–1840 in Rome. Hensel, who had spent five years there as a young painter, all the while courting Fanny through his letters to her mother, now was able to escort her around to the relics, ruins, and museums he knew so well. Quickly the Hensel-Mendelssohn entourage, installed in comfortable quarters, became the center of a group of young artists and musicians from abroad also living in the city. One of the latter was Charles Gounod, then twenty-one years old, who like Berlioz had won the Prix de Rome. Fanny took a liking to the young Frenchman; he for his part admired the way she played Bach and Beethoven and listened to her performance of *Fidelio* excerpts almost as if intoxicated. Later on he made a trip to Berlin for the express purpose of visiting the Hensels there. Fanny thought he had unusual musical gifts as well as a keen appreciation of things German; she would have been even more impressed if she could have known that twenty years later, he would give Germany's most famous play, Goethe's *Faust,* the most popular musical setting it has ever had.

Rebecca began her pilgrimage to Italy in 1843. She and Dirichlet had undergone tragedy a few years previously when their youngest child had died at the age of thirteen months; for a time they even considered moving away to Paris, where Dirichlet had been offered a professorship. In the end they remained in Berlin, and when they left for Italy, they took their two other boys, Walter and Ernest, with them. Rebecca always was the most vivacious and impish of the Mendelssohns, and the Italian trip at first gave a tremendous lift to her spirits. She was delighted by the scenery, the people, and the language, which, she said, was "so comfortable, and at the same time a bit scurrilous and Jewish." For example, she wrote home triumphantly that the Italian word *poverino* ("poor fellow") meant the same thing as the Yiddish *nebbisch* ("a nobody").

Rebecca's stay in Italy was marred by a mysterious illness she contracted in Naples that was serious enough to bring Fanny down from Berlin to be at her side. The principal symptoms were jaundice and a general weakness, and she was also discovered to be pregnant at the same time. Gradually the symptoms of sickness cleared up, and a seven-month baby girl was born to her, perfectly healthy, in Florence and promptly named Florentina. Between her illness and her travelings up and down the peninsula, Rebecca's Italian sojourn stretched into a second year before she and Dirichlet came back to their old home in Berlin.

To Felix, comfortably settled in Leipzig, reading his sisters' letters from abroad was like reliving his own grand tour of the previous decade. He sent them instructions on what to see and whom to visit, directed them to various museums and monuments, did all he could to supervise their travels from afar. But he himself was well content to enjoy the local scenery around cities like Leipzig and Frankfurt without seeking anything more exotic and to spend his vacations in a little rural village named Soden. It might not be Palermo or Sorrento, he admitted in a letter to Rebecca, but he liked it just the same. It was wrong to enjoy only one kind of beauty to the exclusion of all others, he explained: "I never can bear to hear people say they appreciate Beethoven only, or Palestrina only, or again, Mozart or Bach only. Give me all four, or none at all. . . . this life at Soden, with its eating and sleeping, without dress-coat, without visiting cards, without carriage and horses, but with donkeys, with wild flowers, with music-paper and sketch-book, with Cecile and the children, is doubly refreshing." Cecile, for her part, spent much of her time painting, for she was, like her husband, an accomplished artist. He did most of his landscapes in water color; she preferred oils.

Unfortunately for Mendelssohn, he enjoyed few respites like this interlude at Soden. His compositions, his conducting chores, his administrative responsibilities at the Gewandhaus, his teaching schedule at the conservatory, his trips to England, and his activities at various festivals turned him into the most active, not to say overburdened, musician in Europe.

On top of all, in 1840 came what was in effect a royal summons to return to Berlin. A new king had ascended the Prussian throne, Frederick William IV. He was forty-five years old, and although he had no idea of furthering the sovereignty of the people, he did plan to establish a kind of paternalistic monarchy in which each class—nobles, peasants, burghers—would be encouraged to make its own contribution to the state. It was a concept of government that looked back to the eighteenth century rather than ahead to the twentieth, and Frederick William did not go down in history as a very successful or enlightened ruler. But he did attempt to establish culture and the arts as a cornerstone of his regime, and to that end he invited poets, painters, and philosophers to his court.

It disturbed Frederick William IV that the most famous musician in Germany, Felix Mendelssohn, had chosen virtually to exile

himself in Leipzig although he belonged to one of the great families of Berlin. Similarly, the king thought it unseemly that another
Berliner, Meyerbeer, should be composing his operas in Paris.
Invitations were forthwith extended to the two wanderers to return. Meyerbeer was appointed director of the opera in place of
Spontini. Mendelssohn's position was to be even more exalted
because he was designated as the head of the Music Division of
the Royal Academy of the Arts, charged with establishing a great
new conservatory that would become a center for German musical
activity.

Mendelssohn's family eagerly urged him to accept the post. His
mother Leah, aging rapidly since the death of her husband,
wanted him back in Berlin; his sisters were pleased by the project;
and his brother Paul, who had been asked by the king to act as
intermediary, also supported the idea.

Everybody, in fact, favored it, except Felix himself. He had had
his fill of the Prussian nobility, and he retained his ancient dislike
for Berlin. Besides, he knew of the king's general reactionary
outlook; whereas he himself was a steadfast political liberal. A few
years before, for example, he had with his brother-in-law Dirichlet
worked actively on behalf of the "Göttingen Seven," a group of
liberal university teachers who had been dismissed from their
posts at the orders of the king of Hanover. The Göttingen professors never regained their original positions, but Mendelssohn was
among those who stood by them until they found teaching posts
elsewhere.

But despite these misgivings, Mendelssohn found it difficult to
reject the royal summons completely. A long and vexatious correspondence ensued regarding the exact terms of the agreement. It
never was a monetary issue; the stipend of 4,000 thalers ($3,200)
was higher than his Leipzig salary. What bothered Mendelssohn
was that he never could pin down the king's emissaries as to what
his exact duties or authority would be. For weeks he worked over
a lengthy memorandum detailing his views on musical conditions

in Berlin, emphasizing the need for a complete revamping of musical education there. Upon delivery to court officials, the document was pigeonholed and the recommendations ignored. What the king really wished was to have Mendelssohn as an adornment for his court, thus restoring Berlin as the musical capital of Germany; the elevated titles and grandiose projects never had any real meaning.

Mendelssohn understood this perfectly—his letters of the time are full of bitter references to the delays, obstacles, and frustrations he encountered, but in the end he accepted the king's offer and in 1841 moved himself and his family to Berlin. Nevertheless, he prudently kept one foot in Leipzig, working out an arrangement whereby he retained his affiliation with the Gewandhaus and was able to return there from time to time to conduct. Leipzig was his lifeline in case anything went wrong in Berlin—as, indeed, almost everything did.

Mendelssohn's five years in Berlin proved to be an unending misery for him. The orchestral musicians were hostile; even worse, they were far less skilled than their Leipzig counterparts. However lofty the king's intentions may have been, his court officials were evasive and dilatory when it actually came to putting the royal plans into effect. Mendelssohn's principal musical satisfaction in Berlin came from Fanny's Sunday musicales, a throwback to the days of his youth that brought back all the old stimulation and pleasure. Plagued as he was by administrative vexations, he also managed to write one of his finest works for piano solo, the *Variations Sérieuses* in D Minor, op. 54.

As if to add to the gloom and grimness of those years in Berlin, on December 12, 1842, Leah Mendelssohn died. As the head of his own family, Felix could face his mother's death with more security and strength than his father's; nevertheless, he was greatly affected. Leah's death came without warning, and Felix happened to be in Leipzig at the time; when he heard of it, he went into his room and wept. Shortly afterward, he wrote to his brother Paul of the difficulty of carrying on his regular conducting duties and that he was glad he had some "half-mechanical work" to do—transcribing, copying, instrumentation. He found relief from sorrow, he said, in "the pleasant intercourse with the old familiar oboes and violas and the rest, who live so much longer than we do, and are such faithful friends."

In 1844, Mendelssohn decided to give up his royal service in Berlin as a bad job. He had made several attempts during the years, with some success, to lighten his duties in the Prussian capital, but he kept on traveling to England and various musical festivals in Germany. He felt weary much of the time and developed a cough; "in fact," he wrote, "everything that I do and carry on is a burden to me, unless it be mere passive existence."

When Mendelssohn told Frederick William IV of his desire to leave, the king, in the immemorial manner of monarchs, was puzzled and a little hurt that so highly esteemed and liberally rewarded a royal servant should prefer freer air elsewhere. Nevertheless, he acquiesced, on condition that Felix be available for future commissions and performances on special occasions. Mendelssohn, at the point of exhaustion, gave his promise. "The first step out of Berlin," he told Devrient, "is the first step toward happiness."

Mendelssohn's unhappy association with Berlin is reflected in much of the music he wrote there during this period. Whether because he found the city oppressive or was uninterested in the subjects suggested to him, he composed rather empty and formal incidental music for presentations in Berlin of Sophocles' *Antigone* and *Oedipus at Colonus* and Racine's *Athalie.* These scores are largely forgotten today, save perhaps for the War March of the Priests from *Athalie* which, as musical historian Philip Radcliffe notes, "does not now sound either warlike or priestly."

And yet posterity, which has its own way of looking at such things, can well conclude that Mendelssohn's Berlin sojourn was time well spent if only because it was there, also on commission from King Frederick William IV, that he completed his incidental music to *A Midsummer Night's Dream*. Seventeen years before, Mendelssohn had composed only an overture; now, at the age of thirty-four, he was asked by the king to write a full set of incidental music for an actual performance of the play. Ludwig Tieck, the court poet on much the same basis that Mendelssohn was the court composer, had made a new German translation of *A Midsummer Night's Dream;* Felix was to provide interludes, entr'actes, dances, marches, and a nocturne to go along with his Overture.

No artist has ever recaptured his youth more perfectly than Mendelssohn in the *Midsummer Night's Dream*. The seventeen years that separated the Overture from the rest of the work seemingly had never existed, so seamless was the finished work. Mendelssohn took some of the themes from the Overture and restated them at various points of the complete music, but most of the score was completely new, with numbers like the Scherzo and Wedding March as subtle and original in their ways as the Overture is in its. Schumann criticized Mendelssohn for concluding the Finale with a repetition of music from the Overture, but to us today the four ethereal woodwind chords that begin the work also seem the perfect music for ending it, a portal that closes as magically as it opened.

Even in Berlin, the *Midsummer Night's Dream* music was an instant and overwhelming success. The whole family was in attendance, scattered through the theater, for adjacent seats were hard to find. There were two rows of "Mendelssohn and Company" in the balcony, Fanny reported; and Paul said that when the audience began calling for "Mendelssohn" at the conclusion, he stood up and took a few bows himself. Shortly afterward the score was performed in Leipzig, London, and elsewhere in Europe, creating for itself in the world's musical consciousness a place that it has never lost.

Perhaps it was Fanny Mendelssohn who once again best put into words what Felix had accomplished:

We were mentioning yesterday what an important part the *Midsum-mer Night's Dream* has always played in our house, and how we had all at different ages gone through the whole of the parts from Peaseblossom to Hermia and Helena, and now it has come to such a glorious ending. We really were brought up on the *Midsummer Night's Dream,* and Felix especially had made it his own, almost recreating the characters which had sprung from Shakespeare's inexhaustible genius. From the Wedding March, so full of pomp but so thoroughly festive in its character, to the plaintive music of Thisbe's death, the fairy songs, the dances, the interludes, the characters, including such creatures as clowns—all and everything has found its counterpart in music, and his work is on a par with Shakespeare's.

As for Felix himself, for once he seemed satisfied with a work he had written, for he did not attempt to revise or rewrite the *Midsummer Night's Dream* music, as he did with so many of his other scores. He, too, felt that he had written music not unworthy of Shakespeare. A few weeks after the première, he reported to Fanny, a courtier at a royal supper at Frederick William's palace remarked to him: "What a pity that you wasted your beautiful music on such a stupid play!" He was at first startled, then amused at the remark, but he did not take it as a compliment.

This portrait of Felix was commissioned by Jenny Lind from Magnus in 1845.

Contemporary artist depicted Mendelssohn playing at Buckingham Palace for a slim Queen Victoria and an elegant Prince Albert.

Jenny Lind in a portrait by Magnus. When she met Mendelssohn she was twenty-three and he thirty-five. He guided her singing career, spent hours with her, lauded her "upper F-sharp."

The Leipzig Gewandhaus auditorium during a concert by Felix and Jenny. The women in the audience sat in rows facing each other, sideways to the orchestra, while the men stood crowded behind them, against the walls.

My dear Madam

I shall be most happy to accept your kind invitation for Tuesday the 14th & to partake of that fine dish of Politics of which you have given me hopes. Although I think I shall leave London on Tuesday night, I hope yet to be able to avail myself of your kindness. I was extremely sorry to hear Mr. Taylor has been so seriously unwell and hope to find him better very soon. With my best regards to him believe me Dear Madam

very truly yours

10 Gt Portland St.
7th May.

Felix Mendelssohn B.

Mendelssohn displays his command of English in letter to a London hostess accepting her invitation to partake of a "fine dish of politics."

Felix was an accomplished artist but had difficulty drawing people. He made picture above of his Leipzig living room in 1840, but Cecile, also a fine painter, added the figures of herself and her children Carl and Marie. Below is a watercolor of a scene near Interlaken in Switzerland, Felix's last painting, completed in the summer of 1847.

Mendelssohn's workroom at Leipzig in a painting made after his death. In lower right-hand corner stands his spinet piano, covered by cloth.

Typical of British adulation of composer after his death is torchlight procession at Crystal Palace, London, during Mendelssohn Festival in 1860.

Deathbed drawing of Felix Mendelssohn by his brother-in-law Wilhelm Hensel.

The Mendelssohn statue in front of the Leipzig Gewandhaus, removed and melted down by the Nazis in 1937 over the protests of Leipzig's mayor.

Mendelssohn's music has found new relevance in use by modern choreographers. Above, one of the most successful recent productions, George Balanchine's A Midsummer Night's Dream *by the New York City Ballet Company.*

XXI *Felix and Jenny*

Mendelssohn's departure from Berlin in 1844 brought him a tremendous sense of release and was followed, perhaps not coincidentally, by the completion of one of his supreme masterpieces, the Violin Concerto in E Minor. Mendelssohn had had such a work in mind for many years, but it was only in the quiet surroundings of Soden that he was able to put it on paper. In 1839, he had written to Ferdinand David: "I should like to write a violin concerto for you. . . . One in E minor runs through my head, the beginning of which gives me no peace." He kept consulting David about the technical problems of writing for the solo violin, to achieve a work that would be not only beautiful but playable.

The Violin Concerto in E Minor turned out to be one of Mendelssohn's most innovative works, with a cadenza written as an integral part of the musical fabric and a unity of spirit and structure throughout. There even was a unique musical bridge between the first two movements, a sustained B on the bassoon, unfortunately almost always drowned out by audience applause. David, of course, gave the Mendelssohn Concerto its world première, becoming the first of a procession of fiddlers whose end, one imagines, will never be reached as long as there are violins in this world and violinists to play them.

A few weeks after completing the Violin Concerto, Mendelssohn took a brief trip to Berlin on business matters and while there made the acquaintance of a young singer named Jenny Lind, with whom he was to have a tutelary relationship for the rest of his life.

In fact there were those who suspected the bonds between them went deeper, among them Mendelssohn's wife, who was never happy about the time her husband spent with the young soprano.

When Mendelssohn met Jenny Lind, at a social gathering at a friend's house on October 21, 1844, she was not yet the internationally celebrated "Swedish Nightingale," but a twenty-three-year-old girl from Stockholm with ambitions to establish herself in Germany. She had already sung with great success in her native land and had taken lessons from Manuel Garcia, Malibran's brother, in Paris. Meyerbeer heard her there and persuaded her to come to Berlin, where he was now running operatic affairs for King Frederick William IV. It was Meyerbeer who brought her to the party where she met Mendelssohn.

Felix's gallantry invariably produced an effect even on experienced women, and he all but overwhelmed the young singer from Stockholm. At thirty-five, he was at the height of his fame, slender, handsome, a vivacious talker, and full of high spirits when he found the company enjoyable. He seemed to take an instant liking to the singer, by no means a raving beauty, but nevertheless appealing enough with her dark hair parted in the middle, her clear, pale skin, and her simple Stockholm dress. He had not yet heard her sing, he told her, but so many people had spoken to him of her "great talent" that he was certain she must be an exceptional artist. So happy was Jenny at the meeting that the next day she wrote an excited letter to a Swedish friend telling how "indescribably friendly and polite" Mendelssohn had been to her.

They did not meet again until the following year when Mendelssohn, at the behest of Frederick William, returned briefly to Berlin to supervise productions of *Athalie* and *Oedipus at Colonus.* Whenever he could spare time from his own affairs he went to the new Berlin Opera House, which had been built for Meyerbeer, to hear Jenny Lind sing in such works as *Norma, Don Giovanni, Der Freischütz,* and *Les Huguenots.* They encountered each other frequently at the home of a mutual friend, a sculptor named Wichmann. "Mendelssohn is here!" Jenny wrote to her Swedish correspondent. "I see him almost every day at the Wichmanns'. And he is a quite exceptional man."

As they became better acquainted, they spent more and more time alone, often going over Jenny's music together, she singing, he playing her accompaniments or simply improvising for her amusement. Her "upper F-sharp possesses an irresistible charm," he told friends, and presumably she had other attributes that attracted him as well. Many observers concluded that Jenny was in love with Mendelssohn, and he certainly seemed eager to spend as much of his time as he could with her. "If all goes well with her in this world," he said, "it is as pleasant to me as if it went well with me."

Before Mendelssohn left Berlin, he invited Jenny to sing at the Gewandhaus with him. As the departure date neared, he saw no reason why she should travel there separately, so when he returned to Leipzig, he took her along with him. She stayed in the home of a family named Brockhaus, with whom she was acquainted. Cecile Mendelssohn was not overjoyed with her arrival in town; understandably, she had been a bit cool to Felix's enthusiastic accounts of the new singer he had met in Berlin.

However, everybody else in Leipzig was ecstatic over the young soprano. At her Gewandhaus appearance on December 4, 1845, she sang "Casta Diva" from *Norma* and "Non mi dir" from *Don Giovanni,* while Felix conducted the orchestra in Mozart's *Prague* Symphony and Weber's *Oberon* Overture, and finally joined his protégée at the piano in a group of songs. Ticket prices for the concert were increased, leading to a scattering of protests. Mendelssohn thereupon asked Jenny to give a concert the following day for the benefit of the orchestra's Widows' Fund, and she eagerly agreed. This time she sang arias from *The Marriage of Figaro* and *Der Freischütz,* while Felix performed some of his own piano music and accompanied her in several songs, including his own "Spring Song."

That night, a throng of students crowded into a courtyard beneath her window at the Brockhaus' dwelling to serenade her and, on behalf of the orchestra, Ferdinand David came up to present her with a silver tray inscribed from "the grateful musicians." She was still unused to such demonstrations, couldn't find words to reply, and seemed almost terrified; so Mendelssohn, who had been standing quietly by, took her gently by the arm and led her to the courtyard. "Gentlemen," he said, "you think that this is the Kapellmeister Mendelssohn who is speaking to you, but you are wrong. It is Fräulein Jenny Lind who is speaking to you, and she thanks you from her heart for the exquisite surprise you have given her. And now I turn myself back into the Leipzig Music Director again and ask you to wish long life to Fräulein Jenny Lind. Long life to her! And again, long life to her! And for the third time, long life!"

That Christmas, Mendelssohn sent Jenny, now back in Berlin, a gift of an album of his own songs, written out in his own meticulous hand and illustrated with little line drawings. In her turn, she commissioned a fashionable Berlin painter, Edward Magnus, to make a portrait of Mendelssohn. They kept writing to each other through the winter, his letters affectionate and warm, but filled with small talk about his family and musical matters. In April, 1846, he brought her back to Leipzig for another Gewandhaus appearance, with Clara Schumann, David, and himself sharing the program with her. This time Cecile seemed more cordial, and Brockhaus, her host in Leipzig, observed that Jenny was much struck by the happiness and closeness of the Mendelssohn family circle.

In May, both Felix and Jenny were engaged to appear at the Lower Rhine Festival, this year to be held again at Aix-la-Chapelle. They agreed to meet at Frankfurt to take the Rhine steamer down the river together. Jenny traveled with a chaperone, but that did not prevent the two of them from having long talks and taking their meals together. Felix told her he was planning an oratorio about the prophet Elijah and that he wished she could sing in it; she replied that she had sung little sacred music before. So by way of practice they decided to schedule three arias from Haydn's *Creation* on the festival programs. Jenny Lind's appearances made the Lower Rhine Festival of 1846 one of the most talked-about in years, with Felix content to stand by and enjoy her success. When the festival ended, they were reluctant to separate, and so spent a few extra days together on a holiday, visiting the Drachenfels, a mountain overlooking the Rhine, and passing a day or two at Cologne.

After that their principal contact was by letter, although they did have one brief final meeting in London during Mendelssohn's last visit there. To the end of his life, Felix acted as an adviser, almost an agent for her, counseling her to visit London and Vienna, putting her in touch with impresarios, reading over the contracts that were offered to her, suggesting musical programs to her. She relied on his counsel, and one of his biggest disappointments was that she was unable to come to England to participate in the première of *Elijah,* which she only sang after his death.

How much was there between them? Clara Schumann, a shrewd, discerning, and sympathetic woman, was certain that Jenny loved Mendelssohn "no less as a man than as a composer." Others felt that Mendelssohn, although he was strongly attracted to the young girl, and well aware of her feelings toward him, was too loyal and devoted to his own family to set aside the scruples that were part of his own moral code. Still, no one can be certain how far the intimacy went; whatever may or may not have happened between them, there can be no doubt that their two lives touched each other deeply. Some mysteries are at their most attractive when left unsolved, and perhaps the final word on that of Jenny Lind and Felix Mendelssohn can best be spoken in a letter he wrote her not long before his death: "I often think now of your question on the Rhine steamboat, whether I should not like to leave Leipzig again? And your wish that I should not stay in

Leipzig forever, etcetera, etcetera. You were quite right, and I well know what you meant; and in two or three years, at the utmost, I think I shall have done my duty here, after which I should scarcely stay any longer. Perhaps I might prefer Berlin; perhaps the Rhine; somewhere where it is very pretty, and where I could compose all day long, as much as I liked. But really you would have to sing to me sometimes."

XXII *Visiting Victoria*

Felix Mendelssohn has often been described—in no very complimentary sense—as the ideal Victorian composer. In actual chronology, he was a Victorian before Victoria, because he had made four visits to England before her accession to the throne in 1837. From his very first in 1829, his music met an instant response and acclaim in England that it never really found in his native Germany. Much the same thing happened in the United States, as is attested by the Mendelssohn Clubs, Choirs, Societies, and Halls that came into being during his lifetime and after his death, many of which exist to this day.

Why did the British so admire Mendelssohn? There was about his work a sense of control, order, and gentlemanliness that had a particular appeal during the Victorian age. Yet there was more to it than that, for the British musical public, far from being superficial or casual, was as discerning and appreciative of fundamental musical values as any in Europe. Handel, after all, had offered them music with dramatic surge and a strong personal imprint and had become practically their national composer; and Beethoven, almost from the start, had won a wide British audience with his bold and innovative works. The Philharmonic Society enthusiastically programed his Fifth and Ninth Symphonies when musical groups elsewhere were still balking at them; it offered him all sorts of inducements to come to England to conduct; and when he was in his last illness, it sent him a generous gift of money to meet expenses. If the British loved Mendelssohn, it was because they regarded him not as a composer of salon piano pieces but as a true successor of Beethoven.

Mendelssohn also impressed the Victorians for his charm, industriousness, and ability to get things done. If one wanted a man to organize a musical festival, lend it prestige, and bring it authority, Mendelssohn was ideal. Even his Jewish ancestry, which had always been held against him in Berlin, was an asset. Jews were becoming fashionable in London; one of them, Nathan Rothschild, was a leading financier, and another, Disraeli, would later become Victoria's prime minister. For all his Lutheranism, Mendelssohn's Jewish origins and his descent from Moses Mendelssohn were frequently commented upon, almost always in a friendly way, by his British contemporaries. William Makepeace Thackeray told a friend: "His face is the most beautiful face I ever saw, like what I imagine our Saviour's to have been." Sir George Grove, in the first edition of his *Dictionary of Music and Musicians,* published in 1879, wrote in his famous article on Mendelssohn that "his look was dark and very Jewish." Even the fifth edition of that esteemed work, published in 1954 and reprinted in 1970, comprehensively attributed Mendelssohn's "charm of manner . . . his business acumen, his appreciation of domestic propriety . . . his punctuality, his sense of religious duty and a somewhat moralizing attitude" to "his upbringing and to ancient traditions of his Jewish race"—although it would seem that these qualities, if they actually all existed in Mendelssohn, would make him a perfect Englishman no less than an excellent Jew.

With each visit, Mendelssohn found England a more exciting and progressive country, far ahead of any on the Continent. He was especially enthralled by its railroads; on a visit to Liverpool, he persuaded a railway inspector to take him for a private ride through a new tunnel that had just been completed on the Manchester line; he wrote home about mines and mills he had seen with as much enthusiasm as his visits to art galleries. He could easily have settled in England but for three factors—the obligations he entered into with Frederick William in Berlin, his love for his good city of Leipzig, and perhaps strongest of all, the family ties he felt to a clan that since the days of Moses Mendelssohn had always maintained and cherished its German background.

In those times it took a minimum of three days to travel from Berlin to London, with an overland voyage by coach or rail on either end and an uncomfortable passage across the English Channel in the middle. Nevertheless, Mendelssohn commuted to England with almost the same frequency that jet-age conductors travel there today. In 1837, the year of Victoria's accession, he made his fifth visit; and he returned for varying periods in 1840, 1842, 1844, 1846, and 1847.

The 1842 journey, which lasted four weeks, was particularly festive. For one thing, Cecile accompanied him. She had relatives in Manchester, a family named Benecke, and the Mendelssohns visited them. At their home he composed one of the most celebrated of his *Songs Without Words,* the ineluctable "Spinning Song." In London he performed his new *Scotch* Symphony, and the Philharmonic Society was so delighted with it that they wound up their season by giving him a fish dinner at Greenwich "at which we ate whitebait and made speeches," Felix reported home.

But the major event of his stay was his visit to Buckingham Palace, where he was received by Queen Victoria, who was eager to meet the famous "Dr. Mendelssohn," as he was usually addressed by London officialdom. The queen, far from being the matronly figure later made familiar by dozens of portraits, was then a young woman of twenty-three; her husband, Prince Albert, was the same age; they had been married two years. Both enjoyed music. Victoria sang a little, and Albert, of German extraction, was a respectable composer and keyboard performer. For all their exalted station, they were quite fluttery about the visit by Dr. Mendelssohn. Albert was particularly anxious to show off a new organ that had been installed at the palace, for Felix's organ playing had created a sensation in London. While the two men were talking away, the queen came in, a draft from the open door littering the room with music sheets as she did so. All three of them began picking up the loose papers, and then Albert and Felix took turns playing the new organ. Felix played a chorus from his *St. Paul,* "How lovely are the messengers!" and the queen and prince promptly began singing it.

When Mendelssohn expressed his pleasure, Albert told him that Victoria also sang some of his songs, and after some urging she agreed to sing one right then and there. However, the music could not be found; it had all been packed up, the queen explained, for a trip to the country. After a time the party adjourned to the queen's sitting room, where a bound volume of Mendelssohn's first set of songs, opus 8, was discovered; and Victoria promptly sang one, with Felix playing the accompaniment. She sang, he reported in a letter to his mother, "quite charmingly, in strict time and tune, with very good execution," except that at one point she sang a D-sharp instead of a D.

As luck would have it, the song the queen had selected, "Italy," was not by Felix at all but by Fanny Mendelssohn—one of the numbers by his sister that he had incorporated into his published works. Swiftly he explained the situation, and the queen and her consort looked considerably surprised. "Now I beg you to sing one of *mine,*" said Felix, and Victoria obliged with another song from opus 8, after which Prince Albert sang still another. During the impromptu concert, Victoria asked that a large parrot in the room be removed; otherwise, she said, "he will sing louder than I do." Felix himself obligingly carried the cage outside and deposited it on the other side of the door. To conclude his visit to the palace, Felix improvised at the organ. As a memento, Albert presented him with a ring engraved "V.R. 1842." Felix was both pleased and amused with the whole episode: in a lengthy, good-humored account he sent to his mother, he quoted a current quip that Buckingham Palace was "the one really pleasant, comfortable English house in which one feels *à son aise.*" However, he added, "if this long description makes Dirichlet set me down as a tuft-hunter, tell him that I vow and declare that I am a greater radical than ever."

Mendelssohn dedicated his *Scotch* Symphony to Victoria, and he saw the young queen on subsequent sojourns in Britain. On another visit to the palace, when Victoria asked him what favor she could bestow on him in recompense for the pleasure his music had given her, he expressed the desire "to see the royal nurseries and all the domestic arrangements connected with the royal children." It seems like a peculiar request, but it went straight to the heart of the young mother, and for the next hour Victoria gave him a guided tour of her children's apartments, peering into closets, examining wardrobes, and exchanging pleasantries with nurse-maids.

Victoria's enthusiasm for Mendelssohn was seconded by that of her subjects. His appearances with the Philharmonic Society helped keep that organization in a state of solvency; his organ recitals were attended by throngs of cheering, handkerchief-waving enthusiasts who refused to leave the churches where he played; he was approached by strangers in the street who recognized him and wished to shake his hand. Society women doted on him, and he welcomed their attention much more eagerly than that of their Berlin counterparts; he was seen so often with a Miss Louise Bendinen that one of his friends, the music critic James W. Davison, warned him that people were beginning to talk. Back in Germany, Cecile expressed jealousy and wrote: "You must keep nothing from me, until your lungs are worn out." It is doubtful that he complied, any more than other men.

In England, Mendelssohn was invigorated by an exuberance and a sense of well-being that he felt nowhere else. He met Dickens and Thackeray, who each pronounced him their favorite composer; he dined with bishops and noblemen; he enjoyed and reciprocated the esteem of the ordinary British concertgoer and man in the street. "A mad, most extraordinarily mad time," he wrote to Fanny in 1844, on his eighth visit to London. "I never had so hectic a time before—never in bed till half-past one; for three days together not a single hour to myself in any one day. . . . My visit was glorious. I was never received anywhere with such universal kindness, and have made more music in these two months than I do elsewhere in two years."

On only one occasion did the British musicians fail him—when the men of the Philharmonic refused to play Schubert's great C Major Symphony, which Mendelssohn had premièred so successfully in Leipzig five years before. When Mendelssohn had the British musicians try the Schubert work at a rehearsal, they laughed out loud at its harmonies and figurations and said they could not play it. They reacted similarly to a new Symphony in C Minor by Niels Gade, the Danish composer, whose work Mendelssohn admired and who filled in for him frequently as conductor at the Gewandhaus during his absences from Leipzig. Mendelssohn was so incensed at the reaction of the London musicians that he refused to let them play his own *Ruy Blas* Overture, which he had also brought with him to England. Mendelssohn professed never to care much for *Ruy Blas* anyhow; he regarded the Victor Hugo play for which it was written as "perfectly horrible," and since it had been composed to aid the pension fund of the Leipzig theater he referred to it derisively as the "Overture to the *Pension Fund.*" Succeeding generations have found it a thoroughly dramatic, romantic work that catches perfectly the spirit of the play it introduces.

In 1845, Mendelssohn received an invitation to come to America. The Philharmonic Society of New York had been founded three years previously by Ureli Corelli Hill, a Connecticut-born violinist who had studied with Ludwig Spohr in Europe. Hill was well acquainted with Mendelssohn's music; in 1838, he had directed the first performance in the United States of *St. Paul,* with the New York Sacred Music Society.

From the start, Hill also scheduled Mendelssohn's music with his new Philharmonic Society, which played in rented quarters at the Apollo Rooms on Broadway, between Canal and Walker Streets. The *Midsummer Night's Dream* Overture appeared on the third program of the Philharmonic's first season.

Hill was eager for his orchestra to have its own home, and in 1845, the cry of "We must have a Philharmonic Hall!" was raised for the first time in the society's literature. As a fund-raising scheme, Hill decided to follow the example of Düsseldorf, Birmingham, and other cities by staging his own festival in New York and inviting a living composer to direct it. His first impulse was to build it around Spohr, his old teacher, but the sixty-year-old violinist-composer declined. So he turned to Mendelssohn, who had just severed his connection with King Frederick William and was taking a brief rest in Frankfurt. Mendelssohn answered him almost immediately, and in English:

Frankfurt, January 20, 1845

Dear Sir: I beg to return my best and most sincere thanks for your letter. Indeed, I may say that I felt truly proud in receiving so kind and so highly flattering an invitation, and the offer itself, as well as the friendly words in which you couched it, will always continue a source of pride and true gratification for which I shall feel sincerely indebted to you.

But it is not in my power to accept that invitation, although I am sure it would have been the greatest treat to me if I could have done so. My health has seriously suffered during the last year, and a journey like that to your country, which I would have been most happy to undertake some three or four years ago, is at present beyond my reach. Even the shorter trips which I used to make to England or the south of Germany have become too fatiguing to me, and it will require a few years' perfect rest before I shall again be able to undertake the direction of a musical festival even in my own country. I need not tell you how much I regret to find it utterly impossible to come and to thank you in person for all the kindness and friendship which your letter contains.

Accept, then, my written thanks, which are certainly not less sincere and heartfelt, and pray let the committee know with how

great a gratification and how thankfully I heard of their kind intentions toward me, and how deeply I regret not to be able to avail
myself of so much kindness. Should you ever visit Europe and my
country again, I hope you will not forget me and give me an
opportunity of renewing your acquaintance and of expressing to
you once more how deeply I feel indebted to you. I shall always
remain, dear sir, yours most truly,

FELIX MENDELSSOHN BARTHOLDY

Although Mendelssohn did, in fact, direct other music festivals
in Europe without availing himself of "a few years' perfect rest,"
there is no reason to doubt his sincerity in pleading exhaustion as
a reason for undertaking a trip to New York. Two weeks after his
letter to Hill, he wrote to a friend: "I myself am what you know
me to be; but what you do not know is that I have for some time
felt the necessity for complete rest—not traveling, not conducting,
not performing—so keenly that I am compelled to yield to it and
hope to be able to order my life accordingly for the whole year.
It is therefore my wish to stay here quietly through winter, spring
and summer, sans journeys, sans festivals, sans everything."

Mendelssohn kept thinking about traveling to the United
States; whenever he met an American in Europe, he talked about
the idea. One such visitor was Bayard Taylor, later to become
famous as a novelist, poet, and the translator of Goethe's *Faust,* but
then a youth of twenty on his own grand tour of Europe. Mendelssohn made a deep impression on Taylor, who thought he resembled Edgar Allan Poe, with dark eyes "shining, not with a surface
light, but with a pure, serene, planetary flame" and a nose that
"had the Jewish prominence, without its usual coarseness. . . . the
nostrils were as finely cut and flexible as an Arab's."

"As I looked upon him," Taylor confided to his memoirs, "I
said to myself, 'The Prophet David!' and, since then, I have seen
in the Hebrew families of Jerusalem, many of whom trace their
descent from the princely houses of Israel, the same nobility of
countenance."

One can only speculate on how Mendelssohn might hav
reacted had he known the thoughts that were running through his
young visitor's mind; as it was, he politely bade him welcome and
said: "You are an American. I have received an invitation to visit
New York, and should like to go, but we Germans are afraid of
the sea. But I may go yet: who knows? Music is making rapid
advances in America: and I believe there is a real taste for the art
among your people."

Taylor gravely assured him that this was so and then presented
him with a poem he had written about Beethoven. Mendelssohn
read it aloud while its author listened, pronounced it very good,
and asked whether he might keep the copy. In return he gave
Taylor the manuscript of a chorus in his *Walpurgis Night.* Taylor
went his way, rejoicing that he had met so great a man, and
believing that he would some day visit America. Perhaps if he had
lived long enough, he would have done so.

XXIII *The Second Elijah*

To the nineteenth century, the work that set the cap on Mendelssohn's fame was his oratorio *Elijah,* which was performed for the first time on his ninth trip to England, in 1846. Aside from its inherent qualities, *Elijah* filled a void in Mendelssohn's own pattern of musical achievement, for it recompensed him to some extent for his failure ever to write a successful opera. Ever since the debacle of his youthful *The Wedding of Camacho,* he had thought about composing a stage work; but despite a few false starts, nothing ever developed. He kept talking about the possibilities to the end of his life. He told Jenny Lind that he wanted to compose an opera for her; he wrote another friend: "Give me a text I can use and I'll start working on it at 4 A.M. tomorrow." Shakespeare's *Tempest* was one of the subjects he considered and discarded; Emanuel Geibel's *Loreley* was another, and in this case he actually wrote the finale of one act, in the form of a vintner's chorus and an Ave Maria which were published after his death. An English publisher tried vainly to interest him in a libretto called *The Siege of Calais.* The most startling possibility of all was nothing less than the *Nibelungen* legends, which Mendelssohn read in a version by Ernest Raupach, and about which he corresponded thoughtfully with his sister Fanny. On December 5, 1840, she wrote to him: "I am heartily glad to hear that you are entering into the idea of the *Nibelungen* with such zest. . . . The conclusion strikes me as the greatest difficulty, for who would finish an opera with all that horrible carnage?"

Elijah was far from an opera, but it did afford Felix a certain scope for vocal dramatic writing and musical characterization, while remaining within the religious framework that his father had always regarded as the ultimate musical form to which a composer could aspire. It certainly was a far different work from *St. Paul,* written ten years earlier; that was obviously derived in form and style from the Passions of Sebastian Bach; whereas *Elijah* was a kind of dramatic landscape on which a good man, the prophet himself, battled for the souls of the people with such evil forces as the prophets of Baal, finally rising to heaven himself in a fiery chariot.

Mendelssohn apparently had *Elijah* in mind as an oratorio subject almost from the time of the completion of *St. Paul;* he even asked his friend Klingemann to provide him a libretto, but the diplomat never did so. Ferdinand Hiller recalled the genesis of the idea this way: "One evening I found Felix deep in the Bible. 'Listen,' he said; and then he read to me, in a gentle and agitated voice, the passage from the First Book of Kings beginning with the words: 'And behold, the Lord passed by.' 'Would that not be splendid for an oratorio?' he exclaimed—and it did become part of *Elijah.*" In fact, Hiller might have added, it became one of the most powerful choruses Mendelssohn ever wrote.

Elijah was actually completed in response to an invitation from the city of Birmingham, the site of an annual music festival. Mendelssohn had been there before in his visits to England, conducting his *St. Paul* and his *Lobgesang* ("Hymn of Praise"), a choral symphony cast in the mold of Beethoven's Ninth, except that its choral finale was twice as long as its first three instrumental movements combined.*

Mendelssohn enjoyed Birmingham and its festivals; he called the city "Brummagem" in the British humorous manner, and its

---

*The *Lobgesang* constitutes the Symphony No. 2 in B-flat op. 52 in the Mendelssohn canon. Once widely played, it has now fallen into a state of disuse from which it might profitably be rescued from time to time.

affection for him was equaled only by London's. When the Festival authorities asked him for a new work in 1845, he resolved to give them *Elijah.*

But completing it was no easy task. By now he was back in Leipzig with a full schedule of preparing and conducting concerts and looking after other musical affairs. The work on *Elijah* went carefully and deliberately; he himself had the feeling he was producing something extraordinary, even writing to a friend: "If it only turns out half as good as I think it is, I will be glad indeed."

The *Elijah* libretto was provided by Julius Schubring, a theologian who came from Moses Mendelssohn's old town of Dessau. It turned out to be rather awkward in structure and, of course, had to be translated from German into English; but Mendelssohn, for all his misgivings, found it reasonably workable.

The first performance was scheduled for Birmingham on August 26, 1846, and as the date approached, Mendelssohn's pace grew hectic. Since he was to supervise the Birmingham Festival as a whole, with the assistance of Moscheles, he had not only to complete *Elijah* but also to designate singers for the solo roles and oversee the selection of the orchestra, not to mention conduct the rehearsals, which began in Leipzig and continued in London, prior to the final sessions in Birmingham itself.

Among the most vexatious tasks was the selection of the soprano soloist. Mendelssohn had wanted Jenny Lind and had written the part for her, but when her commitments on the Continent made it impossible for her to come, he had to rely on the recommendations of the Birmingham authorities. They advised him to take Maria Caradori-Allan, who was Alsatian by descent, Italian by birth, forty-six years old, and had been singing in English oratorio for many years. This popular but slightly worn veteran was, in Felix's eyes, not much of a replacement for the youthful Jenny Lind, and she did not endear herself further to him when she immediately began demanding changes in her part. She particularly objected to the aria "Hear ye, Israel." Mendelssohn, with

Jenny in mind, had made it a strong aria featuring the F-sharp he found so irresistible; Mme. Caradori-Allan, after trying it out, told Felix that it "was not a lady's song" and requested him to transpose it down a whole tone. Felix refused and told her bluntly if she was too much of a lady to sing the aria, he would ask the festival authorities to replace her. She sang it as written, but Felix saw to it that she was not re-engaged when *Elijah* was repeated the following year in London in a revised version. The other singers satisfied the composer eminently, especially the baritone Joseph Staudigl, who sang Elijah, and a young tenor named Charles Lockey, who was making his first important appearance and sang so beautifully that he made a career for himself on the spot as one of the outstanding British singers of the nineteenth century.

The excitement in England was tremendous as Mendelssohn arrived in the country for the final preparations. Somehow the word spread that Britain's favorite composer had outdone even his past achievements and that a masterful work was to be expected. It was also noted that Mendelssohn did not look well; although he was only thirty-seven, his dark hair was streaked with gray, and he seemed haggard and weary. A pupil watching him at a preliminary rehearsal in the Hanover Square Rooms in London reported that he "looked very worn and nervous, yet he would suffer no one to relieve him, even in the scrutiny of the orchestral parts, which he himself spread out on some of the benches . . . and insisted upon sorting them out and examining for himself."

On August 23, a Sunday, Mendelssohn went by rail to Birmingham. He always took delight in trains, then still a novelty; and now he had his own, for the trip was made in a "Mendelssohn Special," which carried the composer, his assistant Moscheles, the soloists, many of the musicians, and a full complement of music critics. Several of these last had had a look at parts of the score and attended the rehearsals, so that laudatory notices of *Elijah* began to appear even before the first official performance.

The première was to be given at 11:30 A.M. on a Wednesday, and the streets around the Town Hall auditorium, which seated 3,000, were jammed with ticket holders, onlookers, and vendors of various sorts. No one could complain the program was too short for, over Mendelssohn's objections, his full-length oratorio was to be followed by three other numbers; an aria from Mozart's secular cantata *Davidde penitente,* a recitative and aria from Cimarosa's *Il Sacrificio d'Abramo,* and Handel's coronation anthem "The King Shall Rejoice." For these the famous husband-wife operatic duo of soprano Giulia Grisi and tenor Giovanni Mario had been engaged; there were those who regretted they weren't singing in *Elijah* as well.

When Mendelssohn entered the hall to take his place, baton in hand, before the assembled forces of 125 instrumentalists, 271 choristers, and 4 soloists, a tremendous shout went up from the packed hall. The room was lined by two rows of high windows along the sides, and several journalists who were present noted that just as the frail-looking composer raised his baton to begin, the sun broke through some morning clouds and—to quote one one of the more effusive reporters—"seemed to illuminate the vast edifice in honor of the bright and pure being who stood there the idol of all beholders."

The music itself was an enormous success. While Grisi and Mario cooled their heels in an antechamber, eight numbers—four arias and four choruses—had to be repeated. At the end, the *Times* reported, there were "shouts of exultation" and "a long-continued unanimous volley of plaudits, vociferous and deafening." Mendelssohn, overwhelmed, left the podium quickly, but was called back time and time again. "Never was there a more complete triumph—never a more thorough and speedy recognition of a great work of art," said the *Times.*

Mendelssohn himself was more than satisfied with the performance, except for the unfortunate Mme. Caradori-Allan. His criticism of her is interesting because he himself has sometimes been accused of writing music that is superficially smooth but wanting in underlying feeling. "The worst was the soprano part," he wrote afterward to a friend in Leipzig. "It was all so pretty, so pleasing, so elegant; at the same time so flat, so heartless, so unintelligent, so soulless, that the music acquired a sort of amiable expression about which I could go mad even today when I think about it. . . . Nothing is so unpleasant to my taste as such cold, heartless coquetry in music. It is so unmusical in itself, and yet it is often made the basis of singing and playing—making music, in fact." On the positive side, as if to demonstrate how an interpreter can add luster to music even for its composer, he wrote to his brother Paul of Lockey's singing of "Then shall the righteous break forth": "A young English tenor sang the last air so beautifully that I was obliged to collect all my energies so as not to be affected, and to continue beating time steadily." His deepest feelings of all he conveyed in a letter to Jenny Lind: "It was the best performance that I ever heard of any of my compositions. There was so much go and swing in the way which the people played, and sang, and listened. I wish you had been there."

Despite the general satisfaction, there were sections in the original version of *Elijah* that did not completely please Mendelssohn, and he immediately began working on changes, most of them minor. Eight months later, on April 13, 1847, he was back in London for the tenth time, bringing with him the score as we have it now. He directed no fewer than six performances of *Elijah* within two weeks in three different cities: London, Birmingham, and Manchester. Although most critics were agreed that none of these matched in quality the première of the previous year, again the reception was tumultuous. Prince Albert, attending one of the London performances, wrote out an effusive commendation for Mendelssohn, hailing him as "a second Elijah" who had "employed his genius and his skill in the service of the true."

While in England for, as it turned out, the last time, Mendelssohn by no means limited his activities to conducting *Elijah.* He had brought with him his fifteen-year-old violin protégé Joseph Joachim, whom he wished to introduce to the British public; he also gave a concert at the Philharmonic Society, conducting his *Midsummer Night's Dream* music and *Scotch* Symphony and appearing as soloist in his favorite piano concerto, the Beethoven G Major. There was a particularly distinguished audience on hand, and when a friend commented on the splendor of the performance Felix commented: "I was desirous to play well, for there were two ladies present whom I particularly wished to please, the Queen and Jenny Lind." A few evenings later, the positions were reversed, for Felix went to Her Majesty's Theater to hear Jenny make her British operatic debut in Meyerbeer's *Robert le Diable.* For himself there was a final round of musical appearances, calls on friends, receptions at the Prussian Embassy and Buckingham Palace. Everyone agreed that when he played or conducted he appeared to possess all his old vigor and freshness, but that when he was not actually making music he seemed careworn and prematurely aged. When friends pressed him to stay longer in London he replied: "Ah! I wish I may not have stayed here too long! One more week of this unremitting fatigue, and I should be killed outright!"

Mendelssohn left England on May 9, 1847, via the Dover-Calais ferry, and headed toward Frankfurt, where he hoped for some months of repose with Cecile and his children. But at the frontier town of Herbesthal near Cologne, an unfortunate incident occurred. The police mistook him for another Dr. Mendelssohn, who was being sought for radical activities and association with the notorious political activist Ferdinand Lasalle. They removed Felix from the train and refused to let him continue his journey. Over and over again, he explained that he was Dr. Mendelssohn the composer, just returning from England, but he was searched, questioned, and made to write out long statements detailing his whereabouts for weeks past. When he finally reached Frankfurt, he was in a state of complete exhaustion. Then as now, musical fame was of little moment to the bureaucratic mind.

XXIV Night Song

For several years now, Felix had seen a good deal less of his sisters than he could have wished, although the three of them maintained a steady correspondence through the mails. First each girl had taken her trip to Italy, then Felix had finally abandoned Berlin for Leipzig, and always there were the repeated voyages to England. All the Mendelssohns, including his brother Paul, kept writing to each other about a time when the families could all again live in a proximity that might recapture the days of their youth; but it did not seem to be getting any closer. In the meantime, each eagerly awaited and anticipated every communication from the other.

So when Felix, on his second day home in Frankfurt after his journey from London, received a message from Paul, he had no cause to suspect anything was wrong. When he opened it, he stared at it incredulously, gave a cry, and fainted. Fanny was dead. The news had been almost equally staggering to Rebecca and Paul, for they had no indication anything was seriously amiss with their sister. Fanny, who was forty-one years old, had been living a busy, happy life in Berlin for the last few years; she had been running her Sunday musicales with unflagging energy and, encouraged by the publication of her music, had been working hard at composition. In retrospect there were, as there always are, disquieting signs. For three years, Fanny had been subject to repeated nosebleeds. They were difficult to stanch, and one had lasted intermittently for thirty-six hours. She had a particularly severe attack in the spring of 1847, which again was stopped with difficulty. On May 14, she was conducting at home a choir rehearsal of Felix's *Walpurgis Night,* which was scheduled for that Sunday afternoon. Suddenly, at the piano, she became ill and felt her arms grow numb. She was quickly put to bed, and her son Sebastian, then sixteen, was sent rushing through the streets for a doctor, just as Joseph Mendelssohn had raced sixty years before when Moses Mendelssohn lay dying. "I ran with all my might," Sebastian later remembered, "and kept saying to myself: 'It can't be anything serious; nothing bad can happen to us.'" But at 11 P.M., Fanny died. The doctor gave a cerebral hemorrhage as the cause.

Fanny's death had a fearful effect upon two men: her husband and her brother. Hensel went to pieces almost immediately; he managed to complete a sketch of his wife as she lay on her deathbed, and it was almost his last picture. Fanny had run the household, looked after the property, and supervised the education of their son; after her death, Hensel found himself unable to cope with any of these tasks. Overnight, he lost all interest in his painting and shunned the artist's studio on the grounds where he had previously spent his days. Although he had commissions on hand and several paintings well under way, he never finished any of them. Even his son Sebastian failed to rouse him, and when Rebecca and Dirichlet suggested that the boy come to live with them, Hensel raised no objection, so that Sebastian remained with his aunt until his own marriage. Hensel himself wandered about for some fifteen years, dabbling in politics and doing little else. He was hit by a vehicle in a street accident in November, 1861, and died of his injuries.

Felix did not lose command of himself in the same way, yet the effect of his sister's death was evident to everyone who met him in the succeeding months. He tried to continue his work, kept on composing, maintained all his family activities. Yet there seemed little heart in what he did; the best that his wife and friends hoped was that in time he would work off his grief. He and Fanny had been not only brother and sister; they had been linked by bonds of musical and spiritual compatibility such as few human beings ever experience; in their minds and in their hearts, they were identical twins.

Felix could not even bring himself to go up to Berlin for the funeral or to visit with Rebecca and Paul. He managed to write a long letter to Hensel attempting to comfort him and also thanking him for having given Fanny happiness in her marriage. "This will be a changed world for us all now," he wrote, "but we must try to get accustomed to the change, though by the time we do, our lives may be over, too."

That summer it was decided that a trip to Switzerland might be beneficial to everybody, so Felix and Paul, with their families and Hensel, all set out for the Alps, where so many years before Felix had proudly written down his analysis of yodeling for Zelter. This time, though, it was not easy to find solace in mountains or in music, and after a month Paul and Hensel returned to their homes as dispiritedly as they had come.

However, Felix and Cecile decided to remain in Switzerland with their children for a while and settled temporarily in Interlaken. There Felix began to compose again, writing a remarkable Quartet in F Minor that, although it is not labeled as such, stands unmistakably as a memorial to his sister. It was his first string quartet in nine years, and it struck an impassioned, agitated note that he seldom expressed so openly.

It so happened that Henry Chorley, the British music critic and historian, was in Interlaken at the time; and he spent a good deal of time with Mendelssohn, who seemed grateful for the opportunity to talk about musical matters. Previously Mendelssohn had not been known as a warm admirer of Italian opera, but now Chorley found him praising Rossini and even speaking kindly of Donizetti, whose operas were then at the peak of their popularity, although some academicians derogated them. Of *The Daughter of the Regiment* he said: "It is so merry, with so much of the real soldier's life in it. They call it bad"—this with a smile—"but it is surprising how easily one can become used to 'bad' music!"

He also asked Chorley about a new operatic composer named Giuseppe Verdi who, he heard, was achieving some remarkable effects in his finales. Since the best-known of Verdi's operas was then *Ernani* (*Rigoletto, Trovatore,* and the others still lay in the future), Mendelssohn obviously was aware of the rising new talent quite early. He asked Chorley to show him a Verdi finale as best he could on the piano; he also complained about the way Handel's organ concertos were currently being misplayed, and talked wistfully about some day writing an opera himself for the Grand Opera in Paris.

Mendelssohn had little opportunity to play music that summer of 1847 in Interlaken; the piano he had in his rooms was an old and much abused instrument. But, he confided to Chorley, in a little village called Ringgenberg on the Lake of Brienz, so isolated there was no proper road leading to it, he had stumbled upon an organ in a little church and, finding it empty, had gone in to play it. He asked Chorley if he would like to go to the church with him, and the Englishman eagerly assented. They traveled there by boat, the only way the village could be reached, on a cold, gray, rainy day. Once again the church was empty with its door open, so they walked in. They found a peasant boy who was willing, for a few coins, to operate the bellows. And so Mendelssohn, whom Chorley had last heard play the organ before an audience of thousands at Exeter Hall in London, now played it for him in the deserted church at Ringgenberg—first some Bach, then improvisations of his own, "long and rich chains of sound," which seemed to the English critic, reminded of some lines in Milton, to "bring all heaven before the eyes." "Such things must come to an end; but they are never forgotten," wrote Chorley of this strange concert, the last ever given by Felix Mendelssohn.

Chorley left this farewell picture of him: "My very last [remembrance] is the sight of him turning down the road, to wind back to Interlaken alone; while we turned up to cross the Wengern Alp to Grindelwald. I thought even then, as I followed his figure, looking none the younger for the loose dark coat and the wide-brimmed straw-hat bound with black crepe, which he wore, that he was too much depressed and worn, and walked too heavily. But who could have dreamed that his days on earth were so rapidly drawing to a close?"

In time, conceivably, Felix might have shaken off the effects of Fanny's death, immersed himself in his work, and pulled together the threads of his life. Certainly he had projects underway. He had been asked by the Philharmonic Society in London for a new symphony for 1848; the city of Liverpool wanted a piece written for the opening of a new concert hall; Cologne Cathedral commissioned a work for a dedicatory ceremony; a new cantata had been requested by Frankfurt. The opera *Loreley* was still very much on his mind, and he had started work on a new oratorio to be called *Christus.* Immediately ahead were performances of *Elijah* he was scheduled to conduct in Berlin and Vienna.

But before he plunged deeply into these projects, Felix decided to go to Berlin for a week to discuss business matters with his brother Paul and to visit the old dwelling at 3 Leipzigerstrasse. The trip turned out to be a disaster. Nothing had been touched since Fanny's death; her own rooms were just as he remembered them, as was the great hall in which she had been preparing her Sunday musicale when she was stricken. The score of his *Walpurgis Night* was still open on the piano where she had left it. The familiar sights and the memories they evoked were too much for Felix. He collapsed all over again and reverted to the disheartened state he had been in before the summer trip to Switzerland. In this condition he returned to Leipzig, although he was not yet able to face the prospect of resuming the conductorship of the Gewandhaus. He seemed, noted one friend, "much changed in look and . . . often sat dull and listless without moving a finger."

On October 9, Mendelssohn walked over to visit Moscheles, who had settled in Leipzig at his invitation to head the piano department at the conservatory. Both Moscheles and his wife Charlotte noticed that Mendelssohn's step lacked its former elasticity, and when Charlotte asked him how he felt, Felix shrugged and replied: "Gray on gray." Moscheles suggested a walk in the Rosenthaler Park in Leipzig, and Mendelssohn acquiesced without much enthusiasm.

"Will you take me, too?" asked Charlotte.

A touch of Mendelssohn's old playfulness seemed to return, and he said to Moscheles with a smile: "What do you say? Shall we take her?"

They all walked over to the Rosenthal, and Mendelssohn reminisced about his days in London, where the Moscheles had also lived, and his last visit to Queen Victoria. For a time, they thought, he seemed almost gay.

Later that day he called on another old friend, a singer named Livia Frege, who was married to a Leipzig lawyer. Mendelssohn had composed a new group of songs he intended to have published, and he asked her to sing them through for him to help determine their order. One of them, a mournful "Night Song," had been written for the birthday of a friend a short while before; he told Frau Frege that it was a strange sort of birthday present but that he was very fond of it, as it expressed his own weary frame of mind.*

The soprano sang the songs through for him, and then Mendelssohn asked if she could go over some of the *Elijah* score with him in view of its forthcoming Vienna performance. By now it was late afternoon and growing dark, so she went to fetch a light. When she returned she found that her visitor had suffered some sort of an attack; he was stretched out on the sofa shivering, his hands cold and stiff, and with a violent headache. In a little while he

*According to Sebastian Hensel, this "Nachtlied" was Mendelssohn's last composition.

recovered sufficiently to walk home, where Cecile, alarmed by his appearance, put him to bed.

He failed to improve much during the succeeding days, and none of the remedies that were tried by the doctors—bleeding by leeches, various medicines and tonics—seemed to do much good. At times he felt well enough to be visited by friends like Moscheles and Hiller; once he even left his bed to get dressed and take a walk with Cecile—a mistake, for he had an attack when he got home. On October 25, he wrote an affectionate letter to Paul, expressing fear that he would not be able to go to Vienna for *Elijah* after all, although, he said, he felt stronger that day, and concluding that a visit from his brother would do him more good than all the "bitter medicine" he was taking.

What was ailing Mendelssohn? Modern physicians, examining the pattern of attacks he suffered in the last days of his life, along with the medical history of his family, conclude that he had a vascular deficiency, perhaps stemming from a congenital weakness of the blood vessels. He suffered a series of what are now called "little strokes" or "little apoplexies"—bleeding episodes from ruptures of small vessels at the base of the brain. Possibly one of these occurred when he learned of Fanny's death, and a series of them evidently took place during his final illness. Medical authorities differ as to whether this sort of vascular weakness is inherited, but certainly the history of the Mendelssohn family seems to point in that direction.

In any event, the death of Felix Mendelssohn was not quite as sudden or as easy as that of his forebears. Between October 7 and November 3, he suffered three strokes, each leaving him noticeably worse off than the previous one. After the second, he was partially paralyzed. With the third, he lost consciousness, but began emitting cries of pain without awakening. Ferdinand David sat with the dying man for a while and saw him "hum and drum" as if music were passing through his head. Later his consciousness returned briefly, and he recognized the people in the room with him, although he did not speak to them. Cecile asked him if he was in pain, and he replied "No."

"Are you tired?" she said.

"Yes, I am tired, terribly tired,"* he replied. These were his last words, for he then fell into a deep and motionless sleep, not unlike those he had had as a boy.

At 9:24 P.M. on Thursday, November 4, 1847, Felix Mendelssohn died, aged thirty-eight years and eight months. With him were his wife Cecile; his brother Paul, who had arrived from Berlin; David; Moscheles; and Conrad Schleinitz, head of the Board of Governors of the Gewandhaus. When the gravity of his condition became known, groups of people began congregating outside of his dwelling awaiting news, and regular bulletins were issued by the doctors.

News of his death stunned the city of Leipzig. "An awful stillness prevails," wrote a young English student at the Leipzig Conservatory. "We feel as if the king were dead." Burial was to be in Berlin, beside the grave of Fanny; so after a church service, a ceremonial procession moved through the streets to the Leipzig railway station, while church bells tolled throughout the city. The funeral train traveled at night, but stops were nevertheless made at several towns where the inhabitants marched to the station, their way lit by torches, to sing choruses of farewell. One of these stops was Dessau, Moses Mendelssohn's old town, where the local choirmaster had composed a special part song for the occasion.

The death of Mendelssohn led to a series of obsequies, observances, and commemorations such as few musicians had ever received. Even Beethoven's death in 1827 brought no such universal demonstration of grief, for its solemnities, heartfelt as they were, were pretty well centered in Vienna. In the case of Mendelssohn, it was almost as if cities and nations were trying to outdo each other in their exhibitions of mourning. Queen Vic-

---

*"Ja, ich bin müde, schrecklich müde."

toria wrote condolences to Cecile and her family, as did the kings of Saxony and Prussia. The Gewandhaus canceled its regular concert and gave a special program consisting of the *Eroica* Symphony and of compositions by Felix. One of these was the "Night Song," which Livia Frege sang beautifully. In London, *Elijah* was given in memoriam by the Sacred Harmonic Society. And on November 12, in Vienna, the *Elijah* that Mendelssohn was to have conducted was finally presented, with a symbolic conductor's desk draped in black and the participants clad in mourning garb. A year later, Jenny Lind organized a special memorial service in London and sang at last the soprano part Mendelssohn had written for her in a performance of *Elijah* at Exeter Hall. The proceeds went to a Mendelssohn Scholarship established to commemorate the composer's activities in England.* Jenny told friends that Mendelssohn's death had so affected her that she found it difficult for several years to sing any of his songs.

Memorial concerts and observances were also held in Birmingham, Manchester, Paris, Berlin, Hamburg, Frankfurt, and other cities. One of the most impressive of all took place in New York. There, on February 14, 1848, a massive "Solemnity in Honor of the Deceased Mendelssohn" was organized by the city's major musical organizations—the Philharmonic Society, the Sacred Music Society, the Euterpean Society, the Liederkranz, and the Concordia. It was held in the black-draped Castle Garden at the Battery, admission was free, and 8,000 New Yorkers jammed the hall. On the program, given by the city's leading instrumentalists and singers, were the Funeral March from the *Eroica,* the *Recordare* of Mozart's Requiem, and many excerpts from Mendelssohn's *Lobgesang, Elijah,* and *St. Paul,* concluding with the chorus "Awake, thou city of Jerusalem!" from the latter work. There was no other music in New York that day.

*Its first winner was Arthur Sullivan.

XXV *The Turnabout*

The real drama of Mendelssohn's music began after his death.

Of the thousands of people who marched in the mourning processions, attended the memorial concerts, listened to the eulogies, and clipped out the obituary articles, virtually every one was certain that one of the greatest composers of all time had been forever enshrined. Possibly no other composer's music had ever spread through the world so quickly. It took the Philharmonic Society of New York until 1846, twenty-two years after its composition, to perform Beethoven's Ninth Symphony (and then it was a failure); but within a few years of Mendelssohn's death, the Philharmonic had presented the *Midsummer Night's Dream* and *Hebrides* Overtures, the G Minor Piano Concerto, the *Scotch* Symphony, the *Italian* Symphony, and other works.

In England, Mendelssohn for a generation after his death all but monopolized the nation's musical life, from private drawing rooms where young lady pianists tinkled the *Songs Without Words* as best they could to the great concert halls where leading musical organizations bent their efforts to massive productions of such works as *Elijah, St. Paul,* and the *Lobgesang.* When Queen Victoria's daughter Vicky, the Princess Royal, was married in 1858, it was to the Wedding March from the *Midsummer Night's Dream;* but that was hardly a distinction, for few English girls marched down the aisle to any other music. For more than a quarter century after his death, Mendelssohn's fame seemed unassailable.

And yet it proved to be quite otherwise. Gradually a reaction set in against the composer who had seemed to so many people the heir of Handel, Mozart incarnate, Beethoven's successor. For almost any great composer some period of reassessment after death is inevitable, but for few was the process as drastic as for Mendelssohn. All the reaction against Victorianism in the arts seemed to center around his frail figure. In 1877, the editor of the *Musical Times,* a conservative British journal, found it necessary to write a leading article entitled "Is Mendelssohn in Danger?" denouncing the critics who took delight in "throwing mud at popular idols." When Sir George Grove's new *Dictionary of Music and Musicians* appeared in four volumes in 1879, it was roundly criticized for including an article on Mendelssohn by Sir George himself that was sixty pages long (Mozart got only thirty-two); the piece was, wrote a reviewer for the Edinburgh *Quarterly Review,* "a drag on the book." All things considered, it was remarkable that the original article lasted through four editions of Grove's, giving way only in 1954 to a thirty-one page replacement distinctly cooler in tone.

The outlook of the younger generation of critics was summed up by John F. Runciman, who became music editor of the *Saturday Review* in London in 1894: "The last generation of critics firmly believed in the existence of some strange rules which they termed the canons of art. What these commandments precisely were, what Moses brought them from the Mount, where the Sinai was situated, are facts that may never come to light. Judging by the results, the Moses may have been Mendelssohn (though not Moses, but Felix, of that ilk), and the commandments are, Whatever Mendelssohn did not authorize is wrong."

The journalistic assault on Mendelssohn in England attained its most persistent, and certainly its most readable expression in the writings of George Bernard Shaw, then an unknown journalist in his early thirties. Shaw spent six years, from 1888 to 1894, as a music critic, first on the London *Star* under the pseudonym of "Corno di Bassetto," then on the *World,* where he introduced his

"G.B.S." trademark. Throughout these years, Shaw never lost an opportunity to denounce Mendelssohn and Mendelssohn-worship, although he conceded there were certain qualities in his music that he rather liked. The *Scotch* Symphony, for example, he characterized as "a work which would be great if it were not so confoundedly genteel." But he regarded much of Mendelssohn's product as elegantly superficial, and in particular he expressed an aversion to the oratorios, which were repeated endlessly at that time. In a typical English season, 1886–1887, there were twenty-two performances of *Elijah* and twenty of *St. Paul.** "*St. Paul* next Saturday," wrote Corno di Bassetto in his column of November 11, 1889. "I shall go expressly to abuse it." Which he did.

"We now see plainly enough," Shaw wrote on another occasion,

> that Mendelssohn, though he expresses himself in music with touching tenderness and refinement, and sometimes with a nobility and pure fire that makes us forget all his kid glove gentility, his conventional sentimentality, and his despicable oratorio monger-ing, was not in the foremost rank of great composers. He was more intelligent than Schumann, as Tennyson is more intelligent than Browning: he is, indeed, the great composer of the century for all those to whom Tennyson is the great poet of the century. He was more vigorous, more inventive, more inspired than Spohr, and a much abler and better educated man than Schubert.† But compare him with Bach, Handel, Haydn, Mozart, Beethoven, or Wagner; and then settle, if you can, what ought to be done to the fanatic who proclaims him "a master yielding to," etc., etc., etc.

Shaw's mention of Richard Wagner in this connection was no accident. Indeed, the Wagnerian upsurge constituted one of the major factors in the late nineteenth-century decline of Mendelssohn's reputation. For Mendelssohn's music, with its classical

---

*By the 1926–1927 season, the totals had diminished to twenty performances of *Elijah* and two of *St. Paul.*

†Shaw also had an aversion to Schubert, whose music he characterized as "brainless."

sense of clarity, form, and tidiness, was held up—both by its proponents and by its detractors—as the antithesis of the massive, sprawling music dramas with which Wagner was creating, as he and his supporters believed, "the music of the future." In Germany the attack on Mendelssohn was spearheaded by Wagner himself and led eventually to the total disappearance of Mendelssohn's music during the Nazi era.

Almost single-handedly, Wagner turned Mendelssohn's music into an artistic national issue in Germany. Wagner himself was too acute a musician to be ignorant of Mendelssohn's technical talents; so he based his attack on the argument that Mendelssohn, having been born a Jew, was inherently incapable of making high artistic use of his powers.

Actually Mendelssohn and Wagner had been well acquainted personally. Wagner, who ironically was born in Leipzig, was only four years younger than Felix and, as did most other German musicians, sought out the older man from time to time to seek advice and guidance. In 1835, Wagner, then twenty-two, submitted to Mendelssohn a symphony he had written for possible performance at the Gewandhaus, but it was never played there. In 1843, however, Mendelssohn was in Berlin when Wagner's *Flying Dutchman* had its première and went backstage to congratulate the successful composer. Over the years that followed, Wagner called frequently on Mendelssohn in Berlin, had dinner with him, wrote him cordial notes such as: "My dear, dear Mendelssohn: I am really happy that you like me. If I have come a little closer to you, it is the nicest thing about my Berlin expedition." Actually there was no reason, musical or otherwise, for Wagner to have disliked Mendelssohn. In music each mined different veins, and in politics, Mendelssohn, who could so easily have settled permanently in England, never regarded himself as anything but a good German. That Wagner knew and appreciated Mendelssohn's music very well was demonstrated in his prelude to *Parsifal*, whose opening motif is repeated note for note (though at a much slower tempo) from Mendelssohn's *Fair Melusine* Overture—presumably an unintentional resemblance but nonetheless a striking one.

Only once did the two composers come into anything resembling competition, when both were among those asked to write a festive song for the unveiling of a statue in Dresden of Frederick August I. Neither achieved a very durable or important piece; nevertheless, Wagner went about telling people privately that he had outdone the famous Mendelssohn. In his public utterances, Wagner was always careful to join in the general homage to Mendelssohn.

However in 1850, when Felix had been dead three years, Wagner wrote a diatribe called "Judaism in Music" that set the tone for nearly a century's campaign against Mendelssohn's music in Germany. Wagner published his opus in the *Neue Zeitschrift für Musik* (no longer edited by Schumann) under the pseudonym of "Karl Freigedank" (free thought). He withheld his name not out of respect to the dead Mendelssohn but from fear of the still-living Meyerbeer, whom it also attacked and who then held a position of considerable power. In 1869, after Meyerbeer had also died, Wagner brought forth his "Judaism in Music" under his own name, and it later became part of his published prose, being issued in London in 1894 in a translation by William Ashton Ellis.

In this remarkable document, Wagner denounced all Jews as enemies of true art. Although they might at times excel as executants,* they were totally incapable of true creativity and could only steal other men's work: "The Jew-musician hurls together the diverse forms and styles of every age and master."

Wagner acknowledged that he had a certain regard for Mendelssohn, but "a like sympathy, however, can no other Jew-composer rouse in us." He charged Mendelssohn with turning Leipzig into a Jewish "metropolis of music," stocking it with Jewish musi-

---

*Wagner often made use of Jewish performers, such as Hermann Levi, who conducted the first *Parsifal*.

cians like David and Joachim at the expense of true Germans. His ultimate appraisal of Mendelssohn was: "He has shown us that a Jew may have the amplest store of specific talents, may own the finest and most varied culture, the highest and the tenderest sense of honor—yet without all these preeminences helping him, were it but one single time, to call forth in us that deep heart-searching effect which we await from Art. . . ."

A number of Germans rejected the Wagnerian tirade. Mendelssohn's descendants reacted angrily, and eleven faculty members of the Leipzig Conservatory protested to the editor of the *Neue Zeitschrift* when the original Freigedank article appeared. But his insinuation that Mendelssohn was an outsider, an interloper, and a very minor composer pervaded the German musical atmosphere and contributed to the reaction against the previous adulation. Wagner did not let his denunciation rest; when friendly memoirs of Mendelssohn by Hiller and Devrient were published, he attacked them, too. And when he left off, there was no lack of disciples and camp followers to carry on the work.

Nor was this attitude confined to Germany. As recently as 1932, an Englishman named Percy Colson, in a book entitled *Victorian Portraits,* offered this appraisal of Mendelssohn: "He wrote too easily; he had the fatal facility of the talented Jew. Now it is a remarkable fact that the Jewish race, in spite of its great artistic gifts, has never in modern times produced either a poet, painter, writer or composer of the very first rank. Its genius is executive rather than creative and, even so, is distinguished more for its showy qualities than for depth of feeling and interpretation."

It remained for the Germany of Adolf Hitler to produce the most comprehensively scurrilous book ever written about Felix Mendelssohn. The work of one Karl Blessinger, it was published in 1944, long after the Nazis had totally banned Mendelssohn's music and erased him from the roster of German composers. Blessinger's book, also entitled *Judaism in Music,* denounced the "Three M's" of Jewish music, Mendelssohn, Meyerbeer, and

Mahler. The entire Mendelssohn line was attacked: Moses for being a wily "assimilationist" who wormed his way into German society as the first step in a campaign for Jewish world domination, and his daughters as practitioners of "perverse eroticism" who led unsuspecting young German intellectuals astray in their salons. Felix himself was the greatest "cultural parasite" of all, achieving his reputation only through his father's wealth and the machinations of an international syndicate of Jews. Mendelssohn, Blessinger concluded, "is not to be judged as a single person, but only with the aim of all Jewry; he came of a family that did much damage to the entire German people."

Significantly, Blessinger found it necessary to give a warning to those Germans, apparently a substantial number, who felt themselves deprived of Mendelssohn's music: "If many people say now it is a pity they cannot hear their pet compositions like the *Midsummer Night's Dream* music, the *Hebrides* Overture and the Violin Concerto in E minor, we have to tell them that it is even sadder that great works of German composers like the Schumann Violin Concerto might have been lost through Jewish manipulations. . . ."

The eradication of Mendelssohn from Germany by the Nazis reached into all phases of musical life, starting in 1934, when performances of his music were barred. A standard musical textbook issued in 1936 omitted mention of his name. His scores were included in the public book burnings. Other composers were invited to write replacements for his *Midsummer Night's Dream;* among those accepting commissions to do so was Carl Orff. A prolonged battle broke out over a statue of Mendelssohn in Leipzig, erected in front of the Gewandhaus after his death. The Nazis wanted it down, but the lord mayor of Leipzig, Carl Goerdeler, resisted all attempts to remove it. Finally, toward the end of 1937, while Goerdeler was out of the city, Nazi officials ordered the statue dismantled and turned into scrap iron. Goerdeler was so incensed that when he returned to Leipzig, he resigned his office in protest—the first step along a road of defiance of the Nazis that was to lead this courageous man to execution for complicity in the anti-Hitler plot of July, 1944.

With the end of the war and the downfall of the Nazis, the restrictions on Mendelssohn's music were terminated and a campaign begun to rehabilitate the composer. The Prussian state government restored Mendelssohn scholarships for outstanding musical students originally established in 1878 and eliminated during the inflation of the 1920s. In 1964, the Prussian State Library in Berlin became the home of a Mendelssohn Archive that today is one of the world's great repositories of Mendelssohn scores (by both Felix and Fanny), documents, letters, and pictures, and that includes a special subdivision devoted to Moses Mendelssohn. Berlin also became the seat of the Mendelssohn-Gesellschaft, a society founded in 1967 by Cecile Lowenthal-Hensel, great-granddaughter of Fanny Hensel, aimed at furthering research into the composer and his family. On November 4, 1970, the 123d anniversary of Mendelssohn's death, the City of Leipzig dedicated a Mendelssohn Room in the Old City Hall, in which were placed on permanent display furniture and *objets d'art* from the Mendelssohn family estate.

Most important of all, it again became possible to hear Mendelssohn's music in Germany. Immediately after the war, he became a very fashionable composer, whether because his works again seemed fresh and new after so long an absence or because listening to them in public was a convenient way of demonstrating that one had never been a Nazi at heart after all. Today they continue to play a large part in German musical life both through concerts and recordings; even the Mendelssohn songs, vocal duets, and romantic choruses, once so beloved of many Germans, are resuming their former place. Karl Blessinger's fears have proved justified after all: not even the Nazis, who did so many fearful things to Germany, could expunge Mendelssohn from its musical life.

XXVI *The Mendelssohn Succession*

The vicissitudes of Felix Mendelssohn's music after his death were paralleled by the fortunes of his family, which continued to produce men and women of extraordinary ability during the nineteenth and twentieth centuries, but which did not escape the German upheavals of modern times.

Cecile Mendelssohn survived her husband by only six years, dying of consumption in Frankfurt on September 25, 1853. Hearing she was ill, Ferdinand Hiller had come to pay her a call on that very day; when he rang the bell, Cecile's mother opened the door and, speaking with the calmness of grief, said: "Oh, it is you, Herr Hiller. I have just lost my daughter."

With Fanny as well as Felix gone, life in Berlin lost much of its attraction for the remaining sister, Rebecca. She and her brother Paul sold the great house at 3 Leipzigerstrasse (it later became the hall of the upper chamber of the Prussian parliament). Rebecca's husband Dirichlet accepted a position succeeding the celebrated mathematician and physicist, Karl Friedrich Gauss, on the faculty of the University of Göttingen, where they moved. At the Dirichlets', there was an occasional musical performance where Felix's works were played, but nothing like those of the old days. "Crumbs from our former feasts," Rebecca called them sadly in a letter she wrote to Sebastian Hensel. Rebecca died of an unexpected stroke, like her brother and her sister, on December 1, 1858; and the following May, Dirichlet died of heart disease.

The only Mendelssohn of his generation to live beyond middle age was Paul. With his cousin Alexander, the son of Joseph Mendelssohn, he helped raise the Mendelssohn Bank to new levels of affluence and influence; he also edited a collection of Felix's letters, helped sort out his unpublished musical manuscripts, and served as a financial trustee for his children. If he outlived his brother and sisters, he also underwent a more painful death, after a prolonged illness in 1874, at the age of sixty-one.

Of Felix Mendelssohn's five children, the next to the youngest, Felix, died at the age of eight, four years after his father. Cecile's death in 1853 left the other four, ranging in age from eight to fifteen, parentless. The two boys were taken into their uncle Paul Mendelssohn's household, while Cecile's mother, Mme. Jeanrenaud, raised the two girls.

Felix's eldest surviving son, Carl, became a professor of history at the universities of Heidelberg and Freiburg, the author of a history of modern Greece, and a close friend of Nietzsche. He also edited a volume of memoirs about his father's relationship with Goethe.

Paul, Felix's second son, was a scientist and pioneer in the development of aniline dyes. While still in his twenties he founded a chemical concern called Aktien Gesellschaft für Anilinfabrikation, abbreviated Agfa. The company became a vast enterprise, noted among other products for its cameras and films. In the 1920s it became part of the I.G. Farben chemical cartel, with the name Agfa maintained for the I.G. Farben photographic line. Paul died in 1880 of a heart attack at thirty-eight, the same age as his father.

Both of Felix's daughters, Marie and Lili, married and raised families. Marie's husband was an Englishman named Victor Benecke, who was distantly related to the Jeanrenauds. They lived in England and had two spinster daughters and two sons, one of whom, Edouard, was killed climbing the Jungfrau, and the other, Paul, became a distinguished philologist at Oxford. The English branch of the Mendelssohn family died out in the 1960s.

Lili Mendelssohn was married to Adolphe Wach, a professor of law and a jurist who died in Germany in 1926. Many members of the Wach branch were among the Mendelssohn descendants victimized by the Nazis. In general, the Mendelssohns did not feel the full brunt of the Nuremberg anti-Semitic laws because most of the family had undergone conversion several generations back. However, one member of the clan, a daughter-in-law of Lili Wach, was sent to the Theresienstadt concentration camp; and those who were not personally endangered were nevertheless stripped of university posts, professional memberships, and in general deprived of their honors and livelihood. As a result, the family that had been one of the country's ornaments for a century and a half one by one began to emigrate.

Among this company of exiles was Albrecht Mendelssohn Bartholdy, the son of Carl Mendelssohn. Albrecht had married his cousin Dora, a daughter of Lili Wach, family intermarriage being a characteristic of the clannish Mendelssohn descendants. Like his father, he was a historian, and also a leading authority on international jurisprudence. He served as a member of the German peace delegation at Versailles in 1919, and became co-editor of the archives of the German Foreign Office. Like many of the Mendelssohn descendants, he was a gifted musical amateur, and even composed a youthful opera.

When the Nazis came to power, Albrecht was dismissed from his post as professor of international law at the University of Hamburg. In 1933 he went to England, where a special lectureship was created for him at Balliol College in Oxford. Later he visited the United States to lecture at Harvard University, which conferred an honorary Doctor of Laws degree on him. His book *The War and German Society: The Testament of a Liberal* remains a concise and lucid analysis of Germany from 1914 to 1918. Albrecht died in England in 1936. Another outstanding scholar descended from Lili Mendelssohn Wach was the late Professor Joachim Wach, who left Germany in the mid-1930s to become professor of comparative religion at the University of Chicago.

Paul Mendelssohn, Felix's second son, also produced a distinguished lineage. One of his sons, Ludwig, was killed in the German army during World War I; another, also named Paul, became a director of the Agfa family business, only to be forced to leave Germany for England. A third son, Otto, became a banker who was raised to the nobility in 1905. But despite the "von" he was able to add to his name, he, too, was proscribed by the Nazis and lived out the war in seclusion in a small cottage hidden away in the corner of an estate he owned in Potsdam. Even after the war, he did not get his main house back immediately; the Russians turned it into their headquarters for the Potsdam Conference.

Otto also married a cousin, Cecile (the Mendelssohns had a confusing propensity for repeating the same names in each new generation), who was the daughter of Carl Mendelssohn. They had one son, Hugo, a banker who began collecting Mendelssohn manuscripts in the 1920s and managed to get them to Switzerland, where he established an organization called the International Mendelssohn Bartholdy Society. In 1971, Hugo was the only direct living descendant of Felix Mendelssohn still to bear the name of Mendelssohn.

Paul Mendelssohn had two daughters, one of whom, another Cecile, married an English-born physician named Gilbert, who was residing in Germany. One of their two children, Felix Gilbert, left Germany in 1933 to pursue a distinguished career as a historian in the United States, becoming a leading authority on the Renaissance and a professor first at Bryn Mawr College and later at the Institute for Advanced Study in Princeton. Thus Felix Mendelssohn's descendants have played a part in the academic, cultural, and scientific well-being of at least four countries: Germany, England, Switzerland, and the United States.

Other branches of the Mendelssohn family have made similar contributions. The line of Nathan Mendelssohn, Moses' youngest son, was particularly productive of musicians, notably Arnold

Mendelssohn, who lived from 1855 to 1933. He wrote three operas, three symphonies and many other works, taught at the Cologne and Frankfurt Conservatories, and wrote on musical esthetics.

Probably the most spectacular public career pursued by a Mendelssohn in the United States was that of Eleonora Mendelssohn, the actress. Eleonora came of the line of Joseph Mendelssohn, eldest son of Moses. This was the banking branch of the family, which operated quite differently from the Rothschilds, where all the sons were permitted to enter into the business. Among the Mendelssohns, the family operation was far more restrictive, with control passed down from one eldest son to another. Joseph, an able financier, was succeeded by his son Alexander, who was even abler. Alexander and his wife Marianna were known for their elegant style of living in Berlin; according to one story, when Augusta, wife of King William I of Prussia, wanted to take a bath, she sent over to the Mendelssohns to borrow their ornate portable bathtub, a luxury that the royal palace lacked.

Control of the Mendelssohn Bank was transmitted from one son to another until it reached two brothers, Robert and Franz von Mendelssohn in the twentieth century. Robert, an amateur cellist, married an Italian singer and pianist named Giulietta Gordigiani, whom he had met at the home of Eleonora Duse, the celebrated actress. Their daughter, Eleonora Mendelssohn, who was named for Duse, resolved to become an actress herself and, despite her parents' objections, joined the company of Max Reinhardt, making her debut in 1921 as Jessica in *The Merchant of Venice.*

Eleonora, a woman of striking beauty, had a career on the stage in Berlin and elsewhere, though she never quite achieved the stardom she yearned for. Her first husband was Edwin Fischer, the celebrated Swiss pianist, and her second was a dashing Hungarian aristocrat named Jedre Jessenski, who settled in Austria where he became known as a daredevil horseman and aviator. In the 1930s Eleonora and "Jessi," as everyone called him, occupied a castle on the Wolfgangsee near Salzburg in the Salzkammergut, where they were famous for their hospitality and their parties. Carl Zuckmayer, the German playwright who wrote *The Captain from Köpenick*, remembered an evening musicale in their castle late in the fall of 1937, at which the famous Rosé String Quartet of Vienna played Haydn's *Emperor* Quartet, from which comes the melody that has served both as the Austrian national anthem and the German "Deutschland, Deutschland, über Alles."

"The Viennese artists played it," wrote Zuckmayer, "as Haydn intended it, as a simple pious melody, almost a prayer. Most of the listeners had tears in their eyes. And half a year later most of them were scattered to the winds."

Eleonora was the first Mendelssohn to leave Germany when Hitler came to power. She was politically outspoken, and she belonged to the branch of the family which had retained its Judaism the longest; in fact, she later described herself as half-Jewish and half-Italian. When she sensed the approach of the Anschluss in 1938 she left Austria and again emigrated, this time to New York. With her came her brother Francesco von Mendelssohn, a cellist; and it was not long before the two of them were helping Carl Zuckmayer and his wife, also emigrés, settle in New York.

Eleonora made prodigious efforts to perfect her English so that she could appear on the Broadway stage, and she ultimately succeeded. But she did not have much luck in her choice of plays, for such works as *Daughters of Atreus* and *The Secret Room* were box-office failures. However, she did have a supporting role in *The Madwoman of Chaillot* and later played the lead in the national company. She had a wide circle of friends, from Arturo Toscanini to Alexander Woollcott, many of whom had enjoyed her hospitality in Europe. Her New York home was a small apartment on the East Side, dominated by a portrait of her great-great-great-grandfather, Moses Mendelssohn. Eleonora's one major Broadway success came in 1940 in Elmer Rice's *Flight to the West,* a play about a group of refugees from Nazi Europe traveling by plane from

Lisbon to New York. In the cast were such luminaries as Betty Field, Arnold Moss, and Paul Henried; but it was Eleonora, playing the role of a Jewish woman fleeing Germany, who made the most memorable impression of all in a brief but searing scene. Her greatest stage triumph was one in which she played her own life story.

In 1951, Eleonora Mendelssohn's third husband, a German-born actor named Martin Kosleck, fell from the window of their apartment and was severely injured. A few weeks later, while he was still in the hospital, Eleonora, fifty-one, was found dead in bed from an overdose of sleeping pills, a tragic end to a career that had begun so brilliantly.

Disaster also overtook the Mendelssohn Bank, founded in 1795 by Joseph and Abraham Mendelssohn. Through the nineteenth century, it developed into one of Germany's most important financial institutions, dealing heavily in state loans. In 1920, sensing the coming German postwar inflation, Mendelssohn and Company opened a branch in Amsterdam, which gradually became dominant in its affairs. With the rise of Hitler, the Berlin office receded further in importance and was liquidated altogether in 1938. By now control of the bank had passed from the Mendelssohns to Dr. Fritz Mannheimer, an international financier. When he died unexpectedly of a heart attack in August, 1939, the Amsterdam branch suspended operations, too, and the Mendelssohn Bank passed into history. Of the family's legacy, only Felix's music survived the war.

XXVII Mendelssohn Today

And now, finally, what of that music? At the conclusion of his long and laudatory article on Mendelssohn in his *Dictionary of Music and Musicians,* Sir George Grove wrote in 1879: "His genius had not been subjected to those fiery trials which seem necessary to assure its abiding possession of the depths of the human heart. . . . Mendelssohn was never more than temporarily unhappy. He did not know distress as he knew happiness . . . he was never tried by poverty, or disappointment, or ill-health, or a morbid temper, or neglect, or the perfidy of friends. . . . Who can wish that he had been? that that bright, pure, aspiring spirit should have been dulled by distress or torn with agony?"

The same idea, often expressed in a less kindly and sympathetic manner, has been carried over into much subsequent Mendelssohn criticism, giving rise to the common portrayal of Mendelssohn as the boy who never grew up, the snobbish son of the rich upon whom good fortune showered all his life, the talented but superficial musician who never had to deepen his art in the crucible of experience or suffering.

Hopefully, this book has shown such depictions of Mendelssohn to be considerably exaggerated, if not totally unfounded. It is perfectly true that Mendelssohn never underwent the impoverishment of Mozart, the lack of recognition of Schubert, the deafness of Beethoven. But to depict him as a blithe and untroubled musical spirit who was scarcely touched by the world around him is absurd. For all his affluence, his life was passed neither in luxury

248

nor in idleness, nor was it free of the grinding harassments of daily domestic cares; of administrative responsibilities; of the rebuffs and reverses of a profession that then as now abounds in rivalry, bickering, and intrigue; of disappointments and frustrations; of family crises and tragedies; and finally of the gradual weakening of the spirit and forebodings of death itself.

These are the trials that all men face, but they are no less vexatious or exhausting for being the common lot. Sensitive and highly strung as he was, Mendelssohn, who could so easily have remained sheltered from the competitive, contentious world around him, plunged into it with a sense of mission and dedication, and in the end wore himself out in the cause of music as surely as Mozart did.

He also was beset by an inner artistic struggle, for he was in his way a wanderer between two worlds. Mendelssohn's musical instincts reached backward in time rather than forward; his earliest gods were Bach and Mozart, and he never forsook them. Yet he was too much a man of his own time—entranced by its trains, its ships, its factories, its commerce and aware of its political doctrines, its religious currents, its artistic innovations—to remain a musical recluse or antiquarian. The *Midsummer Night's Dream* Overture was, to quote critic Harold C. Schonberg, "the first through-and-through piece of romantic music in history," yet it remained well within the classical tradition in style and structure. All his life, Mendelssohn sought to reconcile the spirit of two ages, at some times succeeding better than at others.

It seems likely that had he lived longer, he would have become increasingly involved in the new musical developments of his day. One can sense this in the deep feeling of personal commitment in his Violin Concerto in E Minor, written three years before he died, and even more in his String Quartet in F Minor, composed after the death of Fanny Mendelssohn, which has a sense of tragedy that is rare in his music. He died, after all, at the age of thirty-eight, when the world and its troubles were crowding in on him more and more; who is to say what kind of music he might have written had he lived another ten or twenty years?

Today, fortunately for Mendelssohn and for us, the post-Victorian reaction against his music has largely passed. Disparagement is no longer the fashion. Critics like Paul Henry Lang and Alan Rich have been impelled in recent years to write newspaper columns reaffirming Mendelssohn's claims not only to skilled craftsmanship but to originality and innovation. The musical public, which never turned away from such works as the Violin Concerto, the *Scotch* and *Italian* Symphonies and the great overtures, no matter what the critics told them, goes right on listening to his music at concerts and on recordings with frank enjoyment. And of late, not only the Mendelssohn staples but some of the more obscure and neglected music has begun to turn up, often in rather surprising locales.

During the months I have been writing this book, I have heard the lovely and seldom-given Symphony No. 1 in C Minor resuscitated by Stanislaw Skrowaczewski and the New York Philharmonic; the ever-fresh and delectable Octet in E-flat played by eight bearded and blue-jeaned young musicians before a crowd of lunch-hour idlers in the nave of the Fifth Avenue Presbyterian Church; a set of six vocal duets, including one by Fanny Mendelssohn, sung beautifully by Janet Baker and Dietrich Fischer-Dieskau in Carnegie Hall, and, not least memorable, the chorus "Be not afraid" from *Elijah,* performed with plenty of spirit and nice balance (considering that the girls outnumbered the boys three to one) by a choir of New York City school children in the auditorium of Junior High School 190, Queens.

I have also found that Mendelssohn's music has benefited immeasurably from the ballet explosion in the United States. Both the *Scotch* and *Italian* symphonies have been incorporated into ballet repertory—the former by the New York City Ballet Company, the latter by American Ballet Theatre. Most important of all, George Balanchine's beautiful full-length production of *A Mid-*

summer Night's Dream with the New York City Ballet at last permits Mendelssohn's complete score to be heard in its entirety in a theater. For some reason, stagings of Shakespeare's play accompanied by Mendelssohn's music tend to be heavy and unwieldy. This was true of Max Reinhardt's famous production in Germany in the 1920s, which later toured the United States, and of an Old Vic version, which played without much success at the Metropolitan Opera in 1954.*

But Balanchine's ballet seems to enhance the music rather than impede or overshadow it. By his own account, he took Mendelssohn rather than Shakespeare as his starting point. "The play in this case does not make a ballet," he says, "but the music does. It is *musique dansante.*" The score of Balanchine's ballet comprises the entire *Midsummer Night's Dream* music, including songs and choruses, and is supplemented by the Overtures to *Athalie, The Fair Melusine, The First Walpurgis Night,* and *Son and Stranger,* as well as an early string symphony. Balanchine says he worked on his *Midsummer Night's Dream* for twenty years, and musically no less than balletically, it has been time well spent, for it restores possibly Mendelssohn's greatest score to life.

Elijah, that much overexercised choral war-horse, is another work that shows signs of responding to modern performance techniques. It remains musically uneven, with a poor libretto; but it has many passages of grandeur and dramatic power that are often smothered by the traditional "oratorio style" of most performances and recordings. In October, 1970, at a concert sponsored not by one of the established musical organizations but by the American Bible Society, Lukas Foss gave it a forceful and invigorating presentation at Philharmonic Hall, conducting four

---

*Reinhardt's production was given in a German translation. When he was asked why he didn't perform it in English during its American tour, he is alleged to have answered with a surprised look: "But then you would lose the beauty of the original." Reinhardt also used Mendelssohn's music in his famous 1935 motion picture of *A Midsummer Night's Dream,* with Mickey Rooney as Puck.

first-rate soloists, the Westminster Choir, and members of the New York Philharmonic, thus raising the possibility that *Elijah* has been suffering all these years from the anemia of its conductors rather than its composer.

Other Mendelssohn compositions that have been permitted to lapse into silence are also worthy of revival or rediscovery: songs, piano pieces, chamber music, choral works. Pablo Casals, who chose to play the Trio in D Minor for Piano, Violin, and Cello with Mieczyslaw Horszowski and Alexander Schneider when he was invited to the White House in 1961 by President John F. Kennedy, described Mendelssohn as "a romantic who felt at ease within the mould of classicism and who was able to solve, with an elegance and imaginativeness peculiar to himself, the most difficult problems of form. . . . I feel sure he will come into his own again."

Above all, one would wish to encounter, as part of the Mendelssohn revival, a performance of his Psalms. Of the nine he set to music, at least one, Psalm 114, "When Israel out of Egypt came," is a masterpiece, a monumental eight-part choral work that impelled Sir George Grove to write: "The Jewish blood of Mendelssohn must surely for once have beat fiercely over this picture of the great triumph of his forefathers, and it is only the plain truth to say that in directness and force his music is a perfect match for the words of the unknown Psalmist."

It is in music like this that Felix and Moses Mendelssohn come together at the last. For they belong together, these two—grandfather and grandson, philosopher and musician, eighteenth-century rationalist and nineteenth-century romantic. Each translated the psalms his own way into his own language. It was Moses who created a world in which it was possible for Felix to live and work. Today, as in their own times, their name, their family, and their heritage all are one.

Bibliography

The following bibliography contains books and articles that have been of direct use in the preparation of this book and those that may be of interest for further reading. A few of the sources included appear on more than one list since they contain information on more than one member of the Mendelssohn family.

·

I MOSES MENDELSSOHN

Auerbach, Berthold: *Poet and Merchant; a picture of life from the times of Moses Mendelssohn* (fiction). New York, 1877.

Berger, Abraham: "New York library honors Jewish savant." *American Hebrew,* vol. 125, pp. 691–694 (October 11, 1929).

Blau, Joseph L.: *The Story of Jewish Philosophy.* New York, 1962.

Durant, Will: *The Age of Faith.* New York, 1950.

Englander, Henry: "Mendelssohn as translator and exegete." *Hebrew Union College Annual,* vol. 6, pp. 327–348. Cincinnati, 1929.

Gottard, L. M.: *Souvenirs de Moïse Mendelssohn.* Paris. 1832.

Graetz, Heinrich: *History of the Jews,* vol. 5, "The Mendelssohn Epoch." Philadelphia, 1895.

Hensel, Sebastian: *The Mendelssohn Family.* 2nd ed. New York, 1884.

Isaacs, Abram S.: *Step by Step; a story of the early days of Moses Mendelssohn* (fiction). Philadelphia, 1910.

Jewish Encyclopedia. New York, 1901.

"Judaism and the Modern World; a tribute to Moses Mendelssohn in celebration of the 200th anniversary of his birth." Union of American Hebrew Congregations, Annual Report Supplement, San Francisco, 1927.

Karpeles, Gustav: "Jewish Society in the time of Mendelssohn," in *Jewish Literature and Other Essays.* Philadelphia, 1895.

Kaufman, Reuben: *Great Sects and Schisms in Judaism.* New York, 1967.

Kayserling, Meyer: *Moses Mendelssohn, sein Leben und seine Werke.* Leipzig, 1862.

Keller, Werner: *Diaspora.* New York, 1969.

Kohut, George Alexander: "200 years ago today Mendelssohn was born." *American Hebrew,* vol. 125, pp. 420–421 (September 6, 1929).

Kopald, Louis J. "The friendship of Lessing and Mendelssohn in relation to the good-will movement between Christian and Jew." Central Conference of American Rabbis Yearbook, vol. 39, pp. 370–401. Detroit, 1929.

Lessing, Gotthold Ephraim: *Nathan the Wise,* ed. by George Alexander Kohut. New York, 1917.

Levy, Felix A.: "Moses Mendelssohn's ideals of religion and their relation to Reform Judaism." Central Conference of American Rabbis Yearbook, vol. 39, pp. 351–369. Detroit, 1929.

Lowenthal, Marvin: *The Jews of Germany.* Philadelphia, 1936.

Magnus, Lady Katie: *Jewish Portraits.* London, 1925.

Maimon, Solomon: *An Autobiography,* ed. by Moses Hadas. New York, 1967.

Marcus, Jacob R.: *The Jew in the Medieval World.* New York, 1969.

Marcus, Jacob R.: *The Rise and Destiny of the German Jew.* Cincinnati, 1934.

Mendelssohn, Moses: *Jerusalem and Other Jewish Writings,* trans. and ed. by Alfred Jospe. New York, 1969.

Mendelssohn, Moses ("a Jew, late of Berlin"): *Phaedon, or the Death of Socrates,* trans. from the German. London, 1789.

Mendelssohn, Moses: *A Thanksgiving Sermon, for the important and astonishing victory obtain'd on the fifth of December, 1757.* London, 1758.

Mendelssohn, Moses (editor): *Ecclesiastes; The Hebrew text with a translation of the commentary of Mendelssohn.* London, 1845.

Pinto, Jacqueline: *The Story of Moses Mendelssohn;* a biography for young people. London, 1960.

Plaut, W. G. (translator): "Interview with Moses Mendelssohn." *Commentary,* vol. 25, pp. 528–430 (May, 1958).

Raisin, Jacob S.: *The Haskalah Movement in Russia.* Philadelphia, 1913.

Rawidowicz, Simon: "Moses Mendelssohn, the German and Jewish philosopher," in *Occident and Orient . . . Studies in Honor of Dr. M. Gaster's 80th birthday.* London, 1936.

Rothman, Walter: "Mendelssohn's character and philosophy of religion." Central Conference of American Rabbis Yearbook, vol. 39, pp. 305–350. Detroit, 1929.

Samuels, M.: *Memoirs of Moses Mendelssohn, the Jewish Philosopher; including the celebrated correspondence, on the Christian religion, with J. C. Lavater, minister of Zurich,* 2nd ed. London, 1827.

Seeliger, Herbert: "Origin and Growth of the Berlin Jewish Community." Leo Baeck Institute Yearbook, vol. 3, pp. 159–168. New York, 1958.

Simon, Maurice: *Moses Mendelssohn, His Life and Times.* London, 1952.

Snyder, Louis F., ed.: *Documents of German History.* New Brunswick, 1958.

Stern, Selma: *The Court Jew.* Philadelphia, 1950.

Ten Hoor, George J.: "Moses Mendelssohn's relation to English poetry." Modern Language Association of America, vol. 46, pp. 1137–1165. Menasha, 1931.

Universal Jewish Encyclopedia. New York, 1939.

Vallentin, Antonina: *Mirabeau.* New York, 1958.

Walter, Hermann: *Moses Mendelssohn, Critic and Philosopher.* New York, 1930.

Wyschogrod, M.: "Some Love Letters of Moses Mendelssohn." *Commentary,* vol. 17, pp. 283–285 (March, 1954).

Zarek, Otto: *Moses Mendelssohn; ein judisches schicksal in Deutschland.* Amsterdam, 1936.

II ABRAHAM, DOROTHEA AND HENRIETTA MENDELSSOHN

Brod, Max: *Heinrich Heine.* London, 1958

Graetz, Heinrich: *History of the Jews.* Philadelphia, 1895.

Grunwald, Max: *History of the Jews in Vienna.* Philadelphia, 1936.

Hargrave, Mary: *Some Jewish Women and Their Salons.* London, 1912.

Hensel, Sebastian: *The Mendelssohn Family.* 2nd ed. New York, 1884.

Herold, F. Christopher: *Mistress to an Age; A Life of Madame de Staël;* New York, 1958.

Jewish Encyclopedia. New York, 1901.

Kayserling, Meyer: *Die Judischen Frauen in der Geschichte, Literatur und Kunst.* Leipzig, 1879.

Key, Ellen: *Rahel Varnhagen; a portrait.* New York, 1913.

Liptizin, Solomon: *Germany's Stepchildren.* Philadelphia, 1944.

Loomis, Stanley: *A Crime of Passion.* Philadelphia, 1967.

Mayer, Hebe Rahel: "Art and the Jewish Woman" in *The Jewish Library,* series III, chap. xii. New York, 1934.

Meyer, Bertha: *Salon Sketches; biographical studies of Berlin salons of the Emancipation.* New York, 1938.

Prawer, Siegbert, ed.: *The Romantic Period in Germany.* London, 1970.

Remy, Nahilda: *The Jewish Woman.* New York, 1916.

Tymms, Ralph: *German Romantic Literature.* London, 1955.

Universal Jewish Encyclopedia. New York, 1939.

III FELIX MENDELSSOHN

Benedict, Julius: *Sketch of the Life and Works of Felix Mendelssohn;* with appendices by Henry F. Chorley and Bayard Taylor. London, 1853.

Berlioz, Hector: *Memoirs.* New York, 1932.

Blessinger, Karl: *Judentum und Musik; ein beitrag zur kultur und rassenpolitik.* Berlin, 1944.

Blessinger, Karl: *Mendelssohn, Meyerbeer, Mahler; drei kapitel judentum in der musik. . . .* Berlin, 1939.

Bulman, Joan: *Jenny Lind; a biography.* London, 1956.

Colson, Percy: *Victorian Portraits.* London, 1932.

Corregidor, J. Ma.: *Conversations with Casals.* New York, 1957.

Devrient, Eduard: *My Recollections of Felix Mendelssohn Bartholdy, and His Letters to Me.* London, 1869.

Encyclopedia Britannica, article "Mendelssohn" (by D. F. Tovey). 14th ed., 1929.

Erskine, John: *Song Without Words.* New York, 1941.

Gotch, Rosamund Brunel: *Mendelssohn and His Friends in Kensington.* Oxford, 1934.

Grove, Sir George, ed.: *Grove's Dictionary of Music and Musicians,* 3rd ed., London, 1929; 5th ed., New York, 1954.

Grunberger, Richard: *The 12-Year Reich.* New York, 1971.

Hensel, Sebastian: *The Mendelssohn Family.* 2nd ed. New York, 1884.

Hiller, Ferdinand: *Letters and Recollections of Felix Mendelssohn Bartholdy.* London, 1874.

History of the Liederkranz of the City of New York, 1848–1947. New York, 1948.

Jacob, H. E.: *Felix Mendelssohn and His Times.* Englewood Cliffs, 1963.

Jacobs, Robert L.: "Mendelssohn, a revaluation." *Penguin Music Magazine,* Hammondsworth, 1947, No. 3, pp. 11–16 (continued in subsequent numbers).

Kaufman, Schima: *Mendelssohn; A Second Elijah.* New York, 1934.

Krehbiel, H. E.: "A letter from Mendelssohn." *New York Daily Tribune,* October 29, 1905.

Krehbiel, H. E.: *The Philharmonic Society of New York, a Memorial.* New York, 1892.

Lampadius, W. A.: *Life of Felix Mendelssohn Bartholdy.* London, 1876.

La Mure, Pierre: *Beyond Desire* (novel); New York, 1955.

Mendelssohn, Felix: *Letters,* ed. G. Selden-Goth. New York, 1945.

"Mendelssohn died November 4, 1847." *Musical Times,* London, vol. 88, pp. 313–317 (October, 1947).

"Mendelssohn in England; a centenary tribute." *Musical Times,* London, vol. 50, pp. 81–90 (February, 1909).

Mendelssohn Bartholdy, Albrecht: *The War and German Society: The Testament of a Liberal.* New Haven, 1937.

Mendelssohn Bartholdy, Carl: *Goethe and Mendelssohn.* London, 1872.

Mendelssohn Bartholdy, Felix: *Letters from Italy and Switzerland.* London, 1862.

Mendelssohn Bartholdy, Felix: *Letters 1833–1847.* London, 1863.

Mendelssohn Bartholdy, Felix: *Letters of Felix Mendelssohn to Ignaz and Charlotte Moscheles.* Boston, 1888.

Merlin, Countess: *Memoirs of Madame Malibran.* London, 1844.

Moscheles, Felix: *Fragments of an Autobiography.* New York, 1899.

Odell, George C. D.: *Annals of the New York Stage* (February, 1848). New York, 1931.

Petitpierre, Jacques: *The Romance of the Mendelssohns.* New York, 1950.

Pleasants, Henry, ed.: *The Musical World of Robert Schumann.* New York, 1955.

Polko, Elise: *Reminiscences of Felix Mendelssohn Bartholdy.* New York, 1869.

Radcliffe, Philip: *Mendelssohn.* New York, 1963.

Runciman, John F.: "Musical Criticism and the Critics." *Fortnightly Review,* London, vol. 56, pp. 170–183 (August 1, 1894).

Schonberg, Harold C.: *The Great Pianists.* New York, 1963.

Schumann, Robert: *Memoirs of Felix Mendelssohn Bartholdy.* Trans. for Schumann Memorial Foundation, Inc. by James A. Galston. Rochester, 1951.

Shaw, Bernard: *London Music in 1888–89 as Heard by Corno di Bassetto.* New York, 1937.

Shaw, Bernard: *Music in London,* 1890–94. London, 1932.

Sterndale-Bennett, R.: "The Death of Mendelssohn." *Music and Letters,* London, vol. 36, no. 4, pp. 374–376 (October, 1955).

Stratton, Stephen S.: *Mendelssohn.* London, 1921

Veinus, Abraham: *The Concerto.* London, 1948.

Wagner, Richard: "Judaism in Music," in *Richard Wagner's Prose Works,* Vol. III, trans. by William Ashton Ellis. London, 1894.

Weinstock, Herbert: *Rossini.* New York, 1968.

Werner, Eric: *Mendelssohn; a new image of the composer and his age;* New York, 1963.

Werner, Eric: "New light on the family of Felix Mendelssohn." Hebrew Union College Annual, vol. 26, pp. 543–565. Cincinnati, 1955.

Werner, Jack: "Felix and Fanny Mendelssohn." *Music and Letters,* London, vol. 28, no. 4, pp. 303–337 (October, 1947).

Werner, Jack: *Mendelssohn's "Elijah"; a historical and analytical guide to the oratorio.* London, 1965.

Zuckmayer, Carl: *Als wär's ein Stück von mir.* Vienna, 1966.

THE MENDELSSOHNS

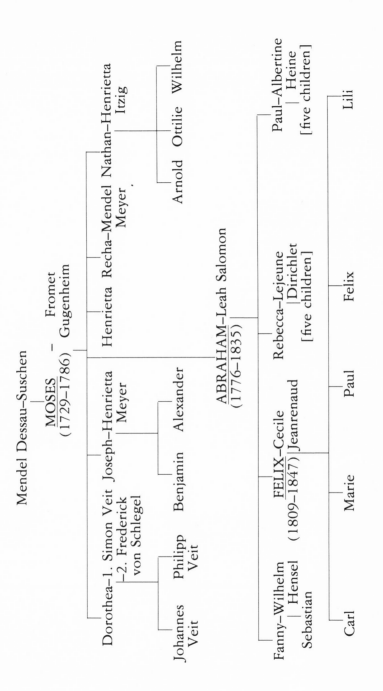

Mendel Dessau–Suschen

MOSES – Fromet
(1729–1786) Gugenheim

Dorothea–1. Simon Veit Joseph–Henrietta   Henrietta Recha–Mendel Nathan–Henrietta
–2. Frederick   Meyer   Meyer   Itzig
von Schlegel

Johannes   Philipp   Benjamin   Alexander   Arnold Ottilie Wilhelm
Veit   Veit

ABRAHAM–Leah Salomon
(1776–1835)

FELIX–Cecile   Rebecca–Lejeune   Paul-Albertine
(1809–1847) Jeanrenaud |Dirichlet | Heine
                                 [five children]   [five children]

Fanny–Wilhelm
| Hensel
Sebastian

Carl   Marie   Paul   Felix   Lili

Index

Illustration Acknowledgments